My beaut[...]

Thank you

up a beautiful world
for me by sharing your
remarkable world with
me.

Thank you for the loving
support that you have
so generously given me.

my love always

Kitana.

Aborted at Birth

Kitana

© 2010 Kitana
All Rights Reserved.

No part of this publication may be reproduced, stored in a retrieval system, or transmitted, in any form or by any means, electronic, mechanical, photocopying, recording, or otherwise, without the written permission of the author.

First published by Dog Ear Publishing
4010 W. 86th Street, Ste H
Indianapolis, IN 46268
www.dogearpublishing.net

ISBN: 978-160844-684-1

This book is printed on acid-free paper.

Printed in the United States of America

SECTION I

Chapter 1

Amman, Jordan: 1970

CALIANA lay in bed with her eyes still closed when she heard the explosion. Her heart clenched as her bedroom shook; her initial reaction was feeling intense fear, uncertainty about the origins of the noise, and the alterations that dawn had brought to her life. She opened her eyes and heard the servants' screams mix with those of her parents, punctuated by the sound of gunfire and explosions. She sat up quickly but felt a blanket of confusion settle over her mind and senses, as if a part of her had gone back to sleep.

She did not remember walking into the living room, only staring at the old white-haired nanny, Jamila, who was unconsciously slapping herself in the face as she screamed uncontrollably that they were all doomed, while another maid shouted at Jamila to stop screaming.

Caliana felt forceful hands on her shoulder and heard her maternal grandfather's rough voice ordering her to follow him. His presence in her parents' house at that early hour was strange. Caliana looked up at her grandfather's face. His brows wrinkled as he gauged which way to cross the battlefield the room had turned into, filled by a family moving fast in a mad dance of fear. He hurriedly dragged her toward the stairway, and, dazed, Caliana wondered if he had spent the night. Her thoughts loomed, inexpressible, a muted voice lost in the cacophony.

The sound of the explosions seemed to be coming from the apartment's front door. Caliana's grandfather flattened himself and her against the smooth plaster of a wall leading to the back exit of the apartment, a route ordinarily reserved for when she played in the garden. The pair traveled down the stairs as her grandfather screamed instructions at every step of the way, to stay against the wall and avoid the windows built at every landing, for fear of a stray bullet entering the stairwell.

Caliana looked at the banister a few feet in front of her. She thought about how grown-ups ordinarily leaned on it, and how they now splayed themselves as far away from it as possible. It had become the most dangerous place on the stairs. She had run up and down these stairs countless times, but this was the first time she had reached the bottom clammy with sweat, despite the slowness of her descent.

It was then that Caliana remembered the paranoid words of her paternal grandmother: their family had always been vulnerable in this country. "The Palestinians have survived here in Jordan, she would say," and she would chant, "*only by the benevolence of the moderate King Hussein, God protect him.*"

Caliana's grandmother was a devout Catholic, a daily churchgoer, and a fanatic. She revered the king and included His Majesty in every prayer and every topic of conversation, no matter how irrelevant. She entreated God to give the king a long life so her family would remain sheltered under his protection. He was their savior, and Caliana's grandmother wouldn't allow her family to forget their debt to him—especially at a time when his life was threatened by persistent assassination attempts. Caliana sometimes wondered if her grandmother was granted a direct audience with her God, for the king seemed to be invincible.

To her grandmother, being Christian, Palestinian, and rich was akin to a death sentence. Only the king could keep the monsters at bay, and her monsters were never fully articulated. They were a vague composite of the people that she kept out of her world: Muslim, poor, and staunch Jordanian nationalists. Caliana couldn't imagine what those *monsters* could do, but she nonetheless had feared the impending civil war between the Jordanians and the Palestinian Liberation Organization. As she stood pressed against the back stairwell with her family, Caliana understood that these fears had finally become a reality. The civil war had begun.

Caliana and her grandfather reached the cellar, which was crowded with the building's machinery. The servants had always warned her not to enter the hot, noisy room, and so she hesitated at the door. When her grandfather screamed at her to hurry inside, Caliana felt anger at the injustice of his reprimand. As she followed her grandfather in, she was surprised to find the neighbors from the upstairs apartment already occupying a section of the dark room.

The cellar was not equipped to house three families. Electric generators and a water heater took up a third of the floor space. Another third was covered by mattresses. The last bit had a small toilet, and a section for food and other supplies brought down by the families in preparation for the possible war. Caliana groped toward a lit candle and tried to slow the panicked beating of her heart.

Her parents entered with two maids, each carrying one of her infant sisters. Her elder sister, Deena, who was eight years old, came in last with her grandmother. Hastily and in the dark, Caliana's father and grandfather spoke to the other men and organized each family over a mattress. As she sat down on her family's mattress, she remembered that she had been sleeping peacefully in her own bed what seemed like hours, but had only been minutes, before. She squinted her eyes and surveyed her dim surroundings.

Her eyes were first drawn to the only source of light: a window one meter by three meters at the top of a wall. The adults congregated in its light. Because the cellar was mostly underground, anyone standing outside would be unrecognizable, seen only from their feet to their knees. Her grandfather shouted that sandbags were needed to block the window, that one stray bullet striking the nearby machinery would be enough to blow them all up. Caliana stopped listening and started counting her heartbeats, worrying that each would be her last.

Within the first days of being trapped in the cellar, Caliana's anxiety increased unimaginably. She was no longer startled at the frequent sound of guns and explosions; instead, her body began storing each jump and ripple of terror into a massive explosion building, churning, within her. She could contain her panic only by clutching her body into a tight fetal ball and shutting out the world of the dark cellar.

She both feared and longed for the combustion that lay coiled inside her, but she knew that once she started screaming, she would be unable to stop. Her grandfather's prophesy became absolute fact in her mind. She vigilantly watched the window for the sole bullet that would strike the machinery and kill them all. Caliana wanted to regain control of her life, even if only by being on guard at the exact moment of her death. Sleep became impossible.

Time ceased to have any meaning. She felt herself slowly asphyxiating in the coffin-like room. Her desire to escape her family compelled her to repeatedly sneak away into dark corners. She was always found and ordered back to the unbearable confinement of the crowded mattress, where she tried soothing her obsessive horror with endless probabilities that reduced the odds of the bullet penetrating the window.

Once, Caliana timidly crawled next to her mother, hoping to get some desperately needed comfort. Her mother was seven months pregnant with her fifth daughter and had begun chain-smoking cigarettes in the cellar. Caliana was finally next to her mother, shoulder barely touching shoulder. Her mother paused in mid-sentence and gave Caliana a withering look. Caliana braved her mother's irritation and, holding her breath, gently lowered her head onto her mother's lap. She was surprised at how clammy and hot her mother's skin was. She felt her mother's legs tense in response, so she tried to put as little weight as possible on them. Maybe if she pretended to fall asleep, her mother would be forced to tolerate her for a little while longer. A few minutes passed, and Caliana felt her mother's hand on her head. Caliana held her breath, longing for her mother to caress her hair and whisper magical words that would make her life bearable. Ever so slowly, her mother lifted Caliana's head from her leg and lowered it onto the mattress, all the while continuing her conversation with the neighbor.

Caliana's throat burned with smothered tears, and she was grateful that the darkness would help hide her humiliation. She waited a few minutes and pretended that the next explosion had woken her up before she crawled back to her designated position on the mattress. Helplessness overwhelmed her and threatened to crush her. She prayed that her parents would die and then immediately felt guilty. She imagined herself dying, and her parents' remorse at losing her. A clear thought crept into her consciousness, and she knew with certainty that she would not be missed. They would be relieved and would only pretend to mourn her.

By the second week, the explosions occurred less frequently. The lull, because it was unpredictable, was in some ways more unbearable than the continual noise, although the boredom of waiting for the next explosion sometimes allowed Caliana the reprieve of a nap. She would wake angry at herself for letting down her guard.

One morning, the men decided to take advantage of the first few hours of silence and dashed outside to fill pillow covers with sand. Caliana was desperate to leave the cellar, and she asked her father if she could join them. She swallowed her disappointment upon hearing his abrupt refusal.

Soon after, she heard her mother telling the nanny to leave the cellar to gather supplies for the babies. Caliana watched the nanny leave with her sister in her arms. She waited a few minutes and snuck out after them. Her need to leave the room overpowered the fear of any possible punishment. She felt elated running up the stairs to her apartment, to be in motion after captivity! She crept into the apartment and into her room. She knew that she had only a few moments yet could not decide what to take back down with her. She grabbed a book that she had meant to begin reading, and her favorite soft pajamas. She reached the babies' room and stood in the doorway.

She watched the nanny frantically gathering items, shoving them into an already-full handbag hanging from one shoulder. In her other arm, the nanny carried Caliana's baby sister. The nanny scurried over to the day bed by the huge bay window and started to lean down to lower her sister onto it.

Suddenly, the window exploded. Caliana watched, fascinated, as shards of glass fell like rain on the nanny's back. The nanny instinctively shielded the infant. Time slowed, and all sounds diffused into the background. Caliana was suddenly calmed. She tilted her head to her left and heard the soft thudding of bullets as they delicately penetrated the doors of a wooden closet. She watched, mesmerized, as the wood splintered and the bullets drew closer. The nanny's screams echoed against the walls, but Caliana barely heard them. Her ears were ringing, and she couldn't look away from the pattern of holes tracing its way toward her. A final bullet wedged itself in the wood a few centimeters away from her. Had the gunman kept firing, she estimated, the next bullet would have found her neck.

It was at that instant that she felt herself fracture. The imaginary bullet had found its mark, and the imagined death allowed her a tremendous relief. Her head disconnected from her vulnerable heart, and she found herself alive from only the neck up.

Energized by the power and speed of her thoughts, Caliana made her way back to the cellar. The nanny was on her knees, surrounded by the adults. Hysterical, she told them about her brush with death. In between frenzied tears, she clutched her hands in prayer and thanked God, six or seven times in a row, for saving them.

Caliana's father raged at the nanny for her stupidity in taking the baby upstairs with her. Her mother, suddenly aware of her negligence, insisted that she had specifically told the nanny not to take the baby upstairs. Even the neighbors joined in unleashing at the distraught woman whom they had met barely fifteen days earlier. In shock and supplication, the nanny was oblivious to them.

Caliana surveyed the scene from a clear, emotionally detached perspective. She saw her parents with a new lens and knew the truth: that her father should be raging at her mother, and that he never would.

Caliana walked to her place on the mattress. She changed into a pair of soft pajamas and opened her book.

All her young life, Caliana had known that her love for her family was synonymous with pain. She carried the pain everywhere in her chest, so that her breath had got used to being only partially drawn. She used her breath to force her feelings deeper down into her body, until she found herself starving for oxygen at times. She pushed aside her desperate feelings of love and wanting to be loved, until her chest froze and stung.

That day in the cellar, she found a new way to control her feelings. She picked up her book, and the world suddenly and implicitly made sense. The pain of her life vanished, and she was submerged into a new reality, where her spirit and imagination joined in flight. The words on the pages fueled a desire to exist that she had never known before. She felt herself fading into an intense silence, and only then did she inhale what felt like her first-ever safe breath.

There, in a loving act, she hid her young soul.

CHAPTER 2

"CALIANA! Khalas! *Enough!*"

The war left Caliana jittering with uncontainable intensity. To combat the feeling of suffocation, residual from the memory of the bullets that had come so close, she remained constantly in motion, running through the halls of her house and her school, squirming and reeling in her chairs when forced to sit. An object of pure motion, she exhausted her family and teachers. Her mother frequently scolded her for fidgeting, and to avoid embarrassment in front of houseguests would joke that her second-eldest daughter was like a drop of mercury, for which stillness was elusive. More than once, Caliana's schoolteachers tied her uniform belt to her chair, preventing her from rocking while class was in session. Her teachers called her dizzying; later in life she would be diagnosed more precisely as having ADHD (combination type).

"Be still! Stop that!"

Caliana's continual movement allowed her to ignore those around her. She never needed to stop and endure the daunting task of trying to relate to anyone. Being still demanded that she exist in a world that she felt excluded from, a surreal world that unfolded around her, uncontrollably, as if in a nightmare. Only when she was absorbed in her reading Caliana could sit still, although her mind continued to function at high speed. She felt safe when the real world around her gave way to the world offered on the pages before her, and this safety made her relax as she knew that nothing was expected of her; she had control.

Caliana felt control slipping when confronted by the daily realities that drove the real world, which was as elusive to her as the mystery of death that she had encountered during the war. She read book after book, searching for information that would better prepare her to guard against humanity encroaching on her alienation. She never wanted to find herself again in a situation whereby she had to depend on others for protection. To regain control of herself, of the fear of death that overpowered her body, she searched in books for new information, answers to questions that she had not yet considered. She wanted to arm herself with knowledge that would help her make better future choices.

Her parents had equipped their main living room with a fully stocked library, an impressive display disturbed only when Caliana needed a new book. She no longer looked to her parents to fulfill the role of guardians and guides. They had become enemies in a smaller war, her war—the indifference of both parents became a weapon more powerful than their scolding. Unbeknownst to them, she waged a private battle for survival, always guarded, training herself to expect nothing from them but averted eyes. To lose her guard was to feel as if she were disappearing, vanishing from the room and the earth without consequence.

* * *

The civil war ended when Caliana was six. By the time she turned nine, she had learned to observe her parents scientifically, detaching all emotion and seeing them truthfully for their flaws. She began to notice the masks they wore in the presence of strangers, anyone not part of the family. Among the wealthiest families in their small society, whom they called their closest friends, Caliana watched her parents turn into caricatures of affluence and happiness, energized by fresh gossip. Watching these shifts in persona and their subsequent interactions left Caliana feeling repelled by the world around her; she learned to make her escape as soon as possible after the perfunctory greeting of kisses and shallow words.

At times, her mother would keep her longer, presenting Caliana as a trophy to her crowd of friends. In her boasting, she sometimes confused details of Caliana's life with those of her other daughters, or invented details altogether. Caliana especially loathed those moments, aware that she was addressed only to make her mother look good. In retaliation, Caliana guarded the details of her life and became miserly in sharing information that could create the appearance of good parenting.

* * *

The frequent performances demanded by a busy social schedule left Caliana's parents with little energy to be humane toward their servants. Ordering servants about precluded the need to say "please," and her parents certainly never felt obliged to thank the servants. Her parents' disdain was deliberate, apparent, and often genuinely relished—their money afforded them a distorted sense of power. Caliana cringed with humiliation when she watched her parents assume license to abuse the poor and destitute.

When both her parents antagonized a servant, Caliana's heart would start pounding and she would quickly look away, afraid of seeing shame and indignance spring into the servant's eyes. In the older servants, this indignance had long since given way to subservience, passivity.

In between their verbal lashes at the servant, her parents would also engage in side comments to express their disdain. Her father usually ordered her mother to fire a servant and would always cite stupidity as the reason.

"Mish maoul! *Unbelievable!* I told him ten times what to do!"

"Fire him!" her father would shout. "He's stupid! Look how slowly he moves!"

Each servant would stand before Caliana's parents, looking from one to the other in terror, waiting for her parents to decide his or her future.

Her mother's only active responsibility in the house was to train the new servants, and she savagely guilted them into further submission. New servants arrived from other third-world countries, usually Sri Lanka. Upon arrival, they were treated as dirty and diseased and first had to undergo delousing, a process about which her mother often boasted and complained to her own friends.

Caliana's mother considered it despicable, having to take time off from her busy schedule of painting, gardening, and reading romance novels to supervise the training of new servants. She always expected servants to memorize, in one take, their microscopic duties. For months afterward, they dealt with her frustrated anger at their inability to follow her specific directions. It was much easier for Caliana's mother to beat the servants' spirits into capitulation than to patiently train them in their tasks. Caliana's mother audaciously reminded the servants of how fortunate they were to live in her home, where they were well fed and cared for, rather than in the abject poverty and misery from which they came.

Caliana grieved for the servants and understood that they were hostages to their poverty. Witnessing her mother's repeated cruelty kept Caliana on guard. Studying her mother's attacks facilitated the death of any love she had ever felt toward her mother. For the first time, Caliana felt embarrassed of her existence, as if her birth had been accidental, anomalous. She attempted to compensate for her parents' behavior by acting exceptionally respectful and polite to the servants.

* * *

Caliana began to view her paternal grandfather in a new light, a surprising and soul-saving discovery. She had always known that he was a powerful man from the constant attention he received. He was addressed only by the title of Basha and was respectfully deferred to. Examining him anew, Caliana was startled to discover that this grandfather nourished the hope of possibility, of a humanity with which she could finally identify.

Her grandfather was formidable, genuinely decent, and kind to everyone. His humility and strong belief in the potential of mankind endeared him to many. He treated everyone with unconditional respect and dignity. The Basha was a self-made entrepreneur who envisioned building a civilized society and country, working tirelessly to create both. He was renowned for his overwhelming generosity and compassion in helping to encourage, and often finance, people into starting their own businesses. He lived in a world dominated by his code of honor and his word, where his vigorous handshake sufficed in closing any transaction.

Her grandfather worked mornings in downtown Amman. He wanted to be located in a place where he could be with the everyday man. The one rule in his humble but large office was to leave his office door open at all times. The Basha's crippled and elderly male secretary adored him and tried to protect the Basha from the constant demands of people waiting to see him. His desk sat outside the Basha's office and was often crowded with people wanting to see the Basha. The secretary always kept an eye and an ear attuned to the Basha's needs. No one entered without his knowledge, and he knew better than to turn anyone away. The secretary tried to get the Basha to adapt to an appointment policy but was always gently reminded that people in need should be able to convey their problems without having to schedule their miseries. The secretary both admired and was frustrated by the Basha's magnanimous attitude.

Caliana's grandfather started insisting that Caliana and her eldest sister, Deena, visit him in his office. On those occasions, he enticed them to write to his daughter in Jamaica by paying them one Jordanian dinar each. Caliana and Deena would sit at the oval conference table in his office and write their respective letters. Caliana loved those times, because she got to observe her grandfather's spirit at work. She never ceased to be amazed by the variety of people who came to visit him.

* * *

One day, a very poor man came into the Basha's office and stood timidly at the door, profusely blessing her grandfather and bobbing in respectful submission.

"Ahlan, Ahlan, *welcome, welcome*," intoned her grandfather as he got up from behind his desk, greeting the man with the same enthusiasm he displayed to everyone. He remained standing when the man shyly refused the offer to be seated.

Her grandfather tried to put the man at ease by inquiring about the man's family and how he was faring in his life. The man shed some tears as he told the Basha about the loss of his job. The Basha reached into his pocket and took out a business card, writing on the back of it a grocery list consisting of a few bags of flour, sugar, and other supplies that the man could collect from the Red Cross. The Basha then told the man to go downstairs to the warehouse and report for work. The man kept trying to kiss the Basha's hand in gratitude, but the Basha deflected it by shaking the man's hand firmly.

As that final exchange took place, a few soldiers entered the office to announce the arrival of His Majesty, King Hussein of Jordan. The Basha greeted the young king with similar enthusiasm and introduced the destitute man to everyone in the room as *Abu* Mohammad. Because the Basha could not possibly remember the names of all the anonymous poor men who visited him, he called them all *Abu* Mohammad, an all-purpose name meaning "the father of Mohammad the Prophet." Caliana's grandfather offered the king and everyone a seat and continued talking as he walked the speechless *Abu* Mohammed to the door. He told *Abu* Mohammad that he expected to hear an update on his family situation and that his door would always be open to him. Caliana grinned with immense pride for her grandfather.

* * *

One day, her grandfather, while working in his office, stood up in a panic and shouted that he had gone blind. He had a history of high blood pressure, and the main arteries in his eyes hemorrhaged suddenly, causing permanent blindness. His handicap limited his activities, and in response, he began working and receiving people at home.

Caliana heard variations of the incident of her grandfather going blind, and her imagination convulsed with painful scenarios. All of them left her feeling frustrated and helpless. She was intimidated by her grandfather's decency and wanted to express her empathy, but in her inept shyness couldn't muster the right words. She longed to let her grandfather know how much she loved him, how grateful she was for his kindness, and how much of an impact he had by making her feel less alone.

It became common to find her grandfather sitting in his garden surrounded by well-wishers and business associates. One summer evening, Caliana saw her grandfather sitting contented and alone on his favorite glider. His eyes were closed, and his face was turned up toward the warmth of the fading sun. She stood anxiously observing him for a few minutes. Hesitant, she walked toward him, feeling like a thief about to steal a few moments of his solitude.

"Who's there?" called her grandfather.

"It's me, Caliana," she responded timidly.

"Come closer so I can see you," he beckoned with a smile. His arms stretched out lovingly toward her, beckoning her closer.

Caliana's heart started racing; she felt nervous. She slowly inched toward his hands, expecting him to lower his arms so she could lean down and kiss him in the accustomed manner of greeting. Her grandfather instead took her in his arms and gently gathered her onto his lap. He tucked Caliana's face onto his neck, and she gradually snuggled into his enfolding arms. With one hand, he started to rhythmically scratch her back, and she tingled with new sensations. Caliana melted into the unfamiliar embrace and blissfully engrossed herself into the serenity of being rocked and caressed. In her grandfather's arms, she allowed herself to be carried away with her most longed-for dream: that he would rescue her from her silence; she would pour out her pain to him, and he would embrace her and love her. She was grateful for the silence between them in that moment, however; she still lacked the courage to expose her feelings through speech.

Caliana's utopia was interrupted by the arrival of a few of her grandfather's friends. Caliana floated out of her grandfather's arms and flew to her alcove, located on one of the numerous levels in the garden. Once there, she huddled in her favorite niche, carved into an old wall. She hugged herself and allowed her elation to flood her face. She felt giddy and faint at the same time. Her heart still raced, and her thoughts whirled fantastic and thrilling, brocading her vision. The depth of the feelings released in her was exhilarating. In her love for her grandfather she had allowed herself to be vulnerable and soothed by the reciprocity of his love for her.

She was so immersed in her thoughts that a few moments passed before Caliana became aware that her body was convulsing. The switch into terror was abrupt. Panic overwhelmed her as she realized it was impossible to breathe. The loud sounds of her labored breathing gripped her. Caliana was suffocating, and images of being buried alive flashed through her thoughts and amplified her dread. She was dying but fighting to live. She was a baby besieged by her mother's birth canal, frantically struggling toward breath, toward life. It was an elongated, surreal nightmare spiraling out of control.

On waking, Caliana couldn't tell if she had fainted or slept, or for how long. She felt drained and acutely isolated. Her loss of control made her shudder. She couldn't figure out how it had happened, only perceived that letting go of her emotions and allowing herself to feel intense happiness had perpetuated a petrifying, deathly reaction. The images of suffocating at birth would not leave her. She felt all the more certain that from the time she was born and until her grandfather had held her, just now, she had never felt real love.

Caliana had learned to bury her emotions to survive her dysfunctional upbringing by her parents. While journeying in her books, she felt safe enough to come to life; she allowed herself to be taken by the emotional ranges of her favorite protagonists. She could question the characters' actions, assess their attitudes, and gain knowledge from them. When she looked up from a book, she was often jolted with disappointment at the world—a world that seemed to crawl along in mirroring and duplicating her family. It was far easier to escape the intolerable monotony of her life and plunge right back into the fictional reality, where she could respond to authors imbedding their lives within their characters and sharing their lives with her. She fervently hoped that these authors who convinced her of grand possibilities were magnificent people in real life, living by the same principles they conveyed through their characters. Even when skeptical of the reality of this hope, Caliana still valued and admired the authors' imaginations in painting a better world into which she could escape.

Books remained her only refuge, a place where she could find characters exemplifying dignity and nobility of spirit, until that day with her grandfather—he was proof that such dignified characters could exist in the reality outside of a book.

CHAPTER 3

TO rear her children, Caliana's mother divided them into manageable groups. As the eldest, Caliana and Deena were always paired. They shared the same room, the same vacations, and the same liberties. The second group consisted of Caliana's other three younger sisters. Split by schedule and location, the two groups of sisters rarely had the opportunity to interact.

Deena was aggressive toward Caliana in private and feigned demureness in front of the rest of the family. Whenever her parents caught an accidental glimpse of these fights they were quick to side with Deena and blame Caliana. It was easier to believe the angel, Deena, than Caliana, the hyperactive, out-of-control tomboy. (To release energy, Caliana had bonded with the wildest group of ten-year old boys she could find, racing motorcycles, crashing cars and dirt bikes, and jumping out of second-story windows.) Caliana had by this time already gained a well-deserved reputation with her family for being the wild child.

Though Deena had failed to be the male heir, she was somehow afforded privileged treatment for being the eldest. Caliana had once felt sorry for Deena, for she clearly saw through Deena's desperate attempts to gain the family's love and acceptance as compensation for her lesser sex, but Caliana's pity quickly turned into rage as Deena vented her own suppressed rage on Caliana.

Deena would start by taunting Caliana for her thinness or alleged stupidity. Caliana would retaliate with angry words, and Deena would respond with blows, which would make Caliana's anger erupt. Their violent fights would inevitably end with Caliana on the floor and Deena straddling her chest, heavy legs pinning down

Caliana's arms. Taunts and insults would spring from Deena with a ferocity that further infuriated Caliana.

Deena used her chubby physique as an instrument of torment against Caliana's skinny frame. She calculated the weight that she held on Caliana's heaving chest, enough to guarantee Caliana's suffocation. She would relieve Caliana for seconds at a time by raising herself from Caliana's chest. When Caliana would buck upward in panicked hysteria, Deena would lower herself to intensify the torture.

Caliana tolerated much of her physical pain by self-anesthetizing. When Caliana refused to comply, admit, beg, agree, or apologize, the slapping would begin. Deena slapped and beat Caliana into submission, stopping only when she was out of breath. The more Caliana fought back, the more she was slapped. Deena developed a ratio system that earned Caliana ten slaps for any act of resistance, and she derived gratification from counting them aloud. The slaps varied in intensity and speed.

Caliana was obstinate, and with her pride at stake, she clung on until she imploded into a claustrophobic attack. She hated these fights because she could never avoid the certain plunge into terror. It was inconceivable for Caliana to cry out for help during any of the beatings, for she understood that she didn't have any protection.

* * *

Her grandfather, the Basha, was having a grand lunch party at his house. Deena and their three older male cousins excitedly beckoned Caliana to follow them into the main guest bathroom. Caliana followed them with distrust.

As soon as the door closed, they produced two glass vials and began to bully Caliana in an attempt to goad her into smashing them. She was so frustrated by the collective pressure that she grabbed the vials and slung them against the wall.

The boys dashed out of the bathroom in hysterical laughter. Caliana heard her sister tell their cousins, "I told you she's crazy!"

Caliana shook from her lost temper and regret when she was overwhelmed by the gagging stench of manure. Her heart raced in fear as she realized that the vials she had thrown were the cause of the odor. Caliana dashed out of the bathroom and firmly closed the door, hoping to contain the stench. She anxiously stood close to the nearest crowd of people and hoped they wouldn't be able to smell the ghastly odor. In horror, she watched as someone opened the bathroom door and recoiled. The stench instantly filled the house, and she watched with shame as people evacuated her grandfather's party.

Caliana was horrified at what she had done. Angrily, she sped down the stairs, looking for her cousins and sister. She found them hiding in one of the bedrooms, and for the first time ever, she lunged at her sister. Deena quickly subdued her in their familiar position and started taunting Caliana, though in front of her cousins, she would never actually strike her sister.

Caliana could only move her head, as her arms were pinned under her sister's knees. Deena taunted Caliana, spurred on by their cousins' laughter. Caliana's humiliation and guilt catapulted her rage to a new, explosive level, and when she saw her sister's exposed inner thigh, she bit it with all her might.

Caliana did not let go, even as her sister's screams reverberated through the house. Relatives stormed into the room, livid at knowing that they had found the culprits responsible for the other disgraceful act.

Her father yanked Caliana's head away from Deena's leg, and Deena screamed even louder. In the slight gap between Caliana's two front teeth, a piece of Deena's skin was lodged. Caliana felt like a wild animal as she stood facing her father and sister, with blood smeared on her face and a torn piece of skin dangling out of her mouth. Contorted faces screamed at her. Her father dragged her out of the room by her arm, hitting and screaming at her the whole way to the car. He threw her roughly in the backseat and ordered the driver to take her home.

Caliana was stunned.

* * *

The following day at school, Deena exaggerated her limp and delighted in showing everyone the evidence of Caliana's savagery. Deena played the perfect victim and loved the attention that she received. Her inner thigh was grotesquely bruised, missing skin, and, as she described it, gouged with savage teeth marks.

As the day progressed, classmates who delighted in expressing their revulsion approached Caliana. Some kids asked her to open her mouth and show her ferocious teeth. Others barked or howled when she walked by. One of her teachers made her stand atop her desk at the beginning of class and admonished her behavior.

Caliana did not speak for a few days after that, a new level of silence. She began to doubt her sanity and was humiliated into believing that she was actually a savage. She was grateful that she had less than two months to finish her last school year in Jordan. Her parents, both products of early-age boarding schools, had signed up Caliana and Deena to begin year-long boarding in September at a British school in Switzerland. She had cherished the respite of spending the past two summers in European boarding schools, and was excited to be permanently leaving Jordan and her family.

Caliana had steadily grown to hate her sister. After the bite fiasco, an unspoken truce was established: So long as they were in the same place at the same time, they split up and spoke only when absolutely necessary. The sisters even managed to spend four weeks that summer in Jamaica visiting their aunt and cousins with hardly a word exchanged between them. Silence was a perfect solution that lasted many, many years. Caliana was glad for the distance. At the age of ten, she understood that certain relationships led to suffocation, and she was determined to protect herself from any such associations.

* * *

In Jamaica that summer, Caliana's dream of living on an island took root. One morning, she lost track of time as she wandered farther away from people on the beach. When she stopped in a secluded alcove, she realized that she was completely alone.

She had always felt a deep affinity with the sea. It left her relaxed and in her element. As she surveyed the beauty surrounding her, her heart swelled with tranquility. She sat on the warm sand and considered her requirements in life. She felt that she had everything that she could possibly need in her backpack: a few books, a bottle of water, sunglasses, an unlimited American Express card, some cash, and her few toiletries.

Caliana was an exceptionally good swimmer, but her real satisfaction came when she succumbed to the ecstasy of floating on her back. Caliana took off her tiny bikini and dove into the water. She kicked her legs up from under her and within seconds floated peacefully on the surface of the ocean. She breathed deeply into her diaphragm and felt her body respond with meditative buoyancy. Surrounded by water, she felt that she truly inhabited her body. It was a womblike homecoming. The gentle warm water caressed her, and she completely gave in to its calming might. Caliana inhaled her dream and promised herself that some day, she would locate and settle on her island.

CHAPTER 4

CALIANA loved being in London. She felt grateful that her parents brought her and Deena on every vacation. In the four years since the war, her parents had stopped pretending to enjoy living in Jordan and were much more vocal about giving their daughters the opportunity of adapting to life in Europe, especially England.

Caliana loved the autonomy and anonymity that London provided. She treasured leaving her apartment in Mayfair and walking everywhere. With her backpack slung over one shoulder, she focused her attention on the crowds and on the paths she planned. Walking intensified her familiar state of defensive mental practice. She kept her mission clear to herself: to be amongst people, yet free to move. Anything less left her feeling stagnant.

Crowds invigorated her. On the always-busy commercial streets, she honed her ability to maneuver rapidly through the throngs of people all while assessing and determining her next few steps. She was irritated when she was forced to slow down. It meant that people came into focus, and she preferred to keep them in a peripheral haze.

When someone accidentally bumped into her, she would immediately replay the scene and orchestrate improved avoidance techniques. She learned to predict people's moves and to execute multiple evasions. She became accomplished at weaving speedily through crowds and congratulated herself on her fluidity. Her child's height was her chief frustration, as it prevented her from seeing clearly ahead.

She hated the unpredictability of being suddenly forced to halt in the tall hordes of people. When momentarily imprisoned, Caliana began to recognize the symptoms of what she had identified as claustrophobia. The sense of danger would escalate, building to anxious suffocation. In spite of this, she was determined to protect herself in these hostile surroundings.

Walking the less-crowded and often-silent neighborhood streets of London gave her joy. On those occasions, she allowed herself the luxury of looking around and breathing in the magnificent safety the city represented. Caliana treasured most of all the freedom of being a nobody: anonymous, invisible, enduring amongst humanity. She could reflect on her ghostly state of being. It reinforced her belief in her budding strength, her belief that she could be the most alone surrounded by people, yet not feel lonely.

As Caliana had spent the past two summers at European summer schools, she had received the glorious taste of living independently from her parents. The fragile political security that had ensued since the civil war, combined with her parents' distasteful endurance of Jordan, gave Caliana a more secure sense of belonging in all of Europe, though she felt the most at home in London. She naturally identified more with the European culture. Living in Europe afforded her the freedom to spend most of her time alone, exploring and developing her passions. She visited museums and galleries; frequently took in movies, theatres and operas; and spent countless hours browsing bookstores. Caliana also learned to appreciate cuisine from the best restaurants and acquired a passion for gourmet foods.

The past two years had exaggerated her sense of separateness, as she became even more immersed in the West and aware of the many differences between herself and her friends in Jordan. Every time she returned to Jordan, it took her a few days to acclimate to their sense of humor, language, and points of references. She couldn't share her new experiences with them even if she tried. She lived in a time when travel was a luxury that few could afford, and the cultural differences between East and West were immense. Her friends could not begin to imagine her other worlds, and therefore Caliana further developed her capacity for introspective silence.

* * *

When Caliana's plane landed in Switzerland, she exhaled in relief. She felt liberated and excited to begin her life at boarding school. She knew that already, at age eleven, she had been granted her sole objective in life up to that point: to never again live with her family under the same roof and preferably never in the same country.

While in boarding school, she perceived her distance from her family as an opportunity to enhance her autonomy, and she valued the reprieve from the emotional barrenness she was leaving behind. Caliana concluded that she could never compete with her father's wealth, which permitted her mother's vacuous emotional outlets: her avid addiction to romance books, her virginal landscaping and vibrant nature paintings, or her dedication to forging and mastering her societal position. Caliana felt sorry for her father. He existed to worship his wife as if she were a goddess. His devotion hid his social ineptness and assuaged his fear of being alone while guaranteeing his wife's captivity. Caliana recognized that their codependency excluded everyone else from their dysfunctional pact.

Her parents were forcefully united in living only for each other. When Caliana paused to contemplate her parents, her numbness often rose to piercing anger. She knew that she needed to escape their company and had added her fervent agreement into finalizing their decision to send her to boarding school.

Caliana had run out of excuses for her parents and could only feel anger toward their choices. Her mother was fluent in English, Arabic, and French; she had received academic scholarships all through her schooling and had graduated Magna Cum Laude from the AUB (American University of Lebanon). Though she had been awarded a Rhodes scholarship, she had chosen a financially secure marriage rather than the pursuit of academia. Caliana's father also spoke English, Arabic, and French fluently, had achieved top grades at all the best private schools, and had graduated from the London School of Economics. Caliana, who never ignored her mind, found her parents' stunted intellectual pursuit appalling. That her mother had graduated as a psychology major, with emphasis on child psychology, gave Caliana pause whenever she heard people rave about the credibility of the AUB and its colloquial title as the Harvard of the Middle East.

* * *

Caliana thrived in Switzerland.

Even though there were only 140 girls in the school, Caliana and Deena rarely saw each other. Deena was totally enmeshed within her group of eight or nine girls, and Caliana deliberately avoided any interaction with those girls. During her first year, she was placed in a large dorm that housed eight girls around her age. Sleeping arrangements were determined by age, so none of them were her form-mates, as her form-mates were at least a few years older. This separation from her form-mates suited Caliana perfectly—she was able to keep them at a desired emotional distance.

Already independent, she quickly adjusted to the school's rigid routine. Her understanding of time was underdeveloped, and in a school that ran on a methodical system of ringing bells, she learned to value punctuality and the potential of living every free moment to its fullest. Within this new structure, she found the school a suitable milieu in which to learn how to take care of herself, by managing her own bank account, sending her clothes to the laundry, and learning to use public transportation. These duties reinforced the lessons she had learned—that she could never allow herself to depend on others, and that if she did not take care of herself, no one else would. Immersed in her new environment, she lived in a constant testing ground of new challenges.

Caliana dedicated herself to every extracurricular activity the school provided. Her P.E. teacher adored her and harnessed Caliana's reckless energy into excellence in sport. Caliana became the school's best swimmer and diver and the captain of the basketball team. She blossomed on both the track field and the tennis court. She distinguished herself on the trampoline, loved learning to control her body's intricate aerial motions. Fearlessly, she learned to ski the black diamond slopes of the Swiss Alps. She embraced athletics without hesitation, and her passion drove her beyond her body's limitations.

Caliana tolerated the uncomfortable attention that partnered her accomplishments and dismissed the awards and accolades she received. She accepted her advantage in athletics and learned to compete only with herself. Her P.E. teacher empowered Caliana by imparting an incredible method: visualization. The teacher emphasized that, to perform a difficult routine or maneuver, Caliana must first see it successfully completed in her mind's eye. Caliana absorbed and utilized this powerful lesson to perfect her techniques. During one particularly boring geography class, Caliana imagined herself performing a difficult trampoline routine she had previously struggled with. She was astonished when, later in the afternoon, she mastered the routine on her first attempt of the day.

The first time she experienced jealousy was when she saw a girl flawlessly execute a "Brownie," a dive that she had never seen before. It was exquisitely torturous—Caliana stayed up all night trying to combat her jealousy with rational thought. Jealousy was an unexpected emotion that needed to be weeded out, and she was determined to understand it in order to rid herself of it, to resume control of her mind. She wanted to rise above her jealousy and to be able to appreciate the egoless beauty of every experience. She felt sorry for the girls who had watched her succeed and had responded with jealousy, considering them petty and insecure. To be guilty of that same response now felt hypocritical, and Caliana's pride was diminished by this unwanted, common emotion.

Within a few days, Caliana was able to prove the success of her efforts as she contentedly observed the other girl during a dive practice.

* * *

Caliana attracted many friendships. She was easygoing and genuinely liked by most of the girls. She learned to be a loyal listener and always felt indebted by the act of receiving, making sure to give back tenfold to compensate her friends for their generosity. On a superficial level, Caliana's relationships thrived, and she was considered one of the most popular girls at her school. Secretly, her sense of isolation grew with her awareness that she would let no one know her true self.

Learning to establish and maintain strict boundaries was necessary in her tightly knit environment and kept her from potential suffocation in so many relationships. Boarding school was her first sustained exposure to lonely, and at times suicidal, girls who desperately wanted nothing more than to be at home with their families. In the boarding school's small universe, more than thirty diverse nationalities were represented. Most of the girls came from broken homes, as an expensive boarding school in Switzerland was the accepted solution around the globe for affluent divorced families. Seeing the girls' pain drew Caliana to them, simultaneously reinforcing her belief that emotions were a universal weakness.

She learned that needy people could be the most draining. They activated her guilt and sense of responsibility, making it harder for her to maintain her boundaries without feeling like a monster. She found herself aggravated by her obligations. Their misery reinforced her feelings of superiority for not needing anyone, for not attaching enough to want anything from anyone. Witnessing their pain also secured her pride in her own uniqueness, in her superiority for having anesthetized all pain, her emotional divorcing of the world.

* * *

Caliana had not considered that she would face a shortage of books. She had arrived her first September armed with only a few novels, fully expecting to purchase many more as soon as she could locate a bookstore. All privileges and rules were determined by age, however, not grade, and Caliana could go out for only two hours on Saturday afternoons to the tiny village that was within walking distance. The village did not have a bookstore. She snuck out to the nearest town one week, but the bookstore located there did not carry any English novels. Her favorite class was English, but the books that were assigned for the year were not books that she would have chosen to read—too adolescent for her tastes.

She remembered reading her last childish book a year earlier upon her return from Jamaica. Deeply struck by the fantasy of island life, she had asked the librarian to recommend a novel about a girl living on an island and had been given the *Island of the Blue Dolphins*.

The novel had been a disappointment. Caliana had hoped to live vicariously through the main character, but instead, the character was not thrilled about living on her own on a beautiful island and spent her time preparing and hoping continually for rescue. Caliana hadn't cared for the details of survival, either—the realities of food and shelter had no place in her private fantasy. The book had been useful, however, in that it helped her refine her island fantasy to include a nearby village that would support her basic necessities. For years to come, Caliana would assess her love of others by her ability to imagine them visiting her on her island.

Caliana enjoyed the enthusiasm that her English teacher, Ms. Barton, showed while discussing the readings. Caliana focused on the differences in the girls' responses, hoping the girls would stimulate her, although she was more often bored with the immaturity and lack of interest of most of her form-mates. Even though she hesitated in volunteering her thoughts, she enjoyed the wonderful questions posed by Ms. Barton. The insights these questions provoked fed Caliana's imagination and activated her mind.

During one period, Ms. Barton was called out of class. She told the girls to read quietly until she returned. Caliana immediately put down the book the class was reading and opened another book. She was so absorbed in reading that she didn't notice Ms. Barton's return until her teacher gently pulled the book from her hand. Caliana's heart skipped a beat when she saw Ms. Barton note that she had been reading the wrong book. When class ended, Ms. Barton asked Caliana to remain behind.

"I noticed that you were reading *Julie of the Wolves*. Are you aware that it is the last book that we will cover this year?"

Caliana's mind raced with impossible answers. "I've read them all," she blurted in anxious honesty.

"Read all ... You mean the assigned books?"

Caliana didn't respond, but from the look of surprise on Ms. Barton's face, she knew she didn't have to.

"But ... when? How? ... You read all twelve books? ... Had you read some of them before?"

Caliana shook her head. Ms. Barton was attempting composure, but Caliana could read confused, unspoken thoughts mapping her face.

"They're short, and I read quickly," Caliana said, trying to help Ms. Barton understand that her progress wasn't a big deal. She became anxious that Ms. Barton might pursue the subject further.

"You've only had the books for ... six weeks! ... Did you enjoy reading them?"

Caliana debated lying. Books meant the world to her, and she didn't want to pollute her passion with lies. She braced herself and surprised herself by answering, "Actually, no. They're too simplistic and easy to read. I mean, I only had to look up a few words. But I didn't have anything else to read, and I was going crazy!"

Ms. Barton burst out laughing, and Caliana was shocked. Her face burned with shame and anger at exposing her thoughts. Ms. Barton was grinning, however, and she asked Caliana to follow her.

Caliana raced to keep up with Ms. Barton's purposeful strides. Ms. Barton stopped a senior, asking the girl to tell the dorm mistress that she would keep Caliana for lunch, the following period. They entered an empty fifth-form classroom, and Ms. Barton took out a set of keys and unlocked a large closet. With a dramatic flourish, she stepped away from it and motioned for Caliana to come closer. Caliana stared at the shelves loaded with books, almost salivating.

"Go ahead, pick one. I will not be responsible for boring my pupil into lunacy!"

Caliana hesitated. In a bookstore, she would have spent hours joyfully going through the selection process. She randomly reached for a book and plucked one from the shelf without looking at the cover.

"Hmm. Interesting. You chose *Mein Kampf* by Adolf Hitler. Do you know anything about Hitler?"

Caliana hesitantly shook her head.

"Any particular reason why you selected this book?"

"It's the thickest." Caliana felt foolish. "I ... just wanted to make sure I have a long book to read," she stammered.

Ms. Barton chuckled. "Okay. Let's try something different. How about telling me the names of a few of your favorite books?" Ms. Barton sat down and waited expectantly.

"I really liked *The Seven Minutes* ... by Irving Wallace, and I..."

"You read *The Seven Minutes*!" Ms. Barton let out a peal of laughter.

At that point Caliana wanted to bolt for the door, now fully convinced that her teacher was insane.

"I'm sorry, I'm not laughing at you," Ms. Barton continued. "I'm just laughing at the absurdity of ... oh, never mind! Please continue."

Caliana was confounded. She wasn't sure what to believe. She was distrustful of Ms. Barton's intentions yet inexplicably drawn to the teacher at the same time. Caliana had never spoken about books to anyone, and she felt defensive and vulnerable.

"Do you want me to tell you why I liked the book?" Caliana wasn't sure if she should prove that she really had read the book, or if she should go on listing the books that she had read.

"Believe me, at some point I will want to hear your thoughts on it. I'm curious though, who told you about *The Seven Minutes*? How on earth did someone your age get their hands on it?"

Caliana was stumped. What did Ms. Barton mean? Her mind raced as she tried to remember where and when she had bought the book. She had a feeling that whatever she answered wasn't what Ms. Barton was looking for, yet she couldn't determine what was being asked of her.

Seeing Caliana's confusion, Ms. Barton tilted a chair and asked the girl to sit down. She gently asked Caliana to share her background, questioning her about members of her family, where she had lived, and so on. Caliana felt nervous at the interest Ms. Barton was showing her. She was being pushed past her standard answers and probed with specific follow-ups. Ms. Barton seemed to want irrelevant details, which increased Caliana's aggravation.

Caliana just wanted a book and couldn't understand the inquisition she was being forced to endure. Finally, Ms. Barton returned to asking her about the books she had read and on her history and habits as a reader. Ms. Barton's transparent face easily reflected ranges of emotions, and Caliana was trying not to edit in response to the shocked surprise that kept fleeting across her teacher's face.

"Caliana, you have read some excellent books, though some of your choices could have used some adult discretion. I can't get over the fact that Harold Robbins has entered your list! Here's what I propose." She walked over to the bookcase and started rummaging through it. "This is not a bookstore with a best-sellers section, but I do have some wonderful books that I believe you will thoroughly enjoy."

Ms. Barton proceeded to choose three books from her shelves. "I think you should take a few steps into some great classics. Here's *Silas Marner* by George Eliot, *Little Women* by Louisa May Alcott, and *To Kill a Mockingbird* by Harper Lee. Take all the time that you need, and return them to me when you're done."

Ten days later, Caliana returned the books, with a copy of the list of words she had looked up. As a result, she was invited to tea and discussion the following Sunday.

Ms. Barton held a quarterly meeting of avid book readers at her house on Sunday afternoons. Caliana was initially intimidated by the girls; she was the only eleven-year-old and by far the youngest student there. In time, however, she learned to relish those meetings and felt validated discussing books. To Caliana, these meetings became a venue wherein she trained and harnessed her intelligence and corroborated her trust in her mental competence.

By the third month of being at boarding school, Caliana was given a copy of the key to the wondrous book cupboard and was trusted to browse and borrow books at her leisure.

CHAPTER 5

PARENTS were allowed to call only on Sunday mornings between ten and noon. Caliana's father called religiously, always varying the order of the same monotonous questions. He never felt compelled to share any news about the rest of the family, and Caliana never asked. He would inform her when he updated her bank account, and assuaged his guilt by encouraging her to use her financial resources to meet her needs.

Despite her anger, Caliana did feel grateful and financially indebted to her father. She had heard many girls complaining about the stinginess of their parents, and yet Caliana always had access to unlimited amounts of money.

During one phone call, around the time Caliana turned twelve, her father informed her that she had another baby sister, the sixth. A sister that would be even more thoroughly abandoned than the first five. At that point in their lives, her parents' actions had reached a newfound level of neglect. Their experiment with the eldest two daughters at boarding school had proven successful, and they made fast preparations to enroll the rest of their herd. In Caliana's second year at school, her eight-year-old sister joined her and Deena. Caliana maintained the same detached distance with her younger sister, who was the equivalent of a complete stranger. Caliana experienced twinges of guilt for erasing her sister but was driven by her justified resolve in maintaining especially strict boundaries with those she was stuck with: her family.

Another morning during her second year at school, Caliana was called out of class to take a phone call in the main office. Her father informed her that her grandfather, the Basha, had been buried a few days earlier. Caliana was stunned. Fait accompli. Wordlessly, she passed the phone to Deena, who had just entered the office, and ran out. Her thoughts raged as her heart shattered. Unprepared for death, losing the only person she had loved was unbearable. Caliana found herself in the school grounds heading toward the chalet that housed the older girls. She went down to the basement where all the ski equipment was stored, to a small section that was known as the smoking room. Caliana's senses were heightened, and she seemed to focus on minute details. The chalet was dead quiet, without the normal echoing of creaking wood. She had visited that room with her smoker friends and had taken occasional drags of their cigarettes. She reached under the couch where she knew that various brands were stashed and inhaled a few dizzying Gitan cigarettes.

She felt hysterical alarm at the intensity of the raw sobs that were bleeding out of her heart, terrorizing her with their intensity and lack of control. Her only spiritual mirror had been shattered into millions of disconnected shards. Each stabbed her with a sharp point. The physical intensity was suffocating. Caliana wanted to crawl out of her body and disappear. All options of suicide were carefully measured by their efficacy in obliterating her mind the fastest. A bullet to the head was the most merciful. She relished the immediacy and finality of the idea that her mind could just ... stop.

Caliana's thoughts staggered her. She had never wanted to die. If anything, she had always braced herself against her fear of death. How had she become such a pathetic, weak creature? How had someone mattered so much? The realization that loving her grandfather had made her powerless plummeted her into instant rage.

Smoking helped her to clench her heart, and she commanded it not to feel. She rationalized that she had not loved her grandfather, and she found some convincing arguments. She couldn't malign his wonderful spirit, so she enraged herself further with cruel accusations against him. She would erase him, feel nothing for him. He had not rescued her. He had failed her. She was not about to fall apart for anyone. She had her mind, and she believed in its power alone. She was her mind. She refused to shed a tear. Eventually, her anger would dissolve into numbed bliss.

Caliana marched back to class, a confirmed smoker.

A few weeks later, she was enjoying teatime when her name was called out. Letters were distributed at that time, and usually a crowd of hopefuls eagerly awaited their mail. Caliana had never received a letter, nor ever expected to. She turned back around, positive that she had misheard, when one of her friends grabbed the letter from the prefect and brought it over. Caliana stared at the letter until it became illegible. Though she had never paid attention to handwriting before, she admired the script used to address her. It was the most beautiful writing that she had ever seen. She tucked the letter in her uniform and hurriedly left the dining hall as if she were carrying a treasured secret.

Caliana headed to her favorite tree, where she could lean against it and admire the picturesque view of Lake Lemain surrounded by the majestic Alps. She was hesitant to open the letter. She wanted to savor all her imagined possibilities and was loath to face the disappointing reality she had come to expect. She had even considered that the letter might have been meant for one of her sisters, her typical defense in a worst-case scenario. Reining in her excitement, she slowly opened the letter. She sighed when she saw that the letter was addressed to her on the inside also, and, unable to contain her curiosity, she quickly scanned through the three pages of beautiful writing to identify the signature. The letter was signed "Rhea," and for a moment, Caliana could not recall who that was. She hoped the letter would give her a clue. What she was unprepared for was that she would be reading a letter of condolence written by a brilliant acquaintance from back home. Rhea expressed her sorrow at Caliana's loss and affirmed what a great man Caliana's grandfather had been.

Caliana cried gentle tears of grief and guilt at having completely erased her grandfather in the past few weeks. On her second read, she felt shamed by the eloquence of Rhea's identification with her sorrow. Caliana was able to mourn her grandfather through Rhea's compassion. She felt a deep, respectful connection with Rhea's ability to expose and share their mutual feelings.

Her critical distrust vanished in the wake of her loving sadness. Caliana reread the letter many times and each time felt more revived. She felt her grandfather's spirit silencing her cynical, distrustful inner voices. Ultimately, she read the letter with complete trust, and in return, she felt nurtured with genuine empathy. God had gifted her by showing her another side of the secretly beautiful world that she believed could exist. Rhea was an unexpected source. Her love of her grandfather did not have to die, for she could continue to cherish those who truly embodied his decency.

Caliana flashed back to the first moment when she had mentally identified her respect for Rhea. They were ten years old, sitting on the steps facing the basketball court at school in Jordan, where a game was underway. Caliana would have been playing with her classmates, except for a knee injury. Rhea was the goody two-shoes with a well-established reputation for being the top in her class and happened to sit next to Caliana. Everyone knew how smart Rhea was, and Caliana was itching to test her during this unusual opportunity. In the middle of an asinine conversation, Caliana asked Rhea what quality she considered important in a friend. Although Caliana was expecting the usual idiotic variations of a friend being someone she would "hang out with," Rhea took her question seriously, staring off into space. Caliana waited, for it was obvious that Rhea was engaged in thought.

"Loyalty." Even though Rhea said it with conviction, she had a goofy, almost romantic, look on her face.

Caliana's interest was piqued, for she considered it a mature answer. She pushed Rhea to explain her definition of loyalty. Rhea wanted someone to love her no matter what and to accept her completely—a friend whom she could confide her whole heart to and a friend who would take the best care of her heart!

Caliana watched Rhea getting called away by some friends. She sat alone and pondered Rhea's response. She told herself that she would keep an eye on Rhea, that she might be a good one.

Meticulously, Caliana folded the letter and tucked it in her uniform pocket. She let her soul fill with the magnitude of Rhea's graciousness and purity of heart and knew that she would loyally love Rhea forever. Caliana was determined to bridge all her defenses to become a true friend to Rhea.

* * *

During the following summer vacation, Caliana made it a point to spend most of her time in Jordan. She intended to begin seriously befriending Rhea. She had never connected with girls in general and often felt alienated from their feminine activities and conversations. Boys, on the other hand, kept up with her hyperactivity and were a challenging physical outlet. She had a well-developed group of male friends for her visits to Amman. Caliana knew that Rhea's family was very conservative and didn't allow her to go to most of the places that Caliana and her friends frequented. Luckily, though, Rhea's parents were from the same social background as Caliana's, and they trusted Rhea with activities that revolved around Caliana's house. Because of Caliana's parents' disinterest, the house was always open to friends without need for supervision, and thus Rhea was drawn into the popular circle of people who congregated there.

Caliana and Rhea spent most of the summer developing their friendship. Caliana wanted to fulfil Rhea's wish and be the one true and loyal friend, and in return, was rewarded with instant trust and unwavering love.

That summer was a revelation. Caliana's determination to befriend Rhea caused her to start paying attention to the girls who spent time with her male friends. She wanted to understand them so she could identify with Rhea, and she found herself somewhat enjoying being with them.

One girl in particular stood out from the rest: Haya. Caliana was immediately drawn to Haya's quiet dignity, a rare quality in anyone so young. Haya had a simple and happy approach to life and seemed genuinely comfortable in her own skin. She was the most natural being Caliana had ever encountered; she was devoid of any form of deceit. Haya's serene intensity magnetized Caliana, and Caliana found herself calmed by her new friendship. Caliana saw her true abilities reflected in Haya's personality, and for once, she allowed herself to begin the journey of being the receiver of genuine and unconditional love. For some strange reason, Caliana did not feel indebted, burdened, or suffocated by Haya's loving friendship—and for the first time ever, she trusted the natural response that flowed between them. Haya was a miracle that was too good to be true, an old, wise angel accidentally living amongst humanity. Caliana and Haya formed an immediate and unshakable bond. They made it a point to spend countless hours away from their respective groups, developing a treasured one-on-one friendship. That pattern continued to build and grow for many years. Caliana had never thought it possible to meet someone she could so profoundly respect. Having Haya in her life was the most uplifting restoration of her spiritual belief in God.

Caliana returned to Switzerland from her summer vacation feeling fortified with two blessings; she had forged strong foundations with both Haya and Rhea.

* * *

1979

Caliana was having her best year yet. She was fifteen, in fifth form, and graduating high school in May. She was the only fifth former in uniform and couldn't wait to turn sixteen in April so she could spend her last month at school in her own clothes.

The first term required much study in preparation for the mock O Levels in December. Caliana had signed up for seven subjects and felt the pressure of having to pass the mocks so she could formally sit for the O Levels in May. She was also having a hard time deciding where to apply for universities and what to do with her life. She wished for a college that would just let her read great books. She knew that she missed living in London, and because she enjoyed clothes, she considered going to a fashion design school there.

In January, Caliana returned from her Christmas break refreshed and ready to focus on an upcoming trampoline competition. She had passed all her mock O-level subjects and had taken a much-needed vacation. With a month to train, Caliana used all her spare time to practice. She knew that she had been neglectful and wanted her body to be primed and ready.

The trampoline had very strict rules. No one was allowed to be on it without four people on each side to spot. Thick foam floor mats had to surround the trampoline to cushion an accidental fall. Caliana often asked a couple of girls to help her open and set up the trampoline, as it was impossible for one person to do.

One afternoon in late January, Caliana pretended that she had a stomachache to get out of skiing in the mountains. She needed those five uninterrupted hours to practice her routines. A few friends helped her open the trampoline before they boarded the bus. A friend of hers with a broken arm wandered in and out of the gym, watching Caliana practice. Caliana stayed on the trampoline for over one hour without taking a break. When she needed to rest, she let her body simply bounce up and down, worried that if she stopped, she would be too sore to get back on. Her P.E. teacher had often warned the team that they should pace themselves and obey their body's exhaustion. Caliana's muscles were quivering, but she was used to that feeling and ignored it.

Her friend, sensing Caliana's exhaustion, told her to take a break. Caliana uttered "one more" from a parched mouth, and bolted upward for her double back somersault. It was a routine that required sufficient height and speed. Caliana had to tuck her legs tightly to her chest and propel her arms in circular motions to ensure a gravitational rotation.

Caliana shot up into the air and, in slow motion, watched her body lose total control. Her legs disobeyed her. She wasn't supposed to be looking at her toes, and they weren't supposed to be that close to the gym's ceiling. Caliana panicked as she realized that her body was frozen. She couldn't take her eyes off her legs, and in terror, she waited for her head to make contact with something.

Caliana landed on her feet on the wooden floor, a few inches away from the trampoline. There were loud cracking noises, like every bone in her body was breaking. She stood upright for a few seconds before crashing straight back on the floor, before her horrified friend. Caliana's head hit so hard that every nerve ending burst with shock painfully reverberating through her body. Disorientated, she believed that she was being severely electrocuted, and she stretched her palms on the wooden floor, hoping that the wood would de-electrify her. She had never imagined such pain. Mercifully, she passed out.

Caliana came to momentarily in the ambulance, screaming from the jarring pain as the ambulance went up a cobblestone road. The next time she regained consciousness, she was being lifted onto an X-ray table.

The following few days passed in a haze of drugged discomfort. The days blended in a surreal nightmare of disjointed, paralyzed fears. She was aware of an IV in each arm, grateful for the occasional oblivion from the pain. Doctors and nurses jabbed, pulled, and handled her. The only word she managed to croak was "pain" when the medications were wearing off.

A few days later, Caliana surfaced into some lucidity and wished she hadn't. Two doctors came in and removed the sheet at the end of her bed to test out the reflexes of her feet. Watching, Caliana realized that she couldn't feel anything, and she suddenly became aware that her legs were paralyzed. She opened her mouth to scream, but not a sound came out of her. Hyperventilating, she grabbed the sleeve of a nearby nurse. The doctor ordered another shot, and blissfully she sank into deep nothingness.

The next time Caliana was lucid enough, she tried to get information from the nurse. She was told that she would have to wait for the doctors to explain her condition. She spent that day in the most prolonged miserable silence, waiting, mortified at the implications of her crippled condition. A league of doctors finally came in to the room and surrounded Caliana's bed. They performed more reflex testing on her feet and legs. They argued amongst themselves. Caliana was unfamiliar with the medical terms they kept using. Finally, a doctor spoke to her in English and clinically began to summarize the medical consensus.

She was told that her tail bone, her coccyx, had been strongly impacted from the fall and had resulted in a fracture and a shift in its positioning. Considering that all her nerve ending to her legs went through her coccyx, he was not surprised that her legs were suffering the shock of adjustment. Apparently, her toes had wiggled a few times in response to their assessment of her reflexes. This doctor strongly believed that with the help of physiotherapy, chiropractics, and a magnetic belt that would activate signals to her spine, Caliana would be walking soon. The damage to her back was more serious. She had torn a few muscles in her back, thus the excruciating pain, and her spine was left with three pronounced curves in it. The doctor also believed that the chiropractor could help adjust her spine and, in time, lesson the severity of the curves.

Caliana was thrilled to hear that she could walk, and she shyly asked the doctors if she could participate in sports. She was told that she should expect to be in significant pain for a while and that she must never strain her back in any physical activity. The doctor wasn't sure if she would ever be able to sustain being pregnant, as it might be more than her weak back could take. Swimming was the only permissible activity, and highly encouraged. The doctor had planned an intensive in-hospital recovery program that included the use of water in her physiotherapy. He told Caliana that she should estimate four to six weeks' stay at the hospital, followed by frequent daily therapies.

Caliana thanked the doctors for their care and for all that they had done for her, and told them that she would be running soon. And she meant it in ways that she couldn't have ever imagined. If she were to continue existing, she would strive for utter independence. She had experienced a mind-altering awakening from her close call with paralysis, and it was a potent-enough dosage to encourage a new wave of resistance against crippling dependence.

Caliana realized the absence of a loving parent, someone who should have been present for that talk. Since her accident, the emotional implications of her parents' absence had awakened new layers of emotional pain and anger. Caliana hated feeling needy, but she was in desperate need of comfort. Despite all that she knew of her parents, she had still expected them to visit her, if for no other reason than to oblige societal convention. Who wouldn't visit their child in a hospital? Even if only for a minor procedure that required a single overnight hospital stay, parents should be with their children. Her parents traveled the world regularly on whims and yet hadn't bothered to stop by to check on her injuries. Caliana concluded two scenarios that could possibly justify their unbelievable cruelty. In her best-case scenario (and there, Caliana had to stretch her knowledge to include a generous dosage of undeserved humanity), they were unaware of the seriousness of her injury. The best-case scenario still included rage at the fact that it was absolutely inexcusable that her parents hadn't called, not once. The more realistic scenario stemmed from a clinical and detached observation of her parents' repeated callousness. Caliana strongly suspected that they had capitalized on the convenience of the accident happening in another country, and thus it was easy to hide from their world. No one would fault them their parental negligence.

The urge to whip out her credit card and pay the doctors at that instant was terrifyingly powerful. Caliana felt the magnitude of her indebtedness to them and was embarrassed by the aloneness that forced her to always assume an adult position. She asked the doctor how to go about making payment arrangements and was told that her father would be taking care of all the bills. Caliana was informed that her father had apparently sent a letter that gave them permission to treat her and had voluntarily added a substantial deposit. Caliana tasted the unmistakable bitter bile of betrayal.

Caliana focused on her daily routine. It was exhaustingly painful. She spent two hours every morning in a huge bathtub wired with various water pulses. She particularly loathed the two fifteen-minute cycles when the whole tub felt like intense needles pricking every pore in her body. She never complained but asked the technician to give her a warning when the "needle" cycle was about to begin. The water therapy was followed by excruciating work with the chiropractor, who cracked and snapped her spine. The pain had her gasping in tears. After lunch, a physical therapist came to her room and massaged and exercised her legs and lower back. Then her bed would be lowered to a flat position and a magnetic box attached to a Velcro belt would be adjusted on her coccyx. She would spend one and a half hours in a stationary position, waiting for the varying signals to strengthen her back and activate the nerves in her legs. Immediately after that, another physical therapist would wheel her to a recovery room, where Caliana practiced using her crutches, gradually learning to put some weight on her feet. Her bed was fitted with a thick wooden board under the slim mattress, and she had to sleep with her legs on a chair placed on top of her bed every night. Her knees formed a right angle with the chair, and a Velcro belt kept them in place. Caliana tolerated every discomfort, including the humiliation of being bathed and cared for. She was grateful that by her third week she was able to use the toilet instead of the bedpan, which had absolutely mortified her.

A few weeks into her stay at the hospital, Caliana came back from her walking exercise to find an Iranian senior student in her room. The nurse had decided that Caliana could use the company of a schoolmate and had put the girls together. Even though Farah's English was weak and heavily accented, Caliana was lonely for company and enjoyed Farah's vivacious personality. Farah had had a boil removed from her buttocks and had many hilarious stories about her vivid history with boils. She spent two days entertaining Caliana with her dramatic stories and wonderful self-deprecating humor. Before Farah was discharged, Caliana asked her if she could borrow the one book the girl had brought to the hospital. Farah gladly gave it to Caliana after a long recital about how much she had struggled in trying to read it, and that she couldn't even pronounce the title of the book and was glad to be rid of it. Having been deprived of reading, Caliana eagerly settled into reading Ayn Rand's *The Fountainhead*.

The book saved her. The main character, Roark, represented every version of her utopist hopes and dreams for perfection. He was a truly noble spirit who defied conformity and unapologetically dominated his soul's mission. Caliana experienced his journey, and her despondent spirits rose. For the first time ever, she felt her whole being powerfully engaged, felt a belief in herself. That she could identify with Roark's beauty empowered her to believe that she must have some of it in herself. His journey was attainable; he was an unwavering moral being surviving in a dysfunctional world. He gave her the strength to decide to join humanity and risk staying whole, uncorrupted by her surroundings. She hadn't thought it possible to be so powerfully impacted into feeling alive. Caliana lived and breathed Roark and didn't care when her stay at the hospital was extended by another two weeks. Roark was the rare fuel that kept her going. She had to believe in both of them. Unlike Roark, she had no idea what she wanted out of her life, but that only made her more determined to discover her true passion.

Caliana left the hospital in mid-March and spent less than four days at school before she left for Jordan on her spring break. Her classmates were frantically cramming for their O Levels, but Caliana hadn't opened a book in more than two months. Even though the headmistress had sent her schoolbooks to the hospital, Caliana's heart had been fully engrossed in Roark and she couldn't be bothered with studying. As she had already prepped herself for the mocks, she figured she would just catch up on the missed readings. Spring break was two weeks long, and she would use her meaningless family time in Jordan to catch up on her studies.

Caliana was slightly unnerved about visiting her parents. The reality of her parents' denial of her condition was frightening, but the fact that they had made arrangements for her travel meant that they were expecting her. The morning of her departure from Switzerland, Caliana received a phone call from her father. Caliana was bitterly disappointed in her father's utter denial. He acted as though he had spoken to her a week earlier and did not even remotely touch on any subject that could be linked to the past two months. He went through his monotonous list of redundant questions and instructions on her travel plans. Caliana listened with mounting resentment but steeled her pride against responding in anger. She monitored the conversation with heightened perception. She heard her father's cowardly scurry to fill in her silences with nervous nonsense. When it was her turn to speak, she gave monosyllabic responses and heard in his tense silence his readiness to cut off any unwanted utterance from her. She got off the phone amazed at what a few seconds of time could teach her. Her high tolerance for pain had been both physically and emotionally tested, and for once, Caliana could not imagine a worse case scenario.

* * *

Caliana's trip was exhausting. She had been met at the airport in Geneva by an attendant with a wheelchair and whisked to the plane. The doctors had made a thin wooden model of a chair to mold her back in place. It was restraining and uncomfortable, and she had to use it on every chair that she sat on. Caliana's back would stiffen every few minutes, and she would have to painfully readjust her position. By the time she landed in Jordan, she felt physically exhausted. The dreaded wheelchair now seemed like a comfort, and Caliana struggled on her crutches to follow the passengers off the plane, then realized there wasn't a wheelchair waiting. Luckily, she didn't have to identify her luggage, as it was the first to arrive on the belt. Caliana barely managed to point out her luggage to the porter. She was reeling in unfocused dizziness, petrified that she might collapse.

As soon as she walked out of the security doors, Caliana was shocked to find herself suddenly surrounded by a huge group of welcoming friends. Haya had called her mother to get the details of Caliana's flight and had informed a "few" friends. Caliana was never comfortable with the relative use of terms in Jordan. A small dinner rarely had fewer than twenty people, and the definition could accommodate as many as seventy. A small wedding (which rarely ever happened) had more than five hundred people. It was a tightly knit community of people who lived in each other's shadows. Caliana enjoyed this way of life only because it was limited to visits. She was always aware that she could never live in a place where she was so highly visible. Caliana generally disliked surprises, but despite her physical exhaustion, she felt grateful for the show of bombarding affection from her countless friends. Everyone kissed her and asked her about the crutches.

On autopilot, Caliana heard herself minimizing her trauma with only a shred of truth. She wished she had a cast and could claim a broken leg. The bitter truth choked her with embarrassment. It was unthinkable to expose her parents, though if she had had the energy, she might have been tempted to scream it out. In a small, gossipy society that prided itself on harsh intolerance to anyone who disrespected family, Caliana's truth was aborted. Her only shame was that her silence forced her to play along with her parents' hypocrisy. Not that anyone would believe her. They had all been duly charmed by her mother's brief appearances and her father's shy and endearing aloofness. Those who had fallen for her mother's well-woven prompts for compliments were rewarded with oozing charm and feigned interest. Even Haya was incapable of seeing through the phony charm. Caliana understood that it came from Haya's genuine inability to imagine evil in anyone. Haya simply assumed decency and love in everyone. A few times, Caliana had become frustrated listening to her mother chatting up Haya, who would unknowingly give innocent information about Caliana. The simplest information threatened

Caliana. She did not want her parents to know anything about her. Every bit of information gave them possible ammunition.

Caliana had to say something to her friends, and the simple truth sufficed: She had fallen off the trampoline and hurt her back. She was exhausted. They could not spend time together because it was her first night back and she had to be at home. She would see them the following day. An argument broke out amongst her friends regarding which car would drive her home. The family driver impatiently waited for a decision. He was petrified of being late for his boss, took her luggage, and urgently implored them to follow him. Caliana couldn't get out of joining her friends in one of their cars, and she told them that she would simply get into the very first car that pulled up. A hilarious gallant dash ensued. Haya was the only smart one who stood grinning beside Caliana.

By the time Haya and Caliana made it to the curve, there were screeches of tires and honking of horns racing toward them. Caliana loved her friends' wildness and laughed at the absurdity of their erratic driving. Sam, who was a particularly skilled driver, got to Caliana first by driving over the road divider and parking against the flow of traffic. A screaming policeman didn't faze him. Sam simply screamed back that he needed to "pick up a cripple!" Amidst the honking, cursing, and humorous remarks, Caliana collapsed into the front seat of Sam's car and burst out laughing. Her back was killing her, but the energetic commotion was typical and reminded her that she had stepped back into a familiar but bizarre universe.

Seven cars raced out of the airport. Every car and every passenger made a point to honk and wave past her furious family driver, who had his arm out of his car, frantically motioning them to slow down. Caliana knew the insanity of driving in a country that had not yet adjusted to the recent invasion of traffic lights. Lanes were nonexistent, and drivers estimated speed limits based on their own recklessness. Caliana had once asked her friends what the speed limit was, and they had cracked up laughing. Police were generally ignored, but in the rare case that a cop bothered to give chase, it usually became a thrilling game of testosterone and ego for all drivers. Caliana had been in a police chase the previous summer, in which both the cop and her friend had ended up slowing down only long enough to holler final destinations to end the chase. That her friend had beaten the cop by a few seconds earned him begrudging respect rather than a ticket. There had been an instant animated replay of their skilled maneuvers.

The drive to Caliana's house was an animated event, to say the least. By the time her friends dropped her home, Caliana had pushed her endurance past collapsing. She promised again to hang out with her friends the following morning. She could see her father pacing just outside the front door in obvious agitated discomfort at having to deal with unwanted people. Caliana awkwardly climbed the few steps leading up to the front door and turned around to smile and wave at the wild group of honking and hollering friends.

She quickly glanced at her father. Her smile froze. Her father wore a tight, hateful glower, and his whole body seemed ready to erupt in barely controlled rage. He entered the house and stood inside, impatiently holding the door, deliberately not looking at her. Caliana hobbled the last few steps, suddenly terrified.

Her father slammed the heavy metal door shut behind her. He quickly yanked her crutches from her and roughly gave them to the timid butler, ordering him to get rid of them. Her father marched off.

Caliana was staggered.

She stood leaning on the counter, mortified at the tears that had sprung to her eyes. The butler disappeared, and Caliana was left shaking at the door, holding onto the entrance table. The silence was heartbreaking. Caliana took a few deep breaths, swallowed the heaving of her tears, and summoned every ounce of pride and inner strength that she could muster. She slowly pressed her body to pace herself to her room. Her heart sank with each unfathomable deathly step, and time collapsed into relative frequencies of pain. She managed to focus on the visual of her bed as her lifeline. Caliana reached her room and buckled in agonizing physical shakes on her bed.

Her exhausted body longed for the release of deep slumber, but her mind demanded urgent satisfaction. She felt like a fraud who had pretended to be crippled to get sympathy and who had been shamefully exposed. Had she not been so active in her pain, she would have been almost ready to excuse her father's behavior and dismiss herself entirely. Her physical pain kept jarring her conscience to look at the horrific reality of what had just occurred, however, and her mind began to clear.

Throughout her life, she had tried to assuage her financial indebtedness by giving her father some leniency in her empathy. Her father had often used the phrase "I'm not a monster" as one of his redeeming qualities. Caliana realized that she had been protecting her father with justifications and excuses and targeting her mother as the primary villain. Now her father was revealed as a monster, and she was throbbing with the pain of his ugliness. Caliana had been unwilling to give up her slim hope for his redemption. She had needed to connect to him to be able to accept his financial generosity, had been resistant to all evidence that pointed to his true persona. She had mistakenly projected her own moral assumption on his generosity to include kindheartedness.

Her father lacked courage and, dominated by insecurities, she had often witnessed his easy acceptance of other people's convictions, which kept him in an acute paranoid state. In many ways, he was a more volatile and dangerous adversary than her mother; his dismal self-esteem made him a dangerous bully who could be irrationally swayed in any direction. Caliana unraveled the last emotional ties of empathy toward her father, knowing now that her parents were equally partnered. She became an orphan, only financed by a father.

Lying on her bed, Caliana thought of Roark, and just before she slipped into twelve hours of unconsciousness, it dawned on her how lucky and blessed she had been in having relied on only herself for guidance. Her parents had actually done her a huge favor by not raising her. They had spared her from being infected by their repugnance.

CHAPTER 6

CALIANA woke up the following morning resolved to correct her drastic misconceptions. Her boundaries had to be readjusted and tightened to seal her certainty of escape. When she had to spend any vacation time with her parents, she would never again spend more than one evening a week in their company, and that would only occur if they bothered to exert any pressure on her. Guilt-free, she would treat their home as she would a hotel. When forced to be in their company, she would passively glare at the ever-present television or read a book. She had the advantage, for they did not know her, and it would be relatively easy to continue to maintain a nonexistent relationship. She formed a plan, to calculate and curtail every moment, every nuance of language that had to be wasted in their presence. She would begin immediately.

Caliana called Haya and made arrangements to spend the next few days in a frenzy of activities that took her away from her house. That Caliana could barely walk and was in unbearable physical agony only strengthened her resolve to shield her vulnerability from her parents.

When Haya pulled up to Caliana's house, she was surprised to find Caliana dejectedly sitting on the pavement and waiting for her. Haya got out of her car and silently walked over to Caliana. Without a word spoken between them, Haya gently helped Caliana stand and shouldered her into the passenger seat. Haya's sympathy and delicate calm almost unraveled Caliana. Caliana's honesty was totally exposed in the stillness, yet she was incapable of saying a single word. She felt grateful for Haya's silence, for it gave her a few precious minutes to compose the reeling emotions that were about to explode in tears.

Within ten minutes, Haya pulled up in front of the house of their friend Rami. She turned off the engine and faced Caliana. "What happened to your crutches?" she quietly asked.

Caliana knew that Haya was giving her the opportunity to pour out her heart. Caliana took so long to answer, her truth disappeared into silence. Caliana averted her face and hoped that Haya would understand and forgive the necessary lie. "The doctor gave them to me only to help me in traveling. He wants me to practice walking without them." Caliana's heart throbbed loudly in her ears. In the tension that followed, she was sure that Haya heard all the lies.

"It's okay. You don't need them. We would all love to have you lean on us."

Haya slowly got out of the car, and Caliana choked up. She felt undeservedly honored and humbled by Haya's omnipotence. Even in Caliana's lie, Haya had unshakable faith and trust in her, managing to intrinsically understand a truth that was far beyond her.

In not divulging her dysfunctional relationship with her family, Caliana had often felt a degree of shame for lying by omission to Haya. She had gotten to spend a substantial amount of time at Haya's house over the past few years and had been privy to Haya's incredibly loving family dynamic. At first, Caliana had been absolutely shocked that Haya didn't alter her personality around her family. All of Caliana's friends reined in their characters around their parents in some degree of fear and formality. Haya was simply herself and was lovingly allowed to be. She had a sister, Lara, who was a year younger and her best friend, and also another younger brother and sister. They were all close in age and actually got along very well. Even when the siblings argued, their love and respect for each other was apparent.

All the members of Haya's family were naturally demonstrative in their affections and had fun being with each other. They often intimidated Caliana, and she quietly observed their interactions. At times, it seemed that they even forgot her presence. Haya tried making Caliana feel at home, but Caliana simply couldn't speak to Haya in this setting with the same openness as she did in private, no matter how wonderful Haya's family. Caliana had distinct boundaries on her personality and couldn't imagine blending her levels of trust, especially in a real familial dynamic. She managed the light banter and conversation that occurred in social settings, though her guard never faltered.

Caliana would never take such bliss for granted and was thrilled that Haya had such an enviable family. Haya's family was universes apart from hers, and Caliana used the drastic difference as an excuse to keep her darkness hidden by continuing her omissions. She understood that Haya's decency stemmed directly from her nurturing parents and believed that Haya could not be able to truly imagine a life lived without love. Caliana, who so longed to have Haya's blessings, and spent countless years imagining the possibility of belonging to a loving family, could barely wrap her mind around the implications of Haya's reality.

Caliana was especially vulnerable around Haya; she had let her trust disarm her into exposing more of herself than she had ever done with anyone else. She had to resist the temptation to reveal her truth, but her terror at the possible rejection that came with being really seen dissipated her temptation. It was inconceivable for Caliana to imagine trusting such safe, loving honesty. It required her to believe that she was truly worthy of being loved and entitled to be loved back. These were contradicting concepts, impossible to entertain. She had barely adjusted to receiving Haya's love and to believing that she had earned it. She lived with a deeply ingrained belief that full exposure would risk revealing that she was weird and unlovable. Caliana was too petrified to risk losing Haya's love.

They had pulled up in front of Rami's house. Besides Caliana's house, Rami's was the only house that also had an open-door policy, where everyone met freely. Rami was the wildest and most popular member of their group, and to Caliana, he represented the easy safety of her friends in Jordan. Rami had always been especially attentive to Caliana, and she knew he had a childish crush on her. She had delicately let it be known that she regarded her group of male friends platonically and that she was not interested in dating. Therefore, Caliana felt comfortable in Rami's house and relaxed enough in his company. He represented a collective whole: one essential piece that kept the puzzle intact.

Caliana was grateful for the unanimous support that her friends gave her over the next two weeks. Guided by Haya, her friends seemed to always be a step ahead of Caliana in predicting and fulfilling her needs. They eased the tension with humorous role-playing of indentured servants and challenged her to let them care for her. They all made huge efforts to curb and plan their activities to center around those that Caliana could join in, without making her feel their sacrifice.

Caliana had often enjoyed conversing with Dr. Habib Nouri, Rami's father, whom she referred to as *Ammo* Habib. Dr. Nouri was a renowned lawyer with an amazing photographic memory and was very well read. *Ammo* Habib made it explicitly clear that he thought Caliana was brilliant, and he would often tease her that she was wasting her time hanging around his son and his ignominious group. *Ammo* Habib loved imparting his wisdom, and Caliana was the only eager recipient who soaked up his knowledge. *The Seven Minutes* was also one of his favorite books, and from *Ammo* Habib, Caliana had learned to discuss the legal and moral implications of the book. He was an avid Somerset Maugham fan and tried to encourage Caliana to read Maugham's work. *Ammo* Habib revered Gibran Khalil Gibran and particularly loved quoting one specific passage from *The Prophet*. He always quoted the first passage from the section "On Children" in Arabic and would then translate it in English for Caliana's benefit, for she did not have a strong command of classical Arabic. *"Your children are not your children. They are the sons and daughters of Life's longing for itself."* Even though he quoted it with heartfelt passion and stirred Caliana's interest, Caliana was reluctant to read *The Prophet,* instead filing Gibran away as an author she would eventually investigate.

* * *

Caliana again returned to Jordan in June, excited that she had turned sixteen and graduated high school. She had resumed intensive therapies after her spring break, and her back was greatly improved, though there were still daily aches and pains and a general stiffness of motion. Caliana planned to enjoy her summer break before heading to London to begin studying fashion at college.

One afternoon, Caliana was hanging out at Rami's house alone. Her back had been acting up, and she had asked Rami and a few of their friends to leave her to take a nap while they ran some errands. She had just settled in to the couch when she heard the front door bang loudly. From the footsteps coming up the stairs, she realized that it was Rami's elder brother, Samir. Caliana didn't know him very well and hoped that he wouldn't see her in the small sitting room that was tucked near the four bedrooms. She heard some opening and closing of doors, and suddenly he was before her. His face reflected surprise and pleasure.

"Now I get why my poor brother was driving like a maniac out of here. Share with me your secret so I can get rid of him when I want to." He plopped himself at the end of the couch and grinned at her.

Caliana laughed, and batted her lashes. "A lady never gives away her charming secrets of seduction."

"God help him! Take it easy on him; he's still figuring out his head from his ass." Samir chuckled and slowly lit a cigar. "So. Tell me. Besides torturing my brother, where do you hail nowadays?"

"Let's see. Until a few minutes ago, I was really enjoying some peace and quiet…"

"She cuts to the core." He clutched his heart and let out a groan. "What the lady is missing is that I am trying to rescue her from her boredom."

She exaggerated a huge yawn. "According to the Talmud, 'the righteous promise little and perform much, the wicked promise much and perform very little.' Wake me up when your humor has caught up with your ego."

Caliana swelled at hearing Samir's boisterous laugher. Her own laugher bubbled out of her in powerful response. Samir's laugh was a vibration of a soul in ecstatic joy. His whole body quivered, unapologetically alive. Just to hear that laugh, Caliana started goading him and sparring with him. They spent an hour exchanging wit and a steady growing respect for each other.

Caliana was hooked. She craved Samir's peaceful spirit and wanted to experience her happiness through him. They forged an instant friendship through their mental sparring. Samir had an incredibly agile wit that kept her mentally challenged, yet carefree. Caliana had always appreciated humor but had rarely experienced herself as humorous. She became so absorbed in the intensity of her exchanges that her mind was forced to fully engage, and her truth spilled out unchecked. Caliana was able to match his mind in humor, and she shocked herself by feeling the absolute joy in the relief of exposing her unedited thoughts. It felt safe. That day, she was given a new nickname: Mighty Mouth.

Her instant connection with Samir created a platonic blending of sibling soulfulness. That summer was memorable for Caliana because of Samir's keen interest in taking her under his wing. Everywhere she went, Caliana ran into Samir and his ever-present groups of friends.

He had unfaltering love and respect for his father, but his friends were his chosen family, and he was fiercely loving and loyal to them. His nature could not be contained, and he was happiest when communicating with people. He loved the intimacy of any gathering.

Caliana was amazed by Samir; he exuded life in its magnificent glory while maintaining a gentle and most sensitive heart. Every time Samir saw Caliana in public, he made it a point to drag her into his jumble of loved ones. Initially, many of his friends ignored her, as she was at least three years younger and crossing a rigid boundary of age-mixing. Caliana snubbed them back and engaged Samir in many asides that were satirical social commentaries directed at his other friends.

Samir became the brother that she had never thought to imagine. It comforted Caliana to witness his mental energy. She felt as though she could see his mind at work, and his processing speed was brilliant. Until she had witnessed Samir's mind at work, she had always assumed that only she had a weird mind that sped so saliently between a few disjointed channels of clear thoughts. Caliana was so used to editing her thoughts that she had developed various inner dialogues that took off in tangential layers of distrust and cautious speculation. With Samir, she was able to directly focus on a free channel of communication.

CHAPTER 7

CALIANA breezed into her parents' apartment and delighted in its absolute silence. She was exhausted from five months of whirlwind courtship with London's nightlife. She kicked off her platform boots and struggled with the layers of sweaters and jackets she was wearing. She had an hour to get ready to go out but was tempted to cancel and spend the night reading. She would soak in a bath and then decide. She grabbed the mail that the housekeeper had left at the entrance and dashed into the bathroom to start her bath ritual.

Through the people she had met at college, she had discovered fantastic clubs, and a party that never ended. Certain clubs were popular on particular nights, and the crowds seemed to frequent the same places. After a short while, strangers turned to acquaintances. Caliana assumed that at some point she had been introduced to someone by someone and stopped trying to figure out everyone's connections to each other.

Her external attitude on the whole became less guarded. She allowed herself to become approachable and gave people more license in assuming that they knew her. She also discovered that most people were not interested or capable of really knowing each other yet spent exuberant amounts of time being physically together. It seemed that the initial meeting of two people required only a minimal application of basic exchanges before turning into quick friendships focused on engaging in the moment. Caliana began to relax and enjoy the easy predictability of socializing. Mixing with people was so much simpler than she had imagined and required very little of her. All she had to do was go out clubbing.

Caliana's thoughts dissolved with her slow emergence into the steaming water of her bath. She sighed and let the tranquility of the delicious heat penetrate the ever-present chill provided by the London winter. With her eyes closed, she used her hand to lazily search for the stereo remote and then hit the play button. The bathroom had a sur-round-sound stereo system; Caliana inhaled the luscious Spanish gui-tars and let them transform her. She knew that she should slow down her outings, but she was still enjoying the careless thrill of simply hav-ing fun. College was surprisingly easy, and she was therefore unable to use school as an excuse to curtail her nights out. Her days were filled with busy fun, fashion-related projects that required minimal studying.

Caliana was also magnetized by her newfound sexuality. She had never really considered her looks; her mother's reliance on beauty had sent Caliana to the opposite extreme. For her mother, beauty was the ultimate measure of a woman's worth, but Caliana hadn't measured her looks as a factor when her male friends asked to date her. She had assumed they liked her for her personality, humor, or some reflection of her mind, and she gently declined dating them. Strangers flirting with her had received curt dismissals. The few who had persisted and dared to push past her icy boundaries had received her controlled dis-dain. In Caliana's mind, the ultimate insult had been to be asked out based solely on her looks. She might have had a shred of respect for men had they at least attempted to first get to know her. An initial physical attraction had been a concept Caliana couldn't rationally jus-tify; it spoke of a deep-rooted depravity that she associated directly with her mother's superficiality.

In the past few months, however, Caliana had begun to feel flat-tered instead of angry when men appraised her looks. She wondered if getting her first period in August had altered her feelings. She didn't know any other female who had gotten her period at sixteen. Caliana's body had had its own agenda, had transformed her into a woman in what seemed like a blink of an eye. She had shot up from an average 5'3" skinny and sexless fifteen-year-old to a thin, sexually aware 5'7" sixteen-year-old woman. Then she had gotten her period. It was as though her body had been protecting her in innocent asexu-ality until she was ready to actively participate in the world.

Falling in love with Roark in *The Fountainhead* had emphasized the rare impossibility of real love to her; she was convinced that no one could match her romantic notions, for they were deeply imbedded in impossible standards. Sex, however, was an issue that she had been curious about and had known that she would eventually want to experience. The hormonal changes in her body seemed to agree. She was interested in her new ability to tolerate flirtation and at times even enjoyed flirting back. She was also curious to note some shyness and silliness on her part.

Caliana was determined to lose her virginity and wanted to experience the stirring illusion that cropped up frequently in the books she read. She felt compelled to glide through that doorway of aliveness. To tread past her curiosity meant that she had to take a leap into unguarded territory. She couldn't very well have sex if she let her primal urge to wither an admirer take over. Hormonally driven, she found it relatively easy to alter her mental perspective on superficiality to allow for sexual frivolity. Caliana couldn't perceive any possible harm in wanting to experience her sexuality. She had only to adjust to a lesser level of distrust that allowed men closer intimacy.

Caliana stretched her body and deeply inhaled the aromatic steam of the bath. It was decided. She would go out. Her recently budding sexuality affirmed that she was normal and needed to continue practicing her initiation into womanhood, into society. Looking into the mirror had become enjoyable to her, and Caliana appreciated the way clothes looked on her. The fact that she was immersed in studying fashion was helping her uncover her femininity, and the dynamic clothing helped her portray her unique and individual expression. Caliana was blossoming in the compliments that she received from many people.

She had also discovered that even though she hated alcohol, a glass of something loosened the edge of her initial caution. When she had first started clubbing, she had attempted to cover the absolutely nasty taste of alcohol with Coke or some very sweet juice but had still loathed it, yet the dulling reaction that alcohol prompted altered her tolerance to physical proximity to people. The anxiety knob turned down to accommodate crowds that would have otherwise unnerved her. Alcohol helped dim her rigidity and allowed her to physically get close enough to a man to be kissed.

Caliana contemplated Jayce. She had gone out on a few dates with him, seen him frequently at the clubs. He always made an effort to hang out with her and had even told some people that they were dating. He was very good-looking, and she hadn't minded sharing her first kiss—and a few afterward—with him. He wasn't Roark, and she had no illusions about falling in love, yet Jayce excited her on a level that was different and new. Caliana had mastered controlling many emotions, but her sense of weirdness had steadily floated into her psyche to keep her alienated. She rationalized that by having sex, she would barge through her oddity and attain the level of normalcy that would allow her to blend in with the world she planned to conquer.

Caliana's exposure to sexual morality was highly influenced by the disparity between the prohibited pre-marital sexual views of most Middle-Eastern cultures, and the sexual liberties that were practised in the West. She had often evaluated and scrutinized the paradoxecal regional views, and had concluded that sex was a choice that no one had the right to judge or interpret. Even when she had had no physical understanding of her sexuality, Caliana had believed the conservative Middle Eastern perspective on virginity and promiscuity to be illogical because it was rooted in religion. She had pretty much dismissed most conservative schools of thought that were derived or rooted in religion. She had investigated the monotheistic religions and concluded that none came close to pacifying her grand image of what God meant to her. Her belief in a higher being was that of unconditional love in its purest form, and purity could not be ingrained in fear-indoctrinated beliefs and ideas.

Initially, Caliana felt vulnerable lowering her defenses to include sexual intimacy. She debated all the societal conventions on sexuality and cautioned herself against conforming to a principle that did not apply to her logic. She rationalized that being compliant to her body's curiosity was relatively safe in that she had the power of choice and control. She realized that she needed to learn from her own experience and figure out her own authority within her sexual terrain. Overcoming her ingrained aversion to physical intimacy required her to control her anxiety. Alcohol enabled her to desensitize her reservations and became her tool in lowering her guard.

Caliana stood back from the mirror and observed her reflection. She felt proud that she was finally able to apply her eyeliner in one attempt. She packed her purse with the makeup that she would need for touch-ups, and she took a few minutes to tidy up the bathroom. She saw the mail still unattended and glanced at her watch. She had five minutes, so she decided to go into the sitting room, smoke a cigarette, and go through the mail. It was mostly bills. One envelop had only her name typed on it. Caliana opened it and started reading the short typed letter. She smiled at the first few lines as she realized that it was written by a secret admirer. The last line wiped her smile. Slight prickles ran down the back of her neck. As she glanced at the envelope, her heart raced with anxiety at the implication of the absence of a stamp.

He knew where she lived.

Someone had dropped the letter through the mail slot at the door. Caliana ran through the logistics of the person being seen. Her parents' flat was on the ground floor of the building, and the tiny cubical where the building's porter sat was halfway between the main entrance and her door. She had always been grateful that the setup within the cubicle was such that the porter had his back facing the hallway and had prevented her needing to chitchat with him every time she entered or exited the building. She also knew that the porter had a mirror angled to face the main entrance door and would often leave his desk to sign for deliveries or escort various workmen to their destinations. The main entrance door was always unlocked on weekdays during the day and closed in the evenings and on weekends. During those times, a key was needed, or guests were buzzed into the building through the intercom system. Caliana crumpled the letter and resolved to question the porter in the morning.

Once Caliana dismissed the letter, she had an incredible night. She ended up spending most her time dancing, flirting, and making out with Jayce. Dancing left her invigorated. By dancing, she found serenity amongst people, and she could blend into a crowd without her ever-present mental anxiety. She learned to relax and lose herself in the music and her body's synchronized response. Sometimes she even challenged herself to close her eyes while dancing to feel the unreserved elation of being fearless. She realized that fear was the one emotion that had kept her from feeling alive, and she became even more determined to fight against it.

Caliana made an important decision that night. Jayce would be the one she would have sex with. She felt comfortable enough with him and had just experienced a higher level of making out. She figured that her birthday was less than three months away and that she would mark her seventeenth birthday with the loss of her virginity.

Caliana and Jayce made plans to spend the following night together going to dinner and a movie.

Caliana began dating Jayce.

A week later while sorting through the mail, Caliana found another envelope with her name typed on it. She cursed herself for her stupidity in not following up with the porter as she had planned. It had been an exceptionally busy week. Now that Jayce and she were a confirmed couple, Caliana experienced literally no downtime. The few minutes that she could snatch by herself, she devoted to reading. Caliana was tempted to discard the letter without reading it. She deliberated over the envelope for a few minutes and then ripped it open.

Ripples of fear washed over her as she read on. The letter contained a detailed description of her outfit, behavior, and conduct at a club two nights earlier. There was no mistaking the fact that she had turned this admirer on. He used sexually descriptive language to portray the effects that she had had on his body. Caliana inhaled a breath that resonated with shameful mortification. She fluctuated between anger at her sultry actions that had unknowingly induced an unwanted reaction, and anger at the stranger who dared to frighten her. Caliana ripped the letter to shreds and resolved that she would not allow this man to ruin her existence.

Her resolve was hard to maintain. She found herself bristling in fearful awareness everywhere she went. At the oddest moments she would imagine someone was watching her, and her heart would clench in fear. She kept telling herself that she was irrationally paranoid and kept reverting to using her anger to subdue her fear. Mostly, she was angry at herself for feeling afraid. In Caliana's world, fear was a concept that reflected her weakness and allowed people to have possible power and control over her. That someone could scare her was unacceptable, and that the person was invisible was disturbingly frightening.

By the time she received the third letter, the full impact of being stalked permeated Caliana's defenses. Enraged, Caliana stormed out of her apartment and stood shaking in the empty hallway. She was poised to kill, and images of her violence clouded her vision. She yearned for the satisfaction of pounding her stalker to a bloody pulp. She heard her harsh heaving of air in the silent corridor and shuddered in agonizing misery.

Shaken by her loss of control, Caliana understood the full extent of her rage. A part of her was thrilled at knowing that she was capable of killing and that she would never be a helpless victim. She would die fighting. She would never allow someone to threaten her. In raging defiance, she swore that she would exterminate her stalker. Affronted on so many levels, she steeled herself for a deadly war. Her rage would protect her; it infused her body with heat and sustained her core being. She slammed the door and leaned against it, breathing heavily.

When Caliana had moved into her parents' apartment, her father had had the wooden door reinforced with steel and had added multiple locks. He had also ensured that every window in the apartment had steel bars to prevent against a break-in. Caliana had always ignored the prison-like feel of the apartment and disregarded issues of safety. Angrily, she now turned every lock, hated knowing that her stalker was getting to her.

She jumped when the phone rang.

Jayce was on the phone. Caliana had forgotten that she had invited him over for a rare night of shared studying. She contemplated canceling but decided that his presence might be the welcomed distraction she needed. She asked him to give her an hour to take a bath, and he offered to bring some dinner over. When the doorbell rang an hour later, Caliana was still unsettled. She had often pressed the button that allowed expected guests to push the entrance door without lifting the receiver to check their identity. That night, Caliana made sure that she heard Jayce's voice before she buzzed him in and then glanced through the peephole of the door—an action she had never before thought to undertake. She heard Jayce's laugh as he teased her about the number of locks on the door. Caliana felt embarrassed by the amount of time it took her to unlock them all.

"Good God. How many locks do you have?"

"Seven." Caliana attempted a smile. She was feeling self-conscious and irritated at him for reminding her of her fear. "I'm starving. Do you mind if we eat right now?"

Caliana's stomach was knotted and she couldn't imagine eating, but she needed the distraction of moving and changing the subject. Jayce followed her to the kitchen and helped her bring the dishes to the sitting room. They casually chatted as they set up on the coffee table, both opting to sit on the floor. Caliana picked on her food and tried to maintain a carefree attitude.

"Are you okay? You seem tense tonight."

Caliana was taken aback at the directness of the question and the concerned look on Jayce's face.

"It's nothing. I'm just pissed off at some idiot that's bugging me." Caliana hadn't thought to discuss the letters with anyone. Seeing Jayce's confused look, she clarified. "Someone has been sending me some disturbing letters. I guess he's some psycho 'admirer,'" she fumed.

"An admirer. Hmm. Should I be jealous?" Jayce gave her a teasing, flirtatious grin.

Caliana fought the strong urge to slap the grin off his face. She regretted her impulsivity in responding to him and giving him any information. Going on autopilot and moved the conversation to another subject.

Internally, she focused on processing her disappointment at Jayce's shallowness and inability to have followed through with his original instinct. She knew that she had hidden her fear, but he had clearly dismissed her expressed anger. She tried rationalizing her own unfair anger at him by justifying that he couldn't possibly know what she was feeling. She replayed what she had told him and realized that if she took away the angry tone, she hadn't really shared much with him. She had even used the word bugging, which could simply reflect an irritation. She had not shared the contents of the letters or described her repulsion and fear. At the most, then, Jayce had simply made an inappropriate or careless comment. Caliana went as far as assuming that he might have felt nervous by her anger, and wanted to smooth the tension with a playful comment. Guilt quickly snapped her out of her distrustful, seething anger, and she offered to clear the dishes and make coffee.

Caliana was determined not to harbor any ill feelings toward Jayce. She began calming down and attributing her uncharitable thoughts to her anxiety from the letters. She tried to really focus on finding Jayce interesting. She managed to give him another half an hour and then insisted that she needed to study. Caliana settled back on the floor, and Jayce sat a few feet away from her on her left.

She tried to focus on her book and take some notes, but her mind kept replaying the letters and seeing the patterns. Her admirer had grown bolder with each letter. He was clearly letting her know that he had been physically close to her. He could be anyone. He had signed off on all three letters with the same sentence. And even though Caliana couldn't quite decipher its meaning, she knew it represented an ominous threat. Caliana visualized her brain scattering around like a frantic mouse trapped in an intricate maze, trying to get out. She wanted to know her enemy so she could prepare for him. The only clue he had given her was that he was a persistent male who had targeted her to act out his psychosis. She sensed that he must derive pleasure from scaring her. She would not let him win; she would not show her fear.

Caliana was so caught up in her thoughts that she had forgotten Jayce. She quickly glanced up and caught him staring at her.

Caliana froze. In that split second, her gut slammed her with the certainty that Jayce was the stalker.

"Caliana, I want you to know that I love being with you... I think I'm becoming ... addicted to you." He leaned over and, ever so gently, touched her face.

Caliana remained frozen. She felt suspended in a surreal moment. Light-headed, all thoughts evaporated, replaced by a feeling of disconnectedness, as if she were suddenly not there anymore.

"I'm sorry," Caliana stuttered, scrambling to her feet. "I've had such a long day, and I need to crash. Do you mind if we stop studying? I really need to go to bed!" Caliana was already at the door, holding it wide open.

"There's nothing to be sorry about." Jayce smiled at her and gathered his things. "I'm just glad that we could spend some time together tonight."

"Thanks for dinner." Caliana forced a smile as she closed the door behind him. Through the peephole, she watched him leave, exhaling only when the entrance door closed after him.

Bewildered, she willed herself to walk back to the sitting room. She felt as though she had gotten a momentary glimpse into a string of sinister thoughts without the capability of seeing them through to a conclusion. She was frustrated that she couldn't remember her exact thoughts.

A few hours earlier, she had experienced the certainty of rage that would enable her to murder her enemy. When confronted with Jayce—and the certainty that he was her stalker—she had frozen. She had failed a crucial test. The doubts in her ability wilted in the face of realizing that she was not that certain that her rage would save her. Images of Jayce striking her with a dagger flashed in her replay of that suspended moment. Freezing in fear, even for a split second, could cost her life. When the crucial moment came, Caliana had to be able to completely control her fear, keep her rage on the surface, and execute a deadly reaction.

Her lower back started having spasms, and she absentmindedly massaged it. She lay down on the couch and rubbed her forehead. She felt the beginnings of a splitting headache, and uselessly, she wished her brain would relieve her, and just stop. Caliana knew herself well enough to know that she was in for an exhausting mental marathon.

She resented the fact that she was forced to engage in defending herself in a war that she hadn't wanted any part of, yet she accepted that she had no choice; she had been vigilantly preparing for a monstrous act her whole existence.

She fervently hoped that she could endure his sick game. Giving in to the temptation to stay home and become an agoraphobe would be to succumb to cowardice. This was not the time to slow down her outings. If anything, she would face his possibility at every moment and practice overcoming her terror by developing resilience and control. She simply could not afford to be paralyzed.

Caliana felt somewhat better at having made a determined plan. She felt guilty at letting her fear and thoughts project onto Jayce. She rationalized that she had been so caught up with her morbid thoughts that she had unfairly projected her demons onto him, simply because he had been present. She would have to work on keeping her feelings toward her stalker from affecting her relationship with Jayce. She had decided to have sex with Jayce on her birthday; it would be unacceptable to alter her plans out of fear.

"Great! He tells me he likes me, and I have him out the door in less than thirty seconds!"

Caliana dreamt. Her beautiful, serene island had the pristine beauty that could only be organically landscaped by divinity. She wandered the deserted white sands in bittersweet sadness, knowing that she was filled with the glorious bounty of God, but being alone, she was incapable of fully experiencing herself in it. She existed in her eternal imagination, and she was forever in the process of discovering her island.

She stopped in front of a weeping willow to admire its grace. The moonlight gave the willow's yellow sweeping branches a golden hue and surrounded it with effervescent light. The tree's soft branches swayed to the gentle music of the sea, beckoning her. Transfixed, Caliana slowly circled the willow, her hand gliding through and caressing its silky leaves. On completing her loop, she saw a dimmed light through a swaying passage of tall feathery stalks.

She walked away from the willow toward the path that seemed to sway open a step ahead of her and gently close behind her, keeping her in a suspended, feathery womb. Her heart raced with expectation, for she was in complete trust that her soul was guiding her forward. The path ended at a narrow inlet connecting her island to a small cove.

Waiting for her there was her angel, her longed-for prayer. With certainty, she glided toward her destiny, knowing that her soul mate would embrace her in loving validation. Caliana stood before her angel, and they marveled in each other's souls, their beauty reflected. A lifetime of Caliana's unspoken pain poured out, and Caliana's heart absorbed the loving acceptance of being seen and acknowledged. She finally experienced the safe elation of trust and comprehended the healthy equilibrium that could transmute from it.

Caliana's lashes fluttered open. She lay in the dark, blissfully relishing her dream over and over. Her dream fulfilled the glory of her spirituality, and sorrowfully, she realized that her impossible vision vastly contradicted her reality.

* * *

Even though Caliana felt positive that her stalker wanted the attack to happen in person, she inwardly shriveled when she stepped out of her apartment. She imagined being targeted through the telescope of his high-powered rifle and felt his itch to pull the trigger. At times she stood boldly and anticipated the relief of a bullet shattering her mind apart, ending his hatefulness.

Her distorted sense of time had kicked into high gear and was exasperated by the loaded tension of every moment. Restless energy spilled from her pores and prevented her from relaxing. When she was at home, she felt the restless suffocation of her captivity and a gnawing need to claw her way to freedom. When she was out in the world, she wanted to burrow into the safety of her cage and never leave. She was incapable of relaxing in any place. Sleep deprived, Caliana felt her physical exhaustion sapping her endurance. The first clear thought of each day was a muted prayer for a confrontation, followed by an acceptance of her death.

Caliana defiantly suffered every terrifying day by forcing herself to resume her daily activities. Her reality blended into an acute state of hovering blindly in a paranoid surreal nightmare. In a flash, she could be dead. Alone in a vortex of rage and fear, she struggled to control her emotions. Her rage fueled her simmering thoughts into boiling readiness. The intensity of every thought led to a sense of horror; she was trapped in an exhaustingly intimate relationship with evil. He occupied every inhaled breath and in turn became her obsession.

With people, Caliana was forced to soberly act out the carefree image that she had cultivated. She could not afford to alter their perception of her, for he existed in their conjoined world. She sensed him revising his view of her, and any change might alert him to smell her fear.

A part of Caliana felt as though she were paying for the five months of careless, somewhat uninhibited, fun she had experienced. She had arrogantly assumed that she was capable of dealing with the world and had ended up attracting a sick monster. She felt exposed and violated that she hadn't seen it coming.

Caliana was convinced that the explicit sexual innuendos in the stalker's letters were meant to only unnerve her and that his ultimate intent was to murder her. That he probably planned to rape her first did not faze her. All she wanted was the ability to tolerate all intensities of the physical pain that he would inflict on her so she could ultimately kill him. She practiced visualizing her body in every conceivable stage of battered and near-dead state. The worst-case scenario would be for her to die in vain.

* * *

The letters kept arriving. Every week there was at least one letter, sometimes two. Caliana pored over them, dissecting every bit of information, in a sense creating a criminal profile of the monster in her aggravated imagination. Her mind, her single most useful tool to her survival, became a tangled, panicked entity dominated by horrifying scenarios. In her attempt to protect herself from her stalker, she had induced relentless anxiety. She was bound and chained in her preparation of her never-ending nightmare, and angrily, she stalked him back. She had to see it coming.

Caliana's entire existence had been based on her certainty in her abilities; she had gotten through life's traumatic events with invisible fists raised in protective readiness, guarding against her emotions. She had achieved an anesthetized state of being that allowed her to operate on an ethically sound journey in a world that had reflected a perpetual necessity for vigilance.

She had also survived by teaching herself to balance her defensiveness with her solitude. Before her monster had become real, Caliana had welcomed the soothing comfort of her aloneness. Her solitude had never been a mere concept; it had always signified a primitive immersion into a divine retreat from a world she viewed as flawed. She could forget the world entirely in this way, and find a measure of peace.

The pressure of living in unvarying heightened anxiety took a heavy toll, drowning her spirit, yet all she seemed capable of doing was slowing her spiral into oblivion. She had to remain conscious, keep swimming against the riptide sucking her under. Her horizon was devoid of the possibility of rescue, and her weary body wanted to succumb to the futility of resistance. She could no longer replenish herself in the comfort of floating peacefully in her isolation, for her solitude was penetrated; evil lived within her. Caliana felt inundated by it.

The stalker's fantasy felt sickeningly frightening. There was an arrogant assumption that Caliana would joyfully engage in his love-making. He assumed a blatant disregard to any semblance of a rational response from her, magnifying his insanity. The game was being played out by a deranged, disassociated mind who arrogantly expected her loving submission.

Very slowly, you will take off your skirt.

You will let me see your garter belt, and very slowly, slide the skirt down to your knees.

You *are naked underneath your skirt.*

Slowly, you will open your legs …

Disjointed sentences, plucked from a hypnotic mantra that permeated his doctrine, rendered her as a powerless sexual puppet at the mercy of his controlled strings.

Caliana dove beyond his mind and submerged herself in his fantasies. In her attempt to test her resilience to his madness, she practiced picturing herself as he saw her: a sex-crazed victim who enjoyed zombie-like surrender.

* * *

One Saturday morning, two weeks before her seventeenth birthday, she found a familiar envelop already waiting for her. She snatched it unopened and angrily picked up the phone and dialed the police. As she was being transferred within Scotland Yard to a detective, Caliana regretted her impulse. She was a split second away from hanging up when a man's voice came on the line. A sense of manners kept her hesitant, and she stayed on the phone long enough to begrudgingly give a brief report on the stalking. She was told that a detective would be arriving at her house shortly.

Caliana paced and fretted. She wished she could erase the past few minutes, and short of sounding insane and calling back to tell them she had been lying, she couldn't think of a reason that was strong enough to cancel. She was still debating a retraction when the doorbell rang forty-five minutes later. Caliana nervously let the two detectives in and silently cursed her stupidity. They declined her offer for refreshments and sat down.

The female detective established Caliana's name and address ownership, and paraphrased their reason for the investigation. Caliana stalled the preliminary chat as far as she could, until the male detective started his line of questioning.

"When did you first notice that you were being followed?" he inquired.

"About four months. Since January." Caliana nervously lit a cigarette.

"Why didn't you report it earlier?" he continued.

"I ... I didn't think it was important." Caliana felt like an idiot. She wanted to tell him that she still didn't want to report it and just wanted them gone!

"You told the officer on the phone that a man has been stalking you. Would you be able to give us a description of him?" he asked.

"I don't know what he looks like," Caliana responded. She sensed that something was going horribly wrong.

"So you have made no physical contact with him? As in, he didn't try to talk to you, touch you, block your way?" asked the female officer.

Caliana started picturing their definition of a stalker. In her mind, theirs was a blessing compared to the anonymity of her fear. "No. I told you I don't have a clue about his looks."

"Then, you weren't followed." The male officer clarified.

"No."

"Did you receive phone calls from him?" he persisted.

"No."

"So, exactly how are you being stalked?" asked the female detective.

"He's written me some letters." Caliana hated that it sounded so intimate when she said it.

"Do you have the letters?" asked the male.

"Here." Caliana handed over the unopened letter, and cringed at what she imagined they must be thinking.

"When did you receive this letter?" he continued as he opened it.

"Sometime this morning. Or it could have been sometime last night. I found it about an hour ago." Caliana hoped that that would satisfy them regarding the reason why she hadn't opened it.

"Where did you find this letter?" he persisted.

"He dropped it through the mail slot at the door. He knows where I live."

The male detective read the letter silently. Caliana watched his passive face and regretted that in exposing the letter she had rashly opened Pandora's box. She should have lied and told them that she had vaguely seen a man following her, given them some lame, inconclusive details.

When he had finished reading the letter, the male detective passed it to his partner and asked, "You said he had written other letters. Can I take a look at them?"

"I don't have them. I threw them out." The lie slipped out easily. Caliana's defensive instinct was fully active. The detective stared at her. Caliana hoped that he was simply waiting for his partner to finish reading.

The phone rang, and Caliana gratefully excused herself. She was relieved that Jayce was on the phone.

"I can't talk right now. Can I call you in a bit?" Caliana whispered.

"Are you okay?" Jayce asked.

"I'm fine. I just have to speak to the police for a few minutes." Caliana cursed herself for blurting out the wrong information.

"The police! Did you call the police?"

He sounded panicked, and Caliana was too flustered to think of what to tell him.

"I'm coming over." Jayce hung up before she had a chance to register or respond to him. She walked back into the silent sitting room with only one alarming thought. She had to get rid of them in about ten minutes, before Jayce arrived. She had already regretted involving two people, who already probably thought she was a spoiled and paranoid rich kid spicing up her Saturday morning.

"Was there anything threatening in the letters that you tore up?" asked the female.

The assumption was that they had obviously not found anything threatening in the one they had just read. Even though Caliana wanted the detectives out, she also felt irrational anger at being totally dismissed. Maybe they would believe her when they found her dead some day soon, she thought.

"Yes there was. Maybe not directly threatening, but he was making a lot of sexual threats about what he would do to me." Caliana wanted to slap herself. She felt as though she had no control over her mouth. She was making it worse. What the hell was she doing? In one breath she was lying and trying to get them to leave her alone, and in the next she was affronted that they didn't seem to be concerned enough about her.

"What kinds of sexual threats?" the female inquired.

"You know." Caliana felt suddenly shy and uncomfortable. Sex was not a topic she had ever discussed. The way they were looking at her affirmed that they expected her to elaborate.

"Things like how he wants to have sex with me. You know, very graphic details. And he knows where I live!" That was the extent of her idea of giving someone a lot of details. She refused to quote her stalker.

"Can you read this letter and tell us if it is typical of the letters that you have received?" The male detective handed her the letter.

Caliana skimmed over the paragraph and cringed in shame. In this particular letter he was only describing how beautiful she had looked at a party and how sexy he thought she was. He used the same signature line.

"That's him," she told them.

"Would you say that this letter is typical of the letters that you had received?" the male detective repeated.

Caliana wanted to scream out her fears and frustrations. She felt petrified that she was being interrogated and that she had lied to them. Each question had disconnected her further from herself. Instead, she dejectedly managed to nod her affirmation.

"So you have received two or three letters from this person in about four months. Is that correct?" The female asked with her pen poised over the notebook. Caliana found it easier to lie than to elaborate on the truth, so she nodded again. The female took a few notes.

The male detective asked a few more specific questions regarding the use of certain words in the letters. Had the person used the word rape or any violent word that might have given her reason to suspect that she might be in danger?

ABORTED AT BIRTH

Caliana disconnected. On autopilot, she responded "no" to all his questions. She tried to resist glancing at her watch. The detective informed her that that particular letter did not warrant an investigation, as it did not qualify as dangerous evidence of someone meaning her harm, then he began a lecture on safety measures.

"Do you mind if we look around the apartment?"

"Sure. But why?" At that point, she wondered why they even bothered to waste another second on her. Before any of them could respond, the buzzer at the entrance door signaled the arrival of Jayce. Caliana let him in and stood awkwardly, waiting for him to get to her front door. Her mind was dazed from exhaustion, and she felt she had no control on any one thought. She somehow managed to introduce Jayce as a friend to the detectives.

"What's going on? Is everything okay?" Jayce looked between her and the detectives, waiting for an answer.

In the tense silence that followed, Caliana wondered if the police were being tactful or simply waiting to see her lie.

She inhaled deeply, questioning her sanity. She pictured herself exploding in combustion of released pressure and relished the fleeting glimpse of her splattered corpse. Dead. Caliana felt herself swell at her certainty that at that moment she understood that she did not fear death. It was life that was horrifically unbearable.

There were times when Caliana had to look at the letters to remind herself that a monster, other than her mind, actually existed, that, irrespective of her heightened paranoia that had twisted her spirit, there was still an actual viable predator who was genuinely targeting her.

"I just overreacted to a letter that I received. Remember Jayce, I told you a while back that someone had sent me a disturbing letter?" Caliana hoped she was pacifying everyone with her response. She just wanted the charade to end. "I need to show the detectives the apartment. Do you mind waiting for me in the sitting room?"

"Okay."

Caliana saw the look of baffled frustration on his face. She didn't mind that she had manipulated the situation to exclude him.

She marched ahead of the detectives and showed them each room. The female detective asked her about the security system, and Caliana admitted that she didn't know how to use it. She caught a glance between the detectives.

She reprimanded herself for not thinking things through before calling the police. How could she explain that when she had attempted to ask her father how to set the system, and he had gone off on a tangent of how sensitive and complicated it was, and that she was never to touch it. They must have concluded that she couldn't be that scared if she hadn't bothered to learn how to operate it. She was handing them evidence to support her irrationality. They found the two red emergency police buttons on each side of her parents' king-sized bed. One of the officers asked her if she knew what they were, and she assured him that she knew to press one only for dire emergency.

She walked the detectives out and stood with them in the corridor.

"Your house is very well secured. I would recommend that you contact the alarm company and have them give you a tutorial in its use. I think it will help you feel safer. You have bars on every window, and your front door is well fortified. I'm sure it's nothing, but it doesn't hurt to be extra alert for the next few days," concluded the male detective.

"And if you receive more letters, don't tear them up. Call us." The female officer handed Caliana a card.

Caliana imagined that she saw the woman give her a look of pure pity. She felt confused and overwhelmed by the last hour. She thanked the officers for coming.

Back in her apartment, she collapsed on the couch and watched Jayce frantically pacing. He was literally firing questions at her, and she found it hard to focus on any one of them.

"Caliana, what's wrong with you? Can you tell me what the hell is going on?"

Caliana sighed. She felt guilty for worrying him, at the same time resentful of his unwanted presence. She didn't have the energy to fabricate any version of the truth. She just needed to be left alone to sort out her jumbled thoughts. There was also the trap of this new obligation: She was his girlfriend and he had the right to question her. Didn't he?

"Like I said, I overreacted. I just got angry at a stupid harmless letter, and I called the police." Her eyes had wandered over to where she had left the letter on the coffee table. She suspected that Jayce must have read it, as he had had ample time on his own while she was inside with the police. "Read it if you like. It's right there." She pointed to it.

Jayce picked up the letter and quietly read it. Caliana couldn't shake her suspicion that he had read it and was doing a good job pretending he hadn't.

She cursed herself for becoming a paranoid wreck. In the past two months, she had suspected everyone of everything and had lost perspective on what was actually occurring versus what she imagined was happening. She had even questioned her wonderful housekeeper under the suspicion that someone might be paying the housekeeper to bring in the letters, as she had the keys to the apartment. Everyone had become a potential villain; she almost couldn't help it.

"Okay. Did the police take you seriously? What did they say?" Jayce's frustration annoyed her.

"Look, it's really none of your business. I didn't ask you to come over!" Caliana snapped. She felt total remorse when Jayce blanched at her tone.

She continued before he could respond. "I'm sorry, I appreciate your coming. I'm just feeling embarrassed that I made such a huge mistake in calling the police. Don't worry; it will never happen again. They are probably laughing at me right now!" Caliana lit a cigarette and clammed down on her anger. She couldn't understand why she fluctuated between affronted rage, uncertainty, and shame.

Jayce sat next to her on the couch and tried to hold her. Rigidly, she allowed him to briefly hug her. Caliana started feeling guilty and compelled to give him information. She abbreviated her irrational fears into an extremely watered-down version of the truth.

"Why didn't you tell me before? I'm disappointed .... I could have helped you. I want to share your fears with you. I love you. You know that, right?"

It was the first time that Jayce had told her he loved her. Caliana stared at him and almost lied and told him that she loved him too. She felt the magnitude of her shame in not sharing anything of significance with him, yet he loved her. He seemed genuine, which only made Caliana feel more guilty and undeserving.

Caliana nodded gratefully. "I'm sorry. I should have." She then took a deep breath and told him that she needed to take a shower and go meet some friends. The "friends" part was a lie, but she needed her space to process what had occurred. Caliana knew that the past hour reflected a disastrous loss of control, and she needed to sort through her irregularity.

Reluctantly, Jayce got up to leave. He offered to wait for her and drop her off. He even suggested that she should cancel and let him take care of her.

"Oh for God's sake, I'm okay!" she snapped. She hated anyone seeing her in any vulnerability, and she hated her guilt that had prompted her to give Jayce any information. "Can we please just forget about it? It's not important." Caliana could have sworn that she felt hate coming out of Jayce's eyes. She gave herself a mental shake and proceeded to the door before she felt another twinge of guilt and blurted out another word.

Caliana locked the door after Jayce. In a daze, she went to the bathroom, stripped, and stood under the hot water in the shower. She didn't have the energy to even reach for the soap, let alone follow the process of washing her hair.

She felt completely drained and could only focus on the sharp tingles on her scalp as the powerful water slammed onto her head. Caliana had no idea how long she stood there. At some point, she turned the water off, wrapped a huge towel around herself, and crawled into bed. Her mind was mercifully empty. Just before she fell asleep, one question popped into her head. *Why would Jayce want to share her fears?*

* * *

When Caliana had her first full-blown panic attack, she knew that she was fighting a losing battle. A week after the fiasco with the police, she dragged herself to go clubbing with Jayce.

Caliana's senses were heightened and overstimulated. She cringed from the disco lights and the loud sounds. In the past few weeks, every time she had entered a club, she had felt she was fighting her descent into claustrophobic anxiety.

Caliana felt marginally safer when she was with Jayce, certain that her stalker would not approach her then. She resented the part of her that wanted to cling to Jayce when he walked away from her. This was a dependence that was absolutely unfamiliar to her. A few times she had felt the temptation to blurt out her fears to him, but she censored them with the same voracity that she used to stifle her fantasies of fleeing the country.

On that particular night, Caliana entered the club in an exhausted stupor and didn't know how she would muster the required energy to maintain her vigilance. She tried to appear nonchalant as she targeted a corner. She had become an expert at surveying every room and situating herself in the most protective position. A wall guarded her back so she did not have to stress about not seeing something coming from behind her. Caliana was grateful for the small space that she found, and for the noise that prevented conversation. She plastered a look of enjoyment on her face, remembering to vary her expression every few minutes.

Jayce went to get them drinks, and Caliana tried to gulp down air without seeming to. She tried to still the panic of her images of being buried alive with all these people, crowding for oxygen.

That she had actually enjoyed these smoky, loud, and crowded clubs seemed repulsively alien to her now. Flashes of those fearless days mocked her. Maybe she had hit normalcy for a few months, but she had allowed terror to throw her into her worst paranoia. Her thoughts created a panicked swirl of insecurities. The fact that she was ready to jump out of her skin and run to her isolated island (now fortified with landmines on the perimeter) was a crude reminder of her weakness. She knew that ultimately, her fear controlled her and had led her to a new level of depravity. She saw how her choices had dissipated in the face of her loss of control. She had been incapable of ignoring the strings that had jerked her around. She was under her stalker's control, and her will was draining her in the fight to maintain her sanity. This was not a war of mercy. Her stalker wanted her utter subjugation; he aimed to break her. Caliana felt the rage of being violated slowly crowd her mind. A part of her knew that she was engaged in fighting against her own mind's perception of evil. Could she still kill her stalker for scaring her?

Jayce came back with her Coke, and Caliana expanded her smile. She had no idea how long he had been gone. It could have been an hour or five minutes. It was yet another reminder that she was functioning within a convoluted sense of time. She ran through the lists of excuses that she had used in the past few weeks to leave clubs earlier. She would wait until he finished his drink, then claim utter exhaustion.

Jayce was mouthing and gesturing for them to dance. Caliana tried to mouth back that she wasn't ready as she got dragged by the hand to the dance floor. She allowed Jayce to lead her while resenting his need to always be at the center of the dance floor.

It took every ounce of energy for Caliana to maneuver through the crowds. Her heart started escalating as she entered the hub of suffocation. Her habit of ignoring people had been her hardest to break; she was now forced into scrutinizing everyone as she pretend to look on casually. Every defensive nuance objectified her and infuriated her. Caliana tried to loosen her body up for one dance. While being stalked, dancing had become an activity she had minimized and was steadily growing to hate. When she had to dance, she felt as though she were on tainted display and being forced to perform.

Caliana focused her energy on her body to simply begin moving. She hoped that it would continue on its own. She began examining the people closest to her. Her body took on a robotic dance, and while simulating slow spins as part of her routine, Caliana focused on scanning the crowds. She circled fully and came back to find that Jayce had vanished.

Sudden dizziness blinded her, and Caliana gasped at the sharp pain in her chest. She felt her heart frantically pounding in pursuit of its ultimate attack. She was dying. Her breath had become smothered in the shakes of her body. Her stomach heaved a nauseating response, and sweat started seeping from her flushed body. Her world caved inward.

Jayce hazily materialized. The music was suddenly blaring again in her ears, and the lights were blinding. She desperately clutched Jayce's arm but couldn't make her mouth work. She felt frozen in panic.

Mercifully, Jayce grabbed her by the arm and started to drag her away. As soon as he was forced to turn his back to her, Caliana clutched his shirt. The only thought that registered was that she had to hang on. He was her lifeline out of hell, and eternity crawled along as Caliana followed behind him.

Jayce led her outside the club. Caliana collapsed on the nearest bench. Gratefully, she gasped in the cold air until it started choking her. Her ears were still ringing, and tears of relief flowed down her cheeks. Jayce took off his jacket and wrapped it around her. It was only then that Caliana registered her convulsing body and chattering teeth. She closed her eyes and tried to slow her breathing.

Caliana was aware of Jayce trying to soothe her. She was too shaken to feel mortification at exposing her fear, her weakness. She could only focus on breathing and calming herself.

"Can you please just find me a cab?" Caliana finally beseeched.

"I'm going with you. Can you wait for me here, or do you think you can manage to walk to the street?" he asked.

"I'll come with you." Caliana did not trust herself to be alone. She felt grateful for the physical support Jayce was lending her, and she was exhausted enough to fully lean on him.

In the cab, Caliana kept her head on Jayce's shoulder. She wanted to tell him that she was grateful that he wasn't speaking, but she didn't want to break the blessed silence. He rubbed her hair in comforting strokes, and Caliana fought falling asleep. When Jayce paid the cab, Caliana took off his jacket, and attempted to return it while thanking him.

Jayce gently wrapped the jacket back over her shoulders. "I'm coming in to put you to bed. Only after I get you settled, and know that you're okay, then, I will leave."

Jayce unlocked her door and led her to her bedroom. Caliana excused herself to the bathroom. She had to feel water. She stood in the shower and allowed the water to pound her nerves back to life.

Caliana wrapped herself in her softest robe and quietly entered the bedroom. Jayce was setting down a mug of some hot beverage by her bedside. He had turned down the bed, turned off the lights, and lit her favorite candle. Caliana stood surveying him and felt the warm stirrings of love begin to grow. In that moment, Jayce had done for her more than anyone else had.

"Thank you so much. I don't know how to thank you. You saved me from myself tonight." Caliana gave him her most vulnerable and longest kiss.

"Any time." Jayce gave her his careless grin, gently helping her into bed. "I made you some herbal tea." He handed her the mug and helped place a pillow behind her neck.

"Thank you. Again." She couldn't help smiling back at him. She was feeling the sudden exuberance of her fear dissipating and of the beginning of her trust in him. He had been patient and kind with her even as she had treated him with polite detachment. He had been sensitive to her needs, and she had barely acknowledged his.

"I can't wait 'til my birthday," she blurted out and blushed. "I mean…" and she actually giggled. Caliana felt mortified. She had already let him know that she wanted to celebrate her seventeenth with the loss of her virginity.

"I can't wait either." Jayce looked at her with a serious expression. "I am the luckiest man alive. Now, try to sleep."

Caliana snuggled in bed and realized that Jayce had made himself comfortable on top of the cover. She wanted to tell him that she was fine and that he could leave. She wanted to tell him so many things, but her body was deliciously comfortable. Caliana felt that she managed a smile before slipping into sleep.

SECTION II

CHAPTER 8

August 20, 1986

"CAN you feel this?" asked the anesthesiologist as he pinched Caliana's right thigh. Caliana reaffirmed that she could and that she was able to feel the numbness only in her left leg.

The anesthesiologist went on to explain that he had already given Caliana quite a large amount of anesthesia and was concerned about how much more he could give her, considering her small frame and weight. He was afraid that even if he attempted another insertion a few vertebras higher, she might still experience the same problem; for some reason, the numbing was occurring on only one side of her body. One-sided epidurals happen roughly 4% of the time, he explained. They can't be reliably predicted, and the causes are not fully understood. He would rather give her the remaining safe dosage in the form of general anesthesia. She would sleep through the surgery, and her husband, under hospital regulations, would have to leave the room during the procedure.

"I broke my back a few years ago; maybe the curve in my spine is affecting the way the medicine is being distributed to my legs. I think it would be best to give me the general anesthesia." Caliana just wanted the ordeal over with. She was shivering on the operating table. The blanket that had been provided was barely thicker than a sheet.

Her obstetrician agreed and told Rami that because the surgery would be performed under general anesthesia, he could not attend the Cesarean section and would have to wait outside. Caliana watched her husband, the man she had patiently planned to divorce for the past eight months, heatedly argue with everyone in the room.

He found their *silly rules* unacceptable and demanded that they alter their policy for him! He insisted that he should be allowed to remain in the room and that he would only compromise to their unreasonable rules by keeping out of their way and standing back against the wall. He refused to accept the hospital's policy, and kept repeating that it didn't make any sense. Caliana could clearly tell that the doctors were losing patience with Rami, yet he remained oblivious and kept arguing.

Rami finally realized that he wasn't going to win his heated, and by then, ego-driven argument with the doctors. In Arabic, he told Caliana to tell them to try another epidural so he could attend the birth of his son.

Caliana, who had been impatiently gritting her teeth at his typical display of selfish bravado, snapped in English, "I can't afford to try for a third epidural that will most likely not work. Please ... just wait outside."

"Okay, okay. I'm going. But I will be right outside. I'm going to look through this window on the door. It's silly and stupid to make me watch it from there." He arrogantly scoffed, "I'm going to be able to see anyway!" as though this action would be the ultimate defiance of an obvious conspiracy to exclude him from the birth of his firstborn.

Caliana tilted her head and observed Rami leaving the room. She felt slightly sorry for him when she saw the ridiculously small size of the window—if it could be called a window—and its distance from the operating table. She knew that Rami would stay glued to it for a minute at the most. He would quickly lose interest as soon as his ego was appeased in establishing whatever point was going through his limited mind.

Caliana exhaled when the door closed. It seemed that the whole energy in the room was one of collective relief. She breathed in the blessed silence. Rami could exude an unbearably irritating force when he was determined to have his way. He resembled what she imagined an overindulgent child would look like while throwing a tantrum. Caliana, who had learned a horrific new level of impatience while living with Rami, wondered how much of her desire to have him disappear had influenced her consent for general anesthesia.

Gently, the anesthesiologist explained the procedure. He removed the epidural and prepped her for an IV drip. He positioned himself behind her head, and Caliana was surprised at the unexpected caressing of her hair and his soothing words. She felt herself starting to drift into a swirling fog and suddenly felt a panicked resistance. His words were fading, to be gently replaced by words that she hadn't thought of in five years ....

April 1981

You will recede; and you will sing for me. Caliana's eyes misted as she stared at the diagram drawn around the sentence in front of her. Why couldn't she figure out its meaning. Every single letter had ended with it, and she had considered every possibility within every context. He wanted her to disappear, to retreat, to ebb away, yet be physically present to perform for him. What the hell could he possibly mean?

Caliana wanted to shred the pile of evidence. She had a childish yet satisfying image of stomping on the letters and screaming out her rage. Instead, she meticulously filed them away in their folder and locked them in her desk drawer. She had to get ready for her birthday dinner with Jayce.

Caliana thought back to the night of her panic attack two weeks prior. Since then, she had existed in dread of its reoccurrence. Her anxiety had grown to an impossible new state of aggravation. The past two weeks had felt like a bombardment; she had received four letters that first week, followed by three letters the next.

Her breakdown seemed to have left a nasty aftermath of involuntary jitters. It was a familiar reminder of her days in the bomb shelter with her family. She felt suspended in absolute panic, and yet here she was, making plans to lose her virginity in a few hours. Nothing seemed real. Her mind was beyond her control. She also felt a certain level of detachment, as though a part of her soul had declared its utter disgust and independence of her and was sitting on the sideline, watching the show. She felt its judgment.

Caliana forced herself to go through the motions. She had exactly two hours to shower, dress, and meet Jayce at the restaurant. She couldn't imagine how she was going to go through having sex, and she didn't have the energy to imagine it. She would just have to survive every minute as she had been doing. It was too late to back out now.

Caliana entered the restaurant punctually at eight o'clock. She quickly saw Jayce seated at a table. He hadn't seen her, so Caliana did a quick survey of the room's setup and measured her table's strategic defenses. "Stop it" she rigidly admonished her mind. She walked toward Jayce, her eyes landing on the bottle of wine already on the table. Salvation bottled up and waiting.

"Happy seventeenth birthday." Jayce jolted her out of her reverie. She smiled and accepted his kiss.

"Thank you for the wine. It's the perfect gift." Caliana saw the look of puzzlement on Jayce's face. She grinned. She was having a hard time containing a bubble of laughter. The temptation to blurt out her thoughts carried an infectious insanity. She had stopped all alcohol three months before for the sake of preserving the mental clarity required for her vigilance, yet she suddenly felt herself lusting after this bottle of wine. She recognized the potential of this moment, that she might become an alcoholic before taking her first sip.

"I wasn't sure what to order. I know you haven't had a drink in months, but I thought ... it's a special occasion and we should celebrate," Jayce clarified.

"Lovely." Caliana discreetly gulped down her first glass and eagerly anticipated the respite from her madness. She knew that by her second glass she could muster the courage to flirt with Jayce. By the third glass, Caliana couldn't remember one solid good reason why she had abstained from drinking.

She was floating on a cloud of an altered perception, a safe reality. She could let go with Jayce. He loved her. Tonight she would begin erasing all pain.

Caliana floated through the lovely dinner. Afterward, in her apartment, Jayce gently stopped her from reaching for the light switch and began kissing her. The darkness, the wine, were simply an overture to the silence of her mind; she melted into the echo of the last note that vibrated in hushed resonance.

Caliana surfaced from the kiss, certain in her ability to love. It was perfectly appropriate that Jayce's face was blurry. Caliana found herself gently seated on the edge of her bed. Through glazed eyes she saw Jayce step back and slowly take off his clothes. Slowly, she peeled off every layer and embraced her exposure.

"*You will withdraw; you will sing for me,*" Jayce's whisper gradually penetrated her universe.

Of course! That's what the psycho wanted. She got it!

He wanted her defenses to disappear, her mind to disappear, so she could sing for him with her body, to surrender herself willingly, like this.

Her joy at unraveling the ultimate puzzle made her wants to stop Jayce and share with him her breakthrough, to have him share her joy ....

Caliana's mind froze in a horrific reality that suddenly spiraled beyond every nightmare. Like a perfect camera, her mind zoomed back onto the time she had suddenly looked up at Jayce while studying and seen his duality. The camera froze on that one moment, that precise millisecond, when she had known—had absolutely known—that Jayce *was* her stalker.

Her mind released the image and resurrected countless other images for analysis, other times when she should have recognized his duplicity. She was amazed at how transparent everything had become in retrospect!

The camera shifted to her body. Caliana couldn't tell if she had been gone for a minute, or hours. Had she just opened her eyes? She was looking at her body moving. Was she moving it? Was she having an orgasm? Who was grunting?

The next few actions occurred as if in a dream. Hysterical, Caliana shoved Jayce and toppled him off of her. She screamed at him and had no idea what came out of her mouth. She was livid, a mad woman with one objective: shoving and screaming him all the way to the front door.

Caliana couldn't remember being in the bathroom. She was huddled naked on the floor, heaving and vomiting. A minute, or hours, passed. She leaned her back on the glass mirror that covered the whole wall. Her cheek was on fire, so she rotated it toward the cool glass, hoping the coolness would relieve the sting.

The distortion of her image blanched her. She slowly reached her hand to her mirror image and started wiping it clean. The mirror was foggy, it had to be. Caliana didn't recognize the person in it. She dragged a towel from its hook and slid it around her. And she slept. For a minute, or hours.

Caliana slowly walked into her bedroom. Her hand hesitated on the light switch. She expected to see evidence of absolute destruction, and had to blink in the harsh reality. Nothing was disturbed. She walked over to the pile of her discarded clothes and picked up each item. One of his socks was on the floor, and Caliana added it to the exhausted bundle that had become her life. She went into the kitchen and trashed her collection of letters and the bundle of clothes.

A minute, an hour, a day. Caliana found herself cleaning the vomit in the bathroom. Naked, she forced herself to turn around and look at the full stranger in the mirror. She leaned in closer, and closer, yet she couldn't see herself. She could only see fragments. Caliana touched her check and felt the scabby dryness of her blood. She reached for cotton balls and used warm water to gently remove the crust. She didn't feel anything, including the long shower that she took. Her body had lost all sensation. She could have been taking an ice-cold shower, or a scalding-hot one. She couldn't tell. It didn't matter.

She walked back to her bedroom and looked at her room. She knew that she would fall asleep. Something caught her eye on the carpet near her bed. Caliana reached down and realized that her Rolex had come undone. She saw a pinkish substance stuck on the clasp and, curiously, she picked it off.

She had a quick flash of memory as she remembered Deena's skin lodged in her teeth. Caliana realized that she was holding a part of the skin that should have been on her own cheek. Calmly, Caliana walked over to the makeup mirror and, stretching the curled skin, tried to layer it back on her face. She looked at her eyes and realized that she had never seen them before. She couldn't remember what she used to look like, but she knew that she hated what she saw.

Caliana slept. A minute, an hour, a few days. She couldn't tell. The incessant ringing of the phone forced her to finally get up. "Caliana. It's Jayce. Please let me come over. I need to…" "Who?" Caliana responded. "Caliana, I …." "She left." Caliana felt she had finally spoken her truth. She gently hung up the phone, and faded away.

CHAPTER 9

August 20, 1986

"CALIANA."

Caliana resurfaced to her name being cheerfully called. She was visually disoriented and tried to focus on the image in front of her. Her sister Deena was jabbering away excitedly and was partially hidden by the video camera aimed at Caliana.

"Is he ... okay?" Caliana managed to ask. The first clear thought that forced itself to the surface was propelled from her body's response to its pain from the surgery.

"You're in the recovery room, and I'm not supposed to be here. They will only let one person at a time ... and, well, *mama* is also here," Deena grumbled. "I saw your baby for a few seconds. He's so cute and, my God, tiny! The pediatrician decided that he doesn't need to be incubated. Apparently, my nephew is a healthy preemie!" Deena proudly boasted.

Caliana tried to focus her eyes past her sister, on her mother's face. An unfamiliar throbbing need rose up in her; she wanted to reach for her mother, to hold her hand out in comfort, to beckon her closer, yet ... she didn't know how. Images of her mother rocking her in her arms were swirling in her mind. Caliana felt her body ache in response. The clarity of her mother's impassive face made such actions an unthinkable request.

"Thirsty. Water ... please."

Deena set down the camera and looked around for water.

"She's not supposed to drink anything for the next two hours. The nurse said she could chew on some crushed ice." Her mother pointed to a paper cup next to Caliana's bed. "You could also wet her lips with a cloth," her mother continued, dispassionately.

For once, Caliana was grateful for her mother's quasi-medical advice. Her mother came verbally alive when she was playing doctor. She had a talent for dispensing medical conditions with authority. Caliana wondered if her mother's suggestion had been prompted because Caliana's lips looked parched and dry. Heaven forbid that Caliana might have looked her worst right after surgery!

Grateful, Caliana savored the coolness of the ice and tried to greedily chew it to absorb its teasing fluid. She felt horribly parched and longed for an ice-cold jug of water.

"Thank you." Caliana heard her own whisper disappearing into the sudden noise. She floated away into the beeping that was getting louder. Her mother's voice rose inaudibly.

Caliana was suddenly jolted into consciousness by the most excruciating pain she had ever felt. The source of her torture was pumping her stomach. Frantically, Caliana grabbed the wrists that were pushing on her and used her might to force the hands off.

"Stop it! Do you want to die?!" the nurse screamed at her.

Caliana slipped in and out of consciousness. She came to in a room crowded with people. Her father came running in after Deena and nervously kept glancing between Caliana and her mother, who had began her performance.

"I knew that she had lost her blood pressure. I saw the monitor behind her head. It started dropping, and then her pulse disappeared. She would have died had she not been in the recovery room. Imagine, in Jordan, she would have been taken straight to her room after a C-section."

Her father, who needed only the visual verification of Caliana being alive, nodded nervously.

The doctor asked her father and Deena to leave, reassuring them that Caliana was stabilized and had been given a mild blood thinner. She would be closely monitored.

"I thought you died. I went running to get *baba*." Deena looked as dazed as Caliana felt, uncertain of where she should be. She finally blurted that they would wait back at the nursery with Rami; his brother, Samir; and Caliana's father-in-law.

"Isn't it dangerous to give her a blood thinner? There was so much blood gushing when the nurse was thrusting on her uterus." Caliana groaned at her mother's question. She knew her mother well enough to know that this would be a lengthy inquisition into all the detailed possibilities. Her mother was hunting after information to savor for the retelling.

The doctor made his escape as soon as he felt he had pacified the demanding questions, and Caliana was left alone with her mother, who promptly practiced paraphrasing the information into a fresher version of how she had saved Caliana's life. Apparently, her mother not only had known how to read the blood pressure indicator but had also known the cause of her blood pressure dropping. She had immediately shouted for help and had even guided the nurse by indicating that her daughter was having a blood clot, which had helped the nurse take the necessary action of pushing on Caliana's uterus to relieve the clot. Caliana assumed that by the time her mother retold the story in Jordan, she would have been the one pumping her daughter's uterus to save her life.

Caliana was used to getting irritated, and at times angry, at her mother's ability to confidently assume herself as the center of any given event, as the source, discoverer, creator, or whatever position had the most venerable impact. Her mother didn't even think to expect a reaction from Caliana, not even gratitude, for it wasn't about saving Caliana's life. The value of the experience was not about Caliana's life, but rather about *how her mother looked*. Her mother sat down, barely facing her, and assumed an indifferent silence.

Caliana focused on her mother's face and tried to guess her thoughts. Was her mother visualizing her heroic deed? Was that slight frown a reflection of a glitch in her imagination? No, that would require an honesty that couldn't be contained in her consciousness. Or maybe it could be that it was occurring to her that her daughter had robbed her of an even mightier performance: Caliana should have given birth in Jordan and died from a clot because of incompetent medical practice, and then Caliana's mother could have been allowed to play the grieving, yet justifiably angry, mother. Caliana could picture the indignant role her mother would create, followed by a dignified resolve to continue her life, unaffected by her grief.

Instead of anger, Caliana felt her heart clench in agonized disappointment. Waves of sadness enveloped her. She looked into her mother's averted eyes and, for once, instead of her usual rapid, disgusted glance, she stared. Caliana had to see the monster within her mother. Maybe the medication allowed her to feel, for Caliana felt the pain of her mother's cruelty burn within her. She welcomed it. She felt vibrant with the first stirring of intense emotions in five years. She thought it ironic that her mother had given her life twice, yet this time around, Caliana was astute enough to witness being aborted upon her rebirth.

She let her thoughts consume her pain. She had almost died—she in fact *had* died briefly—and her mother hadn't considered showing Caliana the least bit of concern, never mind comforting her, soothing her daughter's fear and pain. *What kind of a person is so vacant?* Caliana asked herself. *What kind of creature is so unmoved by the fragility of life and death?*

Caliana guiltily thought back to the past few months of her pregnancy. She had felt absolutely nothing for the child growing in her. She hadn't even thought to imagine its life. She had named him Kareem, as soon as she had known the gender, and that was the extent of her maternal ability.

She also remembered the resignation and fear she had experienced a few weeks earlier; she had seen a pregnant mother sitting in the sun, gently caressing the life within her, serenely beaming at her dream of its existence. In that moment, Caliana's horror at her own detachment had finally struck her. *I'm just like my mother*, she had thought, and then had immediately dismissed that horrible comparison, yet it had crept up and nagged her a few times. In the hospital, the day before her Cesarean section, she had been informed that she had a dangerous condition. This condition, called intrauterine growth restriction, or IUGR, put the fetus at risk of dying from lack of nutrition. For some reason, her uterus had stopped feeding her son, and the baby was dying in her abdomen. Her son was thirty-four weeks old and stood a 10% chance of being incubated. The doctor had scheduled the Cesarian and released her at five PM to return the following morning. She was six weeks early and completely unprepared for a baby. She didn't even look pregnant. Caliana's mind had spun with a mental shopping list of all that she might possibly need to buy in preparation for her son.

Her father, jubilant at the opportunity to feel useful by squandering a sliver of his father's wealth, had accompanied her to a baby store and hurriedly filled her car with all sorts of new purchases for the baby. Caliana had cringed with shame at the realization that she hadn't even thought to be concerned for her son's well-being. She was amazed that, somehow, some instinct had come through to her, prompting her to ask after her son when she had first resurfaced from the surgery.

Caliana glared at her mother, looking for any hint of similarity, desperate to identify it so she could carve that resemblance from her soul.

The aloof detachment that radiated from her mother echoed back in Caliana's heart. Her mother's vacant emotions were almost too easy to identify with; Caliana had lived the void of her mother's absence and had unknowingly duplicated it in her own soul. She had survived the pain of being thoroughly unloved by defending with the same absence, and she saw how the damage had cycled back at her.

The few times Caliana's mother had been asked about her own mother, she had given an instant and unwavering one-word description: *Hitler*. Caliana knew little else about her maternal grandmother, based on her own impressions. She couldn't remember how old she had been when she had first perceived the icy beauty of her grandmother's face. She had died of cancer when Caliana was ten, and Caliana had felt absolutely nothing. Her only real surprise regarding the obligatory funeral was at having accidentally caught her mother sobbing. The image of her mother's humanity had made Caliana freeze in terror, and this image returned to her in the hospital room and made her pity the woman in front of her.

For the first time ever, Caliana empathized with her mother by feeling sorry for her. The body of the woman sitting a few feet away from her was, at best, an empty vessel. Irrespective of where her damage had come from, she was deadened to humanity.

Caliana looked again at her mother and visualized the empty vessel shattering; she never wanted to be like her mother. Even if Caliana was incapable of loving Kareem, she would treat him with all the respect a human being deserved. She wasn't quite sure what that really meant, but she knew that she had a clean slate to start her off on mothering. She had a son, whom she hadn't seen, and she didn't know how much love, if any, she could give him, but she knew with certainty that she could never, ever display her mother's robotic inhumanity.

Caliana cringed in guilt and shame. Had she really been as honorable as she liked to perceive herself? She felt the shame of her accountability as the awful bits of the past five years floated back to her.

She had gone after her mother's monster and had cycled back to find the monster within herself. The past five years had been, at best, a foggy disconnect of a dreamlike existence. She had made life-altering decisions without really feeling or understanding any of them. She had acted like a puppet responding to various circumstances.

In retrospect, Caliana was able to view the massive outline of the comatose layer that had enshrouded her for the past five years. She felt as though she were resurfacing from a coma, except the journey was ascending inward, through the cluttered smog, back into the memories of five interminable human years, toward her essence.

Caliana drifted back, a minute, an hour...

CHAPTER 10

April 1981

IT STARTED a minute, an hour... after her collision with her stalker.

She knew she had to finish the college term in London; she had one month left. She made a call to the president of the college, in which she adlibbed convincing lies to get herself completely out of class attendance. She managed to negotiate all her remaining work in that phone call, arranging to mail in the outstanding work. The ease of disappearing facilitated every choice; nothing could hurt her, for she could not feel.

She called Deena in Texas and asked her for the favor of applying on her behalf to the university there. Her only condition was that she needed to begin immediately: Deena had to get her registered in time for the first summer session. For Caliana to begin the following month, Deena had to fill out the application on the phone with her. Deena read through a list of possible majors, and Caliana gave each one a second's consideration. She felt as though she were impassively choosing from an extensive menu, yet she had no appetite. When Deena got to Theatre, Caliana felt a slightly positive reaction, based on the fact that she had always loved going to the theatre. She told Deena to sign her up as a theatre major and promptly stopped thinking about it. She knew that her parents' only expectation was for her to get a BA, in whatever she wanted, and then to marry well.

Caliana recalled the necessary steps that she had taken to get herself to the United States. She had felt absolutely nothing. Not even the relief at the lack of fear that had terrorized her for the past few months. When she had found a vase with red roses and a note outside her door, she had calmly trashed the flowers. She had opened the note and read Jayce's apology for the months of unforgivable cruelty. He was *not her stalker*, but rather *a loving boyfriend*, one who had *inappropriately tried to help her get over her fear by quoting her stalker.*

A split second of doubt was all she allowed herself.

She had noted her steady hands as she made one simple rip down the middle of the note. She watched it flutter into the garbage.

* * *

Texas was a shocking introduction to America. Caliana's naïve idealism, assimilated from the strength of the images in movies and a few courses in US history and politics, had prepared her to expect a continent unified in a dynamic utopia. She had assumed that Americans had benefited from their diverse worldly ancestry and from their own struggles as they built a heritage as a united people. She had hoped that she would be joining her fantasy of an ideal society.

At the beginning, she would instinctively ask people where they were from. "America," they would reply. She would follow up by asking, "But where are you *really* from? Where are you *originally* from?" She soon realized that this question did not matter to them, as their ethnicities had become uniform: They were American, and nothing else.

The prejudices she witnessed in certain parts of America were rooted in unquestioned ignorance that had fed unreasonable fears. Texans had simply, by isolation of their geography, been unexposed to various ways of living. Caliana thought it ironic that of the hundreds of people she had met in London, few had been British. In Switzerland, she had lived amongst 140 girls who had represented more than forty nationalities. She had lived in a vibrant, cosmopolitan continent forced to assimilate many cultures. She had not fully appreciated the accomplishment in Europe because she had always compared any shortcomings to her fantasies of America as the most culturally integrated place in the world.

Caliana couldn't believe how many times she had to explain to Texans where she came from. Telling someone that she was from Jordan was at times akin to describing a sci-fi planet. It was almost always followed by, "Where is that?" If she answered "The Middle East," it invariably prompted another blank look. Caliana would then list a few surrounding countries, like Egypt, Lebanon, and Iraq, and wait for any recognition. Some people actually came to life when she mentioned Israel, relieved that they were able to identify one country from her list. Caliana recognized that informing people that Jordan was next to Israel was only confirming a tiny bit of all that they didn't know.

Despite its imperfections, America was still the best country to live in, Caliana knew. There were many other reasons for Caliana to want to live in the US, but the most compelling draw was that she could truly disappear. In America, she was a nobody, a number, an unaccounted-for being, and that freedom facilitated her emergence into the collective.

Every difference that she observed between herself and Texans alienated her further. She had never identified with any one culture or group within any society, and in America it became increasingly easier to disconnect in her terminal uniqueness. Her thoughts were suspended in a timeless, lonely void, one that had no relevance to any specific dimension. She surfaced into reality only long enough to plan her next course of action. Caliana was incapable of feeling anything, not even caring enough to appreciate the fact that she had achieved her ultimate goal of deadening her pain. She was only going through the motions of living, and fortunately, no one knew her well enough to know the difference.

To Caliana, time was an elusive construct. Especially when she was absorbed in a book, she felt the severe distinction between her internal time and real time. She would often look up from a book and feel the splendor of lapsing from actual time into the timelessness of engaging with the world of the book. It afforded her relief from her growing frustration with a stagnant reality. Immersing herself in the world of theater sustained her surreal perception of time.

She was able to experience a new sense of living. With her peers, she discovered an exciting way of bringing the written word to life through the freedoms of unleashing her imagination as a director. Unexpectedly, she found that the theatre drew upon a language she was familiar with: a way of joining humanity by discussing, analyzing, and sharing her interpretations of the world of a play. The success of her vision depended on her communication with others, but Caliana felt safe in speaking passionately about imaginary lives.

She devoted her waking hours to the intricacies of making the stage brim with life. She could dissect a play, master its universe, and control its outcome. All she had to do was execute the reality of a script, breathe her imagination into its essence. It was a gift of wondrous possibilities.

A minute, an hour...

Two and a half years later, her intermission in the world of theatre abruptly ended. Her major in theatre was forced, by circumstance, to be reassessed, and her commitment to the theatre was tested. Caliana had been defiantly ignoring the university's policy requiring all students to take a year's worth of required courses, and she was suddenly faced with having to complete courses that would put her back into a dismal reality. She balked at the invasion. As this was happening, the director of her drama department nominated her as a candidate for one of the two coveted openings for a Masters Degree in Directing. Caliana had indulged her interest in drama, but a career in the theatre required an ambition that she did not have.

A few weeks later, back in London for the Christmas break, she casually strolled into the office of the head of her old fashion design school. A twenty-minute conversation negotiated her fate. She would remain in London. Credits transferred from the university in Texas, combined with her one year at the fashion school, would guarantee her a BA in Fashion Merchandising by August. She would graduate college at the age of nineteen.

She called a friend in Texas to arrange for her things to be packed and shipped to her. She then called the director of the theatre department and informed her that she would not be returning to school. The director, flustered at the unexpectedness of her decision, attempted to reason with Caliana to reconsider. Caliana politely evaded the probing, and started to feel the resentment of having to disengage from a confining situation. The more the director pressured her to stay, the more clearly Caliana's resolve to leave strengthened.

Having set her plans in motion, Caliana settled back into the flat in London. Deena, nursing her second broken collarbone in the same shoulder, was in London for a few weeks. Deena had started dating a Jordanian man a month earlier and wanted Caliana to meet him. She pressured Caliana into joining them for the New Year's celebration on the pretence that she needed help for the night.

Caliana was helping her sister dress for the New Year's party when Deena told her that her boyfriend's brother had surprised everyone by arriving unexpectedly in London. Caliana shrugged at the information. She had completely resigned herself to waste an evening with people she didn't care to get to know. She planned to make an effort with her sister's boyfriend, mainly because it would be expected of her. The additional arrival of his brother adjusted her plan, and she promptly decided to allocate a few extra minutes of niceties to him. She figured she could muster an evening of pre-dictable behavior and hoped that she would only have to respond to people until they got drunk and obliterated themselves to her.

Caliana was kneeling on the floor, awkwardly helping her sister put on frustrating panty hose, when the doorbell rang. Leaving Deena entangled Caliana rushed to the door and yanked it open. She felt a jolt as she focused on the smiling handsome stranger literally dwarf-ing her door. She heard him introduce himself as her sister's boyfriend's brother.

"You're so tall!" Caliana blurted. "And huge!" she exclaimed.

Caliana was mortified at her unedited outburst. His reaction totally disarmed her. He burst out laughing and, with endearing self-deprecating humor, put her at ease. He swept into the apartment with complete familiarity and ease and continued chatting with her. Good-naturedly, he joked about his brother's inability to be punctual, and that he was running behind and had asked him to pick up the ladies.

"At least he's a gentleman," he chuckled.

Caliana was amazed by his energy and by her response to him. He was like a giant teddy bear. She found herself smiling back at the gentle sincerity that coated his every word.

"You have no idea how alike the two of them are. It's scary how consistent she is in living by a two-hour late policy! Deena refuses to wear a watch and never bothers checking the time. I've been nagging her for an hour to start to get ready!" Caliana was interrupted by her sister's hollers for help. "And you'd think that having a broken shoul-der might have gotten her to listen to me!" Caliana dashed into the corridor while calling out for him to feel at home.

The brother made the evening unbelievably interesting. Caliana had never met anyone quite like him. He exuded a unique blend of natural masculine mannerisms and strength with an absolutely sweet nature. He spoke Arabic with the classical masculine dialect of a Jor-danian man, and English with the ease of an American, born and bred. That his mother was American was clear not only in his accent but also in the charming ease with which he shared loving stories about his family, especially his mother. He was emotionally fearless because he was genuinely happy and content in his life and loved and respected his family. Caliana was mesmerized by his healthy views and the ease with which he clearly demonstrated his attraction to her. She admired his confidence and his enthusiasm in speaking with her. His charm completely dominated her night. He was refreshingly honest and comfortable in his own skin.

She spent every day of his visit with him. When he left for Jordan, he spent every night on the phone with her. He flew back to see her every few weeks and courted her with an intensity that was heartbreakingly honest and loving. She flew to Jordan that spring, and he rushed her to his home to meet the rest of his family. He proposed, and Caliana accepted. A wonderful man had fallen in love with her, and she had agreed to marry him, though deep down Caliana knew that she had let him grow to love only her exterior shell.

She went through the motions of an engagement and would have married him, but for a slight twist of fate. Her sister, who had been suitably matched to his brother, broke off her own engagement in August.

Tension flared amongst the families.

Her fiancé's serious offer of an elopement jarred Caliana out of her fog long enough to do the right thing and break it off. She loved him, and she had too much respect for him to allow him to sacrifice his life, his family, his home, for nothing. For her façade, he deserved better. She knew that she was breaking his heart, and she couldn't face explaining the truth. She couldn't explain to him that he was in love with a figment of his own imagination, and that she had simply complied with it. She definitely couldn't face telling him that even though her mind had loved him, she had been unable to access the emotions that should have correlated.

Her parents had been fully ignited by the idea of marriage. While Deena and Caliana had been engaged, her mother had savored the attention that had come with having two daughters engaged to two highly eligible men. She had much to boast about, and she had exalted the brothers' virtues to everyone around her too many times.

When Deena had tried to explain that she was not in love with her fiancé and needed to break off the engagement, her mother had become enraged and had viciously criticized Deena's shortcomings. She had tried to shame Deena into going through with the marriage, irrespective of her feelings. It was her father who finally took pity on

Deena and tried to assuage the situation so his wife would not lose too much face in public. By the time Caliana announced that she had broken off her own engagement, her mother had already had a few weeks of venting her disappointment by way of the malicious tributary of gossip.

Rami, Caliana's childhood friend, had swarmed in immediately after the official ending of her engagement with claims of having loved her for years. He proposed marriage a few months later. It took Caliana all of three minutes to agree. She was twenty-one, done with college, and in need of a home. She had dallied in a few masters degree courses but didn't really have a course of action. Marriage was the expected next step. She knew that she did not want to live with her parents, and she considered Rami a safe childhood friend. He represented the collective comfort of having spent time in Jordan on school vacations. He was a part of her familiar circle of friends, and she genuinely cared for him. She liked his father very much, and she adored his brother. Rami knew her as well as anyone could, so she had agreed to marry him.

The public shame of having had his eldest two daughters break off their engagements spurred Caliana's father into a new traditional role. Rami was finishing his last year in a college in Tennessee and wanted to marry her the following year upon the completion of his BA. Caliana's dad metamorphosed into a conservative chameleon who would absolutely not tolerate another "long" engagement by his daughter. He made it clear to Rami that his daughter would not have her name attached to him in a year-long engagement and that he didn't believe in dating. If Rami wanted her, then he would marry her as soon as possible or take the chance that she would be available for pursuing other suitable matches.

Caliana cringed at her father's obvious hypocrisy and at how he prided himself in his ability to conform to a traditional role to accomplish his intentions. It was a calculated gamble that banked on Rami's fear of losing her a second time around. While Caliana was in London and Rami was in the States, speedy arrangements were made to marry them in London at the end of November. She was marrying a man she had not even dated.

Caliana, who shocked her mother by purchasing a ready-made wedding dress, put the reality of the upcoming marriage on hiatus and resumed a few more courses at a new school in London. Guests and extended family started arriving toward the end of November, reminding her of the happy occasion. The reality of the wedding slammed into her a few days before the date. Her mother breezed into town and started accepting the last-minute lunches and dinners issued by her friends.

Caliana couldn't make any of the prenuptial dinners that were in her honor, as she was laid up in bed suffering a horrific flu. Breathing was painful, and every molecule in her body ached. Her mother was irritated at her inconvenient illness and summoned the doctor to give her every medicine known to man to help her recover faster. When it became obvious that her daughter was still incapacitated the morning of the wedding, Caliana's mother bullied the doctor into giving Caliana some kind of a vitamin shot to revive her sufficiently to attend her own wedding.

Caliana hardly remembered getting ready. Literally dazed and drugged in confusion, she made it down the aisle and stood next to Rami. The solemnity of the service at some point broke through her stupor, and the realization that she was getting married had her in muffled tears of laughter. The guests couldn't figure out if she was laughing or crying; they could only see the back of her shoulders shaking and hear the strange noises coming out of her.

* * *

Living with Rami for a month in Tennessee was a crude eye-opener. Her husband was a wild and crazy party animal who smoked marijuana every day and partied with his fraternity almost every night. When he was sober, he jealously bulldozed her with appallingly insecure comparisons and accusations relating to her ex-fiancé.

By early January, she knew something was wrong with her body. She called the GP in London and gave him her symptoms over the phone. According to the doctor, her period had always been irregular, and the fact that she had begun her first course of birth control a week before her wedding could easily attribute to her loss of a cycle or two. To be on the safe side, he wanted her to have a pregnancy test, and if she was not pregnant, then she should resume the pills.

A clinic confirmed her pregnancy. Caliana was stunned to discover that the antibiotics that she had taken for her flu could have minimized the effect of the birth control pill, resulting in a pregnancy. She was twenty-one years old, pregnant, and married to a wild, needy child who was jarringly irritating. She immediately registered at the only college in town to begin some masters-level courses in theatre, escaping Rami.

The pregnancy altered her plans for an immediate annulment and got her thinking of an alternative "polite time" to divorce Rami. At the time, divorce was a rarity in her parents' world, and Caliana began bracing herself for its eventuality. She spent many hours fantasizing scenarios of how she would approach her parents in a firm manner and debated the necessity of having to give them any information at all.

August 20, 1986

A nurse entered the recovery room and jarred Caliana out of her recollections. Her mother came into focus, and Caliana observed her resuming her perfunctory maternal duties by speaking to the nurse.

Caliana knew that she had scanned back through what felt like a lifetime. She didn't bother going past that operational five-year–coma stage to revive her life.

The nurse declared Caliana stable enough to be taken to her room.

As Caliana was being rolled to her room, she closed her eyes in exhausted relief. Even though her body felt the disorientation of the medications, her mind was experiencing a novel and distinctive clarity. Viewing her past actions collectively and, in an odd sense, experiencing them for the first time, had delivered her from her haze. Caliana felt more present than she had in a very long time. She knew with absolute certainty that she had operated on a level that was deceitful and unworthy of her integrity. She knew that she needed to regain her life and take conscious control of her actions. Guilt for her deception with Rami ripped through her as she realized that irrespective of his shortcomings, he had deserved a woman who might have loved him. She battled her shameful accountability with resolve; she would adjust her future actions to repair her blunders.

As soon as Caliana was settled in her room, another nurse brought her son to her, gently placing him in her arms.

Caliana reverently cradled her son. Tears blurred her vision. She felt breathless from the love that poured out of her heart to her baby.

Caliana felt staggered. She was completely unprepared for the indescribable emotional resurrection. Her soul resonated and her heart poured forth, marveling at the preciousness of the gift she had undeservedly been given.

The magnitude of being responsible for loving and guiding her son plummeted her into new fears. An overwhelming sense of fierce protectiveness trembled her soul with panicked new thoughts, and instinctively, Caliana placed her son next to her heart. She wanted him to feel how strongly her heart beat for him.

"My miracle," she whispered in awe.

Humbled by the intense purity of her loving emotions, she surrendered to her profound gratitude, and it calmed her fears. She would be the most incredible mother. She just had to have faith in her courage to love him from the core of her being, from the place she had kept hidden. She needed to un-guard her soul, for him.

Caliana's thoughts finally clarified into a sudden understanding of the extent of her mother's damage: Her mother had chosen to let fear rob her of the privilege, the grace, that came from loving.

CHAPTER 11

IN A culture that kissed at every moment of greeting, Caliana's mother defiantly responded to the invasion into her personal space. Every time she was forced to reciprocate a kiss in a greeting, she would extend a still, emotionless, frozen mask that showed the barren landscape of her soul. In that brief stillness, Caliana found it mesmerizing to see her mother so evidently exposed. It was a singularly profound moment of truth in which her mother became complete.

Strangely enough, those moments would sometimes lull Caliana out of apathy and draw her to her mother's unguarded revelations. At times, Caliana had even felt a protective impulse to guard her mother, for she understood that her mother's inability to disguise her true feelings reflected her vulnerability. Maybe Caliana needed to see residual humanity in her mother, simply because a part of her could identify with her mother's vacancy. Whenever Caliana herself greeted friends with a kiss, she felt her mother's detachment but made the effort to wear a mask of politeness, to engage in the appropriate mannerisms that were expected of her at all levels of greetings. But she felt nothing, even when she wished to feel. Caliana hadn't known to what extent she hadn't felt her sense of touch until she experienced its exact opposite in being present with her son.

Caliana knew that giving birth had affected her body. She felt that she had undergone a dramatic shift with her hyperactivity. At certain times, she even managed to achieve physical calmness. She attributed the decrease in her hyperactivity to the inexplicable biological factors of giving birth, and her calmness to the altered energy that was formed when she held her son. Partly, it was her conscious desire to be serene around Kareem. Caliana would still every fear that lurked in negativity, abolishing it to its designated outlet. She did not want to contaminate her son with the damaged residuals of her own life. She would focus only on loving her son, her *raison d'être*.

Caliana also knew that the mere physical act of holding her son was allowing her to actually feel the sensation of touch. From early childhood, Caliana had visualized an imaginary shield that had silhouetted her in isolation. And when she was forced to touch another, that layer had sufficiently prevented the feel of the contact. Her mind completely backed her by disengaging from the intimacy of any experience. Over time, she had developed a high tolerance to physical pain by desensitizing the space directly surrounding her.

In retrospect, Caliana was able to recognize how unfeeling she had been. The absence of that barrier was now an intoxicating novelty and allowed Caliana to trust the sanctuary that flourished from the contact. It felt right. It fit. Cradling Kareem in one arm, she would often gently rub the outer blankets surrounding him, infusing them with loving thoughts and peaceful prayers. She wanted to fortify her son's shield with the mighty power of her love.

Caliana couldn't help but compare her maternal abilities to those that she knew her mother had lacked. She was utterly astounded in the mystery of how this loving experience had simply bypassed her mother. She found it impossible to imagine anyone not falling madly in love with her own baby, even when she had solid evidence that one woman could resist that feeling.

Suddenly, it came to her: Her mother had stopped loving Caliana before Caliana was even culpable to humanity or human error. Caliana felt the relief of realizing that her mother's response was not due to her at all; so awful a response revealed damage in her mother.

Caliana felt validated for years of not loving her mother, who had been as good as dead to her. She was starting to appreciate the implications of her mother's actions; how could Caliana have loved her? Her mother had been committed to making Caliana an insignificant part of her life. Caliana had not mattered to her mother, and she had been forced to react by making sure that her mother stopped mattering to her. Caliana had been an exemplary child by granting her mother her exact wish: She had proven herself absolutely capable without a mother.

Caliana appreciated the intellectual clarity of her understanding. Though it couldn't replace the pain of being unloved, it put her feelings into perspective. Caliana hadn't earned her mother's indifference, and she was grateful for the knowledge that there was nothing she could have done to make the woman love her. She realized that even if she had given her mother the fantasy of an ideal daughter, her mother would still have not been able to love her. Actually, Caliana doubted that her mother had bothered visualizing a perfect child, or any child. Caliana couldn't remember ever witnessing a genuine loving moment from her mother to anyone, including Caliana's own sisters. It made Caliana feel good to know that a part of her loved herself enough to love her son, that she wasn't as damaged as her mother.

A dramatically opposing layer had been penetrated. In a strange and wonderfully freeing new way, Caliana felt safe and peaceful in trusting in her ability to love her son. She treasured the many miraculous moments when she held Kareem, and continuously marveled at the integrity of her thoughts; she wanted only his happiness. Caliana felt that she was bonding with a lineage of profound shared emotion that connected her to the first mother of all time.

Having missed out on the experience of being mothered, and thus the expression of a mother's love, Caliana had been unable to fully imagine what a mother's love could feel like. Many movies and books containing maternal moments had particularly moved her, made her sad and wishful. At times, she had yearned for a release to the painful smoldering feelings that had sat in her chest. Becoming a mother herself helped her understand the magnitude of the nourishment that she had never had.

CHAPTER 12

CALIANA spent a month recuperating in Texas, and treasuring every novel moment with Kareem. Her mind was solely occupied with a firm purpose: She had to protect him. When Caliana was not with her son, the fears that she managed to suppress while in his presence swam in distorted scenarios behind her closed eyelids. The dread of realizing that her son had come close to dying in her uterus exposed the fragility of his life.

She became an insomniac. Terrifying dreams of Kareem's death kept her in paralyzed alert. Every horror story she had ever heard regarding children's deaths played itself out in her head, and Caliana felt the devastating heartbreak of each imagined thought. Caliana was surprised by the depths of the reverent prayer that she launched at God. Her prayers were adjusted to beseech God to include her own safety, her survival, just until Kareem was eighteen. She understood that no one would be able to replace her in loving him and caring for him as well as she would. She had found her purpose in life, and she was going to live for it.

She knew that Rami loved his child, but she had also witnessed his limitations. Rami was capable of loving but was a simple boy who wasn't on a solid track into manhood and was thus incapable of caring for Kareem. He joked that his turn at parenting Kareem would arrive when Kareem turned twelve years old, for that would be when his son would be ready to be made into a man. Caliana shuddered at the dismal image of her son being molded to resemble his father. It affirmed her conviction that she should eventually become the sole parent.

Rami's parents had rented them an apartment in Jordan, and her parents had gifted them with furniture and appliances. Caliana thought that she would wait until she returned to Jordan in September before she broke the news of a divorce. She figured that she would then spend a few months in Jordan obtaining a divorce and using the time to figure out where she would best raise her son. She was leaning heavily toward the United States; the US offered a culture more accepting of her as a newly divorced single mother than anywhere in the Middle East.

The moment Caliana landed in Jordan, she started feeling uneasy. She felt like a fraud, being greeted by the welcoming family members gathered at the airport to greet them and escort them back to her new house. A few congratulations later and she had to resist the urge to blurt out her massive divorce proclamation.

Caliana entered her new, fully furnished house with dread. She was stepping into the result of an irrational moment in time when she had agreed to be married. She couldn't regret the marriage, for it had produced her son, but she could not imagine prolonging the façade any longer. It was killing her to smile and respond happily to the excited chatter of her in-laws as they showed her around the apartment. Her mother joyfully recited the brand names of every piece of furniture, subtly reminding everyone of her generosity.

Caliana had barely put her sleeping son in his crib when she was summoned to dinner. She returned to the dining room to a table laden with a variety of steaming dishes. Twelve people were seated around the table. Her mother had arranged for Caliana to host her first dinner in her new home by having her own staff prepare and serve the meal.

The talk around the dinner table revolved around the societal etiquette toward planning the gatherings to celebrate the occasion of her marriage and the birth of Kareem. Caliana was surprised to hear her mother and mother-in-law discussing the receptions that they had already planned to begin the following week. Caliana protested as much as she could but was repeatedly told that she had to receive the people who wanted to honor her by congratulating her. Apparently, because she had had her wedding in London, she had deprived their society of participating in the customary traditions.

The next two months were an endless swirl of lunches and dinners hosted by just about everyone within their class in Jordan. Every single family member from their extensive families had booked them in invitations. Caliana met members of Rami's family whom she had not known existed. Rami and Caliana were invited out by friends of both sets of parents, Rami's friends, and Caliana's friends. Caliana was stuck accepting the whirlwind of invitations, which forced her to postpone her divorce plans. The social functions declared the shocking role she was expected to have as a married woman. After two months, she knew that living in Jordan was not an option after she gets her divorce, and was a reality she could never accept.

More than anything, Caliana resented the time away from her son. All she wanted was to be left alone with him. She craved her privacy and started fantasizing about living on her secluded island with Kareem. She knew that she could not maintain the lifestyle requirements of living in Jordan and the accompanying visibility.

In early December, Caliana seized her opportunity. Rami was spending a day in the Jordan Valley with his friends, and she had her first unscheduled lunch. She called her parents and invited herself to join them for lunch. As soon as the butler served them and moved away, Caliana calmly stated that she had to get a divorce. She told them that Rami was a drug addict and was insecure about her ex-fiancé. It was the first time that Caliana had voluntarily shared personal information with her parents.

Her mother wanted details. She asked Caliana if she had informed Rami that she wasn't a virgin before she got married. Caliana nodded, knowing that her mother was beginning her case against Rami. Caliana awkwardly answered every question that her mother could think of. She watched her father anxiously, trying to predict his muted reaction.

The following morning, at eight, her father rang her up and told her to dress conservatively and to be ready by nine to be picked up by his driver and brought to his office. He hung up without giving her a chance to question him.

Caliana entered her father's conference room and saw that the table was crowded with many men, and that a conference was underway. Her father motioned for her to sit next to him and continued talking. He didn't bother to introduce her. Caliana gradually gathered that some of the men were lawyers. One man was a priest of some denomination, and another was a Sheik of the Muslim faith. Some men barely spoke, so Caliana couldn't figure out their roles.

"My whole life, my biggest fear was in knowing that if one of my daughters wanted a divorce, that we would face this situation." Caliana was shocked to hear her father's admission. Surprised at his authenticity, she found it endearing.

Caliana had never seen her father in such a mode of operation. He seemed to have a well-funded amount of knowledge regarding the law. Caliana, who had never heard of the divorce laws of Jordan, was horrified. Apparently, Christians had "backwards" laws—laws that the Muslims at one point had also adhered to. The only Christians who could divorce were Greek Orthodox. Rami would have to willingly convert from being a Protestant, and Caliana would have to shed her legal identity as a Catholic. Only then could they legally divorce. As for custody of Kareem, he was guaranteed to be with her until the age of two, as the time until then was considered an essential stage for a child to be with his mother. Caliana would then have to negotiate keeping him for a few more years, and even then only up to the age of seven. Her very–best-case scenario was to negotiate to keep her son until he was seven years old, when Rami would become the sole legal custodian of Kareem.

Every option was considered, including Caliana's conversion to Islam. A Muslim woman was allowed to keep her male child with her until he reached the age of fourteen. The Imam warned that converting to Islam had its own set of complexities, for if Rami were to also convert to Islam, Caliana would be bound by the lack of protection of a "civil contract." Every Muslim wedding contract included the option of signing a specific permission allowing a woman to be able to divorce her husband in the unforeseeable future. Considering that the contracts were always negotiated by male members of the bride's family, it was more common for the males to honorably waive the idea of divorce and thus dismiss the concept of giving a female a choice. Technically, the fact that Caliana was not originally married in the Muslim faith and had not specified that she had the option to divorce meant that legally she would be treated as a Muslim woman who had declined her right to divorce at the onset of the union. Rami could convert to Islam and, out of spite, might never divorce her.

Caliana proposed a separation and was devastated to hear that by law, she could be made to return to her marital home if Rami so wished. All he had to do was invoke the law, and the police would escort her back to his house. The only way for her to be able to leave his home was if he desired a divorce and gave her something in writing to indicate his wishes.

Caliana started understanding her father's fear, and a new sense of respect and gratitude grew for him. Her father was trying his best to obtain her freedom. He had gathered every available source to discuss a solution, and for his efforts alone she was indebted. Caliana heard every prognosis and quelled her mounting rage. She could not believe that any civil society could have such laws.

Caliana left her father's office dejected. She was chained by a country's regulations, and she didn't even belong in that country or want to live in it. Caliana had always enjoyed visiting Jordan and had dealt with its hectic lifestyle precisely because she had known it would be temporary. She couldn't remember the last time she had stayed in Jordan for longer than a month. She felt suffocated by the weight of having to live with Rami, of having to live in Jordan. She was drowning in thoughts. Her only glimmer of hope was that Rami would be civil and divorce her.

* * *

That night, Caliana calmly told Rami that she wanted a divorce. The venom that poured out of him was totally unexpected. He ranted and raved and threatened every legal action against her.

She would never be allowed to leave him, he threatened, until he decided that he was sick of her and ready to discard her. If she dared leave with his son, he would have her brought back, like a dog, to be held prisoner at his house. He boasted that he could drink, do drugs, whore around, and do whatever else suited him, and she would have no legal claims against him. She would be an unpaid servant to his son. She was under his mercy, and he could treat her however it suited him.

Or she could leave, and abandon her son.

Caliana was shocked by his knowledge of the law, and highly disturbed by the thrill he derived from threatening her with it. Her son was a tool he was prepared to brandish at her, and Caliana realized that her obvious love for her son had become his only valid ammunition. Instead of receiving civility, Caliana was treated to a horrific display of manic verbal aggression that ended with Rami's glazed eyes inches from her face as he shouted that he "would break her."

Caliana held his manic gaze and felt the fury of her physical response to his challenge. Her body shook, yet she kept her gaze locked in defiant hatred. Her heart shuddered uncontrollably with fears that threatened to invade her mind. She held them off and focused on sending a challenging message of fearless energy.

Time stood still, and her intent gaze allowed Caliana to glimpse the monstrosity within Rami. She sensed an unhinged mind and trusted her intuition.

An old, familiar terror erupted within her. She would fight, and she would survive. She had to, for her son.

Caliana leaned in, a fraction closer to Rami's face. She offered him a view of her deliberately exposed soul. She wanted him to read her resolve. She let her face register a slow, challenging smirk. A deathly resignation infused her with cold anger. She held the moment, for she intended that he feel her strength.

"You ... will ... *never* ... break me." Every syllable was enunciated with deliberate composure.

Almost instantly, she regretted her bold confrontation. She saw in Rami a certain flicker into her future within his insanity. She felt the icy dread of knowing that she had provoked his madness. Her combative resolve had inadvertently stimulated an even more perverse psyche, and it was written all over Rami's face. Her heart chilled in terror.

"I will break you. You will come begging. Like a dog. Begging me to leave you!" He grinned, and left the apartment.

Stunned, Caliana's body began to convulse. Rami's words enhanced the madness she had glimpsed. She was at war with a maniac. For the first time in five years, she flashed on an image of her stalker.

At least with Rami, she knew her enemy and could prepare for it. Caliana felt the first rage at herself for having loved Kareem so clearly. She regretted having loved him. She felt an irrational resentment toward her son for having entrapped her in weakness, in love. She knew that her motivation to live and fight had stemmed mainly from loving her son, but by loving him so openly, she had exposed the only weapon that could be used against her.

Horrified guilty tears clouded her vision as she rushed to her son's room. Kareem, who was sleeping in utter serenity, involuntarily smiled. Shame flooded her, and a dreadful sound poured from her mouth. Caliana swallowed back the sobs threatening to gush out of her. Losing control of her ability to still the pain, or control the noise, Caliana rushed to her bathroom and jumped, fully clothed, into the torrent of water that flowed from the showerhead.

She had never experienced such crying. Her body released powerful sobs. Frustrated rage screamed out of her, and she scared herself back into silence. She started heaving for air, suffocating from the abundance of water on her face. Abruptly, she turned off the water and was surprised by the loudness of her heaving. She tried to still her body with controlled missives from her mind.

It took a towel, savagely shoved in her face, to finally control the noises exploding out of her. Enraged, Caliana sat on the bathroom floor for a long time and contemplated her future.

It would have to be a silent war. She would never beg, but she would make Rami rue the day he dared assume ownership of her. And for his abuse, she would do whatever it took to rid herself of him.

CHAPTER 13

CALIANA lived in hell for four months. She continued the façade of a married woman. Their social engagements decreased to a bare minimum. She observed that Rami continued the party mentality he had adapted in the States and his friends were thrilled. Caliana at times counted the days when he had not seen his son because he came in after Kareem's bedtime and had not even been concerned enough to check in on him while the baby slept.

Caliana continued to meet with her father and the lawyers in clandestine gatherings. She informed them of a subdued version of Rami's activities and kept them abreast of the continuous insults and threats that he made. They strongly encouraged her to endure in silence and hope that eventually Rami would shift gears and release her. Caliana found each moment in Rami's presence unbearable. She could barely mask her revolt and dislike of him in front of others. Besides her parents, the only people she had informed of her decision for divorce were Rami's immediate family.

Her mother-in-law's response was simply that Caliana should not defy traditions. After all, thousands of women were miserable in their respective marriages, including herself, and all those women endured. Why should Caliana behave any differently than all those other women? Did Caliana think herself better than those women? The only time it was acceptable to divorce was if the husband was physically abusive, a gambler, a drug addict, or an alcoholic. And even then, a woman should endure.

Caliana was tempted to affirm that Rami fit into one of her suitable categories but realized that it would be a futile and hurtful admission. Her mother-in-law had previously demonstrated an unshakable devotion toward Rami, and had spoilt him rotten. She was a mother who wanted to believe that her baby son was perfect and could do no wrong. Caliana also tried to be respectful toward *Ammo* Habib. Her father-in-law had delicately cautioned her against discussing the divorce with his wife, as it might upset her "fragile nerves."

Ammo Habib had suggested that they give it some time to try to make it work. He dismissed the drugs as a stage wherein all young men experimented. Caliana felt sorry for him, and hoped that she was wrong, if for no other reason than to make him a happy parent. But she knew that Rami could not live up to the trust and genuine faith his father placed in him. In front of his father, Rami downplayed his addiction and claimed that it was a recreational thing he only did when he was in the United States. Caliana could see that, as a parent, her father-in-law willingly believed his son because he wanted to believe the best of his son, and because he was ignorant of the nature of drugs and, therefore, of his son's addiction.

Caliana was very fond and respectful of her father-in-law. He had been an exemplary human being toward her, treating her mind with respectful regard ever since she was twelve. He had been the only adult in Jordan who had taken the time to talk to her. She had shared the better part of her mind in lengthy discussions about topics ranging from the law to religion and spirituality, and had delved into the meaning of humanity and integrity with him.

Caliana respected the fact that her father-in-law was a self-made man. He had graduated high school at twelve, worked as an errand boy for a lawyer for a year, and begun studying law in England at the age of thirteen. At seventeen, he had returned to Jordan and had to sit through another law degree in Arab law to qualify him to work as a lawyer in the region. At twenty-one, he had obtained his doctorate and worked hard at establishing a brilliant career. He had become a workaholic and been reminded by society that he had pushed the extended age limit given to a bachelor, so he had married at the late age of thirty-two to an eighteen-year-old.

His first child, a daughter, had brought him unexpected joy and happiness. He was probably the only Arab man Caliana believed when he claimed that he would have been more than happy had he been blessed only with one daughter. He had also admitted that in his daughter's infancy, he had loved her so very much that he had been petrified to have any more children for the fear of not being able to imagine loving them as equally. But Caliana had the privilege of having watched him be a loving and respectful father to all his three children.

Caliana had learned to tolerate and adapt to the slower speed at which her father-in-law meticulously searched for the precise word during serious conversations. She had learned to replace her natural and immediate irritation at slow-speaking people with respectful and patient restraint. He had helped show her that the speed of conversation was not a measure of intelligence. He had slowed her thoughts down enough that she could absorb and share his leisurely words of wisdom. She owed the man the debt of having shown her civility, and she could not possibly shock and break his heart with the truth about his son.

Initially, observing Samir's energy in conversations with his father had helped model Caliana's patience. She had been surprised by Samir's ability to listen attentively to his father, totally absorbed. She had assumed that Samir would be as impatient as she was. Even when her father-in-law repeated himself, which was quite often, Samir respectively attended his father's words as though it was his first time hearing them.

Caliana had been impressed with Samir's respectful restraint and patience. When faced with certain social situations that had bored them, Caliana had been used to Samir joining her in witty exchanges that invariably ended with them going off on a private tangent, laughing until tears came to their eyes. People got used to Samir and Caliana interjecting their own running commentaries, and in seeing them doubled over in agonized laughter. The trust they had in each other allowed them to exchange the most outlandish sharing of truths. They amazed themselves at how attuned they were to each other's unedited thoughts. Their humor was grounded in bonding their ability to read each other's minds in varying situations. To say the least, they often excluded people in their humor, but their good friends learned to give them loving leeway.

By witnessing the qualities that had inspired Samir's respect and patience, Caliana had developed a new perspective on Samir, his father, and herself.

Samir came over one morning to talk with her. Caliana had always known that to Samir, his friends were his chosen family, but she had never been able to understand his affinity to their collective society. He thrived from being around people and loved company. She also knew that she was, in some ways, his exact opposite.

Throughout their friendship, they had respectfully argued their diversity regarding their views on Jordanian society. Samir wanted her to share his love of belonging and feel some of his exuberance. His views stemmed from a loving concern for her detachment of home, country, and people.

Caliana was happy for him, for his genuine pleasure in his society, but she had none of his attachments. Her only affection to Jordan was her love for him, Haya and Rhea, and a few others she genuinely cared for. To Samir, it was precisely the love of the people that grounded him into his society, and he had a hard time understanding her ambivalence toward her home. She appreciated that this heartfelt perspective came from a person who had integrated into a world foreign to her.

That morning, Samir was torn. He knew that Caliana was determined to divorce his brother, yet he felt duty-bound to clarify the fuller implications of what it could mean within their society. He was concerned for her and, frankly, scared.

He had almost experienced being the child of divorce in a tightly knit society. He had survived the fear of the possibility that his parents might rip the fragile civility of the marriage that they maintained for the sake of their children. He couldn't promote a marriage like that of his parents, who coexisted in separate bedrooms, sharing only the intimacy that was forced from living together. But neither could he imagine how Caliana would cope as the only divorced person in their world. Samir emphasized that divorce was not socially accepted, and he was concerned that she was not fully prepared for its repercussions.

Caliana listened intently to Samir's advice. She knew that he had left out the part about surviving the "unspoken rumors" of his mother's mental illness, and Caliana instinctively knew that surviving that damage had been a significant part of his makeup. She had never discussed his mother with him. The only time Samir's energy was reserved was when he was around his mother; he treated her respectfully but kept his emotional distance.

"What about Kareem? Can you imagine the possible stigma that he would have to survive? At least if he were living in the States, or somewhere where divorce is common, he would not be the only odd child of divorce," Samir added.

"I agree with you, and that's one of the reasons I plan to live abroad. You and I both know that if it wasn't for Kareem, I wouldn't be sitting in Jordan discussing a divorce. I cannot live in this country, and you know better than anyone all my reasons."

Caliana breathed in her anger and frustration. "Actually, living here the past few months has convinced me more than ever that I don't belong here. Besides a deserted island, though, I can't imagine belonging anywhere ...."

"But you can't be your own island!" Samir's eyelashes started the endearing rapid fluttering that conveyed his nervous intensity. Caliana could see his thoughts race. His anxiety for her was escalating. "Think about the future. Think about when you get older. Aren't you afraid of being alone?"

Caliana felt her eyes fill up with tears. "You have no idea how accurately you used the metaphor of island," she choked. Tears ran unchecked. "I am the most alone when I am surrounded by people."

Caliana surprised herself. She had calmly spoken her most profound truth, and it felt safe.

They sat quietly for a while, each absorbed in thought. Caliana desperately wanted to share her frustrations, her pain, and the cruel imprisonment forced by Rami's bravado, but she was frightened. After all, Rami was Samir's brother. Although she believed that Samir loved her and considered her his best friend, he was bound by the loyalty of his blood. She had no right to put him in a position that may require him to pick a side, and she was scared that he might not side with her.

Two days later, a package was hand-delivered. It contained Rami's divorce decree. Caliana didn't even bother reading past the first obvious lines. She called her father and could barely contain her excitement. Finally, she was free, and she instinctively knew that Samir must have helped push Rami to present her with it.

Her father told her that his driver would be there to pick up the document and deliver it to the main lawyer. He wanted to make sure that it complied with the law before she left her marital home. He told her to start packing, and that he would call her as soon as he heard back from the lawyer.

Caliana asked the nanny to pack Kareem's clothes and headed to her room. She looked around the bedroom that she had shared with Rami for the past eight months and realized that there was nothing that she wanted to take with her. Her cupboards in her room at her parents' house were loaded with her clothes. For a moment, she was tempted to scrawl in bright red lipstick some nasty comment on the mirror facing the bed. Instead, she yanked off her wedding ring, cleared space on the commode, and strategically centered the ring in its gaudy center.

Caliana started heading to help the nanny when the doorbell rang. She froze at the thought that Rami might have returned to his house, though she knew she was being ridiculous, as he would have used his keys.

Haya had decided to stop by for coffee before heading to work. Caliana was immensely relieved to see her. Unable to contain her need to blurt out her truth, Caliana rushed through a series of events. She knew that she was all over the place but that Haya would make sense of her jagged explanation. Haya calmly took in her news and didn't attempt to dissuade her.

Caliana's father rang back to confirm that the lawyer had given her the go-ahead to leave. He briefly summarized that the divorce contract clearly portrayed that Rami had no intention of compromising or being civil. Not that the terms mattered. All they needed was proof that he did not want her.

Caliana felt elation followed by indignant anger at having to be forced to feel elated at a freedom that should have been hers by right. She carried her son, and handed him to Haya. She asked the nanny and Haya to precede her out of the apartment, and she gently closed the door behind her. She didn't look back.

In her mind, she saw herself staring straight ahead as she slowly dragged a can of gasoline in the wake of her exit. She calmly paused outside the apartment, and lit a cigarette. She inhaled a deep drag, and flicked the cigarette behind her, starting a trail of flames that ended in an explosion of Rami's house. She smiled a slow smile as she heard the flames catch behind her. She paused a moment and allowed the fantasy to satisfy her.

Haya refused to leave her and told her that she would follow her in her car until she was home. Caliana insisted that she was totally fine and that Haya should go to work, as she was late already.

Haya stayed with Caliana all day. Caliana appreciated her serene support and total acceptance. Rhea, who was too ill to join her but had known about Caliana's plans to divorce for a few days, called often to lend her support.

Haya left when Caliana's father arrived home.

Caliana met her father in his library to review the plan that they had set in motion a few months earlier. Her father informed her that she would be leaving the country the following morning, at five, to go to the bridge to cross over into the occupied Palestinian territories of the West Bank. There, she would be safe, as Rami could not possibly follow. Few Palestinian families had the legal right of passage that gave them the ability to make the crossing. Caliana went over all the directions that she had been given.

She couldn't sleep that night. She knew that she was about to kidnap her son out of the country and that her action would begin an unpredictable avalanche of reactions. She was prepared for all outcomes and knew that if negotiations failed, her father would financially support her permanent disappearance. Caliana hoped that she would have the option to return to Jordan to visit in the future, but she was just as prepared to never set foot on the continent.

It would be up to Rami how he chose to negotiate from a more equal position. She could not delay staying in Jordan, because if Rami got wind of her plans, he could easily have her name blocked at the borders. She had to leave and threaten him with disappearance unless he could provide a more workable divorce agreement. Caliana had clearly emphasized to her father and the lawyers that her only real concern was negotiating the longest possible years of custody of Kareem. She knew that at age fifteen, a boy was given the adult right to choose where he lived. To Caliana, the best-case scenario would be to have Kareem stay with her the first fifteen years, and then she would accept his choice.

CHAPTER 14

May 1987

CALIANA woke Kareem up at four in the morning and dressed him in shorts and a T-shirt. She carried a plastic bag that held a few diapers, two baby bottles with powdered formula, a baby bottle with water, a small zip-lock bag with wet wipes, a small disposable container of smashed vegetables and fruits, a plastic spoon, and a large water bottle—calculated, absolute necessities that Kareem would need for his single day of survival.

She met her father in the sitting room, and he took off all her jewelry. He replaced her watch with a cheap disposable watch and gave her exactly seventy dinars. Caliana was not to carry anything besides the plastic bag. Her father gave her an old thin blazer that had belonged to her mother, as it had wide enough pockets to hold everything she needed. One pocket held the Jordanian passports and Palestinian paperwork proving that she had *Lam Shamel,* proof of residency, to the Palestinian territories that were controlled by the Israelis. In the other pocket, Caliana carried a packet of cigarettes and a book of matches.

Her father walked her to the car, where the driver was holding the door open for her. The butler came running out to the car with a pillow for Kareem to lie on and some sandwiches that Caliana could eat on their trip to the bridge. Caliana appreciated the gesture of kindness and felt tears well up in her eyes.

In the car, Kareem fell back asleep, lulled by the sound of the engine. Caliana was on edge, knowing that she would have to get through the ordeal of crossing the bridge and dealing with the Israelis. Ever since she could remember, she had been forced to make the dreaded trip every few years to renew her Palestinian residency; otherwise, she would risk having it forever revoked. The Israelis were only too happy to have a valid excuse to statistically eliminate another unwanted Palestinian resident from the territories they occupied. Whenever Caliana and her sisters had complained about having to make the crossing, her father had angrily reminded them that there were millions of displaced Palestinians who would have loved to have permits entitling them to live in their homeland. Their father also reminded them that their permits would eventually allow them to inherit the property and business that the family owned in the West Bank.

Caliana descended toward the Dead Sea just as the sun was rising. The steep rocky hills suited the vast desert landscape. She always experienced a proud thrill at witnessing the bold beauty of the landscape. She felt her ears close from the pressure of descending to the lowest spot on earth, about 783 meters below sea level at the bottom of the Dead Sea. Her favorite part of the descent was the first dramatic glimpse of the Jordan Valley spread bellow. She always felt as though she were looking at a mirage, at an unexpected green oasis. The dramatic shift in landscape thrilled her. Her eyes would drink in the lushness, and Caliana would open all the windows in the car, letting the warm desert air greet her.

That dawn, Caliana resisted that magnificent opportunity. She wished that she had been the one driving, as she would have loved to pull over, wake up Kareem, and have him witness the glory of nature. Instead, she savored the stillness of the fertile pride of the River Jordan as they drove through South *Shouneh* on their way to the bridge.

They headed to the part of the River Jordan where a small old bridge lay suspended, separating the borders of the two adversarial countries. Caliana knew that she would soon be at the Jordanian–Israeli border facility where she would receive VIP treatment on the Jordanian side. She would bypass the common Jordanian exit immigration facility where hundreds of people would be lined up to board buses for the crossing, and she would be driven to the small security facility that the Jordanian army had erected on their end of the bridge. It was a small office that served as a lookout station to the other side. The few guards who rotated that station welcomed the rare interruptions to their monotony by also serving as hosting station to the few important people who made a crossing and had the privilege of avoiding the crowds.

During Caliana's grandfather's life, because of his title and frequent crossings, he had established the family's right of passage by generously rewarding the border guards. Crates of fresh fruits and vegetables were a standard accompaniment to whatever other gift was also given to them. The sharing of food was a staple Arab belief of honoring a person.

The tradition of gifting had carried on past her grandfather's death, simply because the remaining family members still wanted the privilege of preferential treatment when they made the crossings. Caliana's father viewed his gifts as bribes that entitled him to a special crossing, whereas her grandfather had actually visited the guards, chatting with them about anything and everything, enjoying hearing about their lives. Often, he would be so engrossed in conversations that he would wave a bus away to continue talking with them. Caliana and her family, on the other hand, barely acknowledged the guards with a few words. As a result, they were received very well, but with much less enthusiasm than the Basha had been.

Caliana had once overheard an older guard regaling her driver with stories about her grandfather. He swore by his children that the Basha had always shared his tea with them and had treated them as kings. The Basha had been "dearer than a brother, more precious than a brother." He had always inquired about their well-being and cared enough to remember the details of their lives. He would have their needs taken care of without them needing to ask him for anything. Within a few days of his return to Jordan, the Basha's driver would visit them with a generous truckload of every provision that they could have wanted or asked for. It was as though God had assessed their needs and the Basha was the chosen angel who had supplied their wishes, the guard had proclaimed. The Basha was always the most thoughtful benefactor, and the old guard would have carried the Basha on his back all the way to Bethlehem, if he had but asked.

He would always be indebted to the Basha for having shown him genuine civility. The Basha had been a great man, the guard proclaimed, and had the highest esteemed position whereby he could have traveled the country unstopped. He was even allowed to cross the bridge with his diplomatic car, as he was exempt from the barriers that other civilians received. He had had the authority to dismiss the guards completely yet had always made it a point to stop and spend some time with them. When the Basha visited, every guard had rushed to greet him, and pay his respects. No one else could replace the Basha's greatness, the guard swore, for there was no one else like him.

Caliana's father's inherited diplomatic plates ensured that she completely avoided the exit immigration hall on the Jordanian side. She was offered a chair and coffee at the facility at the bridge and was told that the very first bus that would be making the crossing of the day would be hailed down especially for her. She tried to compensate for her parents' previous snobbish attitude toward the guards by making an effort but, as always, managed to run out of words past the formal greetings. She didn't know how to speak their formal language, and Caliana sank into the awkward silences.

Caliana tried to pass the time by looking at the disappointing view of the River Jordan. She had been told that the river had sections with vast flowing waters, especially in the upper portion above the Sea of Galilee, but the part where she sat, where the bridge linked the banks, was small and had shallow waters. Here, the landscape was desolate and only served to emphasize the symbolic slowness of time.

This area of the River Jordan had a formidable history. Jesus' baptism site was nearby. The bridge held an even wider appeal to Caliana, however, as it had been originally constructed by Romans, the first to build bridges over the River Jordan between the first and third centuries AD. During the British Mandate, 1920–1948, three bridges had been built to facilitate the crossing of the British Army into Jordan to fight the ruling Ottomans, and General Allenby of the British army had modernized the structure of this Roman bridge, which had then become known as the Allenby Bridge. Caliana loved standing by it, as it grounded her in history. She imagined the millions of Palestinians crossing the Allenby Bridge in 1948 and 1967 as they fled Palestine from the wars. Even after the bridge had been destroyed, it was rebuilt in 1968 and became known as the King Hussein Bridge. The bridge was a crossing point that split the distance between Jerusalem and West Amman, as it was exactly forty kilometers from each destination.

From her side of the Allenby–King Hussein Bridge, Caliana could easily see the features of the Israeli soldiers on the Israeli side. She had often wondered if the soldiers from each country developed a friendship based on the intimacy of their proximity. They would barely have to raise their voices if they chose to converse across the bridge. Caliana liked to picture them meeting at the halfway point to communicate. She hoped that they would be able to bridge humanity.

Eventually, a beaten, bullet-ridden bus squeaked to a dusty stop, a reminder from the 1967 war between the countries. Before she left the Jordanian guards to join the bus, Caliana tried to show the guards sincerity while thanking them for their hospitality. She wanted them to at least feel her gratitude.

Caliana always felt embarrassed at the preferential treatment of joining the crowded bus only at the very last moment and at not having gone through the checkpoints with the other people on the bus. She hadn't had to wait with the refugees, who had often camped out for days, waiting for the opportunity to have their papers prepared for the crossing; or those who simply had had to wait for the limited space that was designated every day. Often, the Israelis would close the bridge for unknown reasons and for whatever length of time they chose, creating a backup on the Jordanian side.

Caliana's embarrassment this day was instantly replaced by the shock of entering the crowded bus that had only standing space by the time she got on. Claustrophobic waves assaulted her as she tried to breathe from her mouth to avoid the horrific smells. She stood out like an alien in her jeans and T-shirt amidst the Bedouin-garbed *Fallaheen* who crowded inside the bus with many of their belongings. She was always stunned by what people brought with them on the bus to take home. Most of the people were simple disadvantaged farmers returning home from visiting their relatives in Jordan and other Arab countries. Arab generosity being especially infamous amongst the poor guaranteed that the Palestinian returning home was usually loaded down with many gifts given to him by many relatives and friends. Items of furniture were not uncommon. As a child, Caliana had been fascinated with what people opted to carry on a rickety old bus.

The bus barely moved the twenty or so meters, which was the length of the bridge, before it was halted by the Israeli soldiers sadistically demonstrating their power. Their aggression was meant to create instant and lasting fear. They began by pushing and shouting their way through the people, demanding their papers from them. The soldiers all spoke a heavily accented Arabic but expected to be understood and responded to immediately.

In past crossings, Caliana had always steeled herself with a seething rage that kept her from having to endure any fear. It had been easy to maintain the anger, as the Israeli guards had provided ample opportunities to ignite hatred within her. But having her son in her arms, inches from the guns surrounding him, sank her into fearful anxiety.

She found herself stuck, blocking the passage of the Israeli soldiers and having to push back into barely inches of spare space. She had been standing next to the bus driver at the very front when the first Israeli soldier came aboard. She edged back and bumped into a family of six packed into a two-seater space. The Palestinian man quickly stood up and hurriedly pushed her into his seat, telling her to sit in his place.

Before Caliana had a chance to react, she realized that the man had traded his seat for a heavy dosage of humiliation, for her sake. The Israeli soldier, having witnessed his action, started screaming at him for daring to move without his specific permission. Caliana knew from the tension of the woman next to her, who had an infant on her lap and three children crowding her, that she was the man's terrified wife. Caliana's pulse pounded in her head as she heard the poor man attempt to justify his kind act by explaining that he was helping a woman carrying a child who needed to be seated.

Caliana cringed for him, for she knew that the first target of the soldiers' humiliation would be used to set an example. The soldier flew at the man with insults, screaming rhetorical questions and interrupting the attempted answers with theories to demoralize the refugee with utter humiliation. He accused the Palestinian man of having been a pig for not having offered his seat *before* crossing the bridge, for having let a woman with a baby stand. The soldier sarcastically taunted his manhood: Maybe his action was an attempt to impress the Israelis, and he was a coward. Verbal bullets reminded everyone on the bus that every single move any of them dared make better be only as a direct response to a given command.

Caliana was frozen in fear. The soldier moved past them, and other soldiers took their place at the front of the bus. None of the passengers dared to speak, except the unlucky ones made to answer the humiliating interrogations. Caliana's hand shook as she offered Kareem a water bottle. She kept her eyes locked on Kareem, but her every nerve was focused on the presence of the soldiers.

The collective energy changed when the soldiers finally left the bus. Pent-up feelings gave way to some cursing, some exhaled complaints, and a few tears. Caliana was experiencing a new level of response and was surprised by it. She absolutely knew that she had conquered her fear of death and had tried her best to react to dangerous situations by fortifying herself with stored-up anger, and yet here she was, inconsolable at the mere image of her son's safety being endangered, and incapable of suppressing her fears, even with all the might of her anger.

Caliana felt vulnerable and realized that this particular crossing would challenge her control of a new fear. Her previous detachment was somewhat shattered from the direct contact that had been forced upon her by the Palestinian man and his family. Well-intended, they immediately inquired after her and her son, and the man refused her offer to give him back his seat. He insisted that he wouldn't hear of it, and he imitated the Israeli soldier by quoting some of his precise commands. Some nervous laughter broke the tension, and people seemed to settle in the waiting.

Caliana wished she had a fan, or something to cool Kareem and herself. The bus felt like an oven, and everyone was sweating profusely, which added to the terrible smell. Caliana tried to talk to the children, but they seemed crippled in shyness and sagged against their mother, their energy drained from the heat.

Caliana soon became grateful for the collective silence that ensued and let her mind wander. She knew that once the papers were collected, the real waiting would begin. It was widely considered a blessing if the bus had only one hour's wait. Caliana had once spent three hours at that first junction of her crossing.

She recalled her frequent outrages. Even though she had often heard that the crossing was "meant to humiliate you" a thousand times and that every survivor of a bridge crossing had a horrible story to tell, she could never cease to be outraged by the deliberate inhumanity the Israelis inflicted. Images of past crossings flooded her mind, and she began a mental preparation for the ordeal ahead. She needed to get through the day.

That Israel was only forty years old baffled many people. Caliana had read a book that preached about the power of suggestion, the power of foresight, and attaining one's goal by keeping the goal in a constant conscious foreground so one could constantly work on the goal and thus attain it. She realized that the Zionist ideology had accomplished this principle through a tenacious vision that had lasted from its inception in 1897. Theodore Herzl had realized that anti-Semitism existed in spite of assimilation and would continue so long as the Jewish people were a national anomaly.

In the second half of the 19th century, European empires began a new wave of imperialism that was, in reality, plundering of the Middle East. The Middle Eastern Arabs had been trying to gain their independence from the British and the French empires. The British promised the Arabs that once the Arabs helped them unseat the Ottoman rile in the region, they would withdraw, and the Arabs would receive their autonomy at long last. Between 1916 and 1918, the Arabs supported the British forces and revolted against the Ottomans. Unbeknownst to the Arabs, in 1916, the British and French had signed the Sykes-Picot Agreement, which partitioned the Middle East between them. Also, the British had promised to support the Zionist movement in creating a Jewish homeland in Palestine via the Belfour Declaration in 1917. Instead of getting back their autonomy, the area of Palestine, which had been largely populated by Arabs for over a thousand years, was split in half: the eastern half became Transjordan under rule of king Abdullah, and the western half under British administration.

The Zionists had seen the opportunity of their promised land being exchanged by different governing hands, and had grabbed the opportunity to rally their cause. Hitler's atrocities had widely emerged for years after WWII, which had given Zionists the perfect examples to incite activism toward realizing their dream: the creation of Israel. Empathy for the displaced Jews permitted a different kind of atrocity, at the expense of the Palestinian people, who had no say in their country being lost. On May 14, 1948, the state of Isreal was established. Only the Arabs remembered the insult, as they were directly impacted by it.

As a people, the Jews had suffered the longest and the worst forms of persecution, which had always drawn Caliana in empathy to their strife and history. She couldn't believe that the descendants of the Holocaust victims, and the Holocaust's survivors, could have the heart to demoralize others. She had assumed that they, more than anyone, should have learned the value of humanity, irrespective of political justifications. She even understood that they were entitled as a people to ensure that the atrocities that had been inflicted on them by the Nazis would never be repeated, and appreciated their need to secure themselves. She had even forgiven them the fact that they had obtained their security at the expense of a weaker people, another's land. She had accepted the existence of the State of Israel, which had really stretched her subjectivity as a Palestinian. But what she could never accept were the inhumane methods that the Israelis applied in controlling the Palestinians, their conquered subjects. Granted, Israel was a tiny country geographically surrounded by a region that hated it and generally intended its destruction; the Israelis needed to fortify with force, but that still didn't justify their aggression.

Caliana also understood the Arab hatred toward the Israelis; the Arabs had to tolerate an enemy responsible for the loss of a substantially meaningful part of their identity, as Arabs, and Muslims, and the added helplessness of knowing that the Palestinian people were mistreated under foreign oppression.

The global monopoly pumped the new country with all the financial support of the latest advancements that would propel Israel out of a third-world piece of land into an enviably Westernized, powerful force. Israel's growing status was a resentful reminder to the Arabs of the allegiance of the US and other powerful Western nations toward Israel. Anti-American sentiment had been brewing for some time. The collective world either deliberately ignored or didn't care about the civil rights of the Palestinians who were forced to exist under occupation.

Finally, almost two hours after the Israeli soldiers had left the bus, a few reentered and motioned for the driver to begin driving. Caliana almost wept at the joy of having some air enter the overheated bus from the broken windows. Everyone stirred in relief.

Kareem was soaked in his sweat and badly needed his diaper changed. Caliana was relieved to see the dreaded immigration hall for the refugees, if for no other reason than to lay Kareem on the floor and change him.

She entered the large hall that was designated for security searches of the Palestinians. Rows of wooden tables were laid out with many military inspectors surrounding them. Caliana found an empty corner and started putting Kareem down on the floor but was screamed at by a soldier who pointed his rifle at her and ordered her to stand in line.

Luckily, as she was the only one out of the bus without luggage, Caliana soon found herself in front of an officer at one of the designated tables. He seemed disappointed that she had only a plastic bag and fired dozens of questions pertaining to the fact that she was ill-equipped to travel with very little. Caliana calmly explained that she had what she needed waiting for her at her home in Bethlehem. She could feel his seething fury at her crippling answer; he couldn't think

of anything else to ask her. With deliberate turtle-like speed, he prolonged the search of the few items she had into a forty-five–minute
examination. With arm and neck muscles protesting Kareem's
weight, Caliana stood shaking, frequently shifting Kareem from one
sticky arm to the other, while every article she had with her received
unbelievable scrutiny.

With gloved hands for protection, the guard meticulously ripped
through the lining of the first five diapers and rendered them garbage-
worthy. He was less brutal with the remaining diapers. They survived
with only minor cuts and probes and were still generally functional.
Caliana wanted to rip the guard apart with a dosage of verbal sarcasm
but gritted her teeth and instead found an outlet through silent angry
thoughts as she was made to observe his creativity in unearthing danger from obviously harmless objects.

With Israel's entire modern infrastructure at their utter disposal,
the Israelis deliberately chose to keep the bridge facilities in primitive
operational conditions. They could have used machines to detect all
sorts of danger but seemed to prefer sadistic hands-on methods. They
wanted the desperate Palestinian refugees to be humiliated and
degraded for their unwelcome return to their homeland. The unbelievable security measures alone kept people sweating through hours
of unreasonably extensive searches that added to their wait time.
Every article underwent Israeli scrutiny.

Caliana's family had long since learned that they should carry
nothing, as that would substantially shorten the clearly understood
"everything is declared and analyzed" immigration policy. Her family
had always avoided the tables and bought everything they needed
when they got into Bethlehem. Naturally, the new items would remain
in Israel, as they too would undergo the rigor of being searched on the
way out. Basically, they entered with nothing and left with nothing.

Glaring defiantly at the guard, Caliana was struck by how differently she felt just by having Kareem in her arms. A fierce protective
pride replaced the symbolic emptiness of her past crossings. She was
entering enemy territory with her most beloved and precious son,
everything that mattered to her, and he was wilting in her arms. Every
delayed moment in waiting increased his discomfort, and Caliana was
incensed for him.

Finally, they proceeded to a room designated for females and
their young infants to be bodily searched. Caliana was ushered into a
small cubicle partially closed with a curtain. While waiting for the

strip search, Caliana was grateful for the opportunity to strip Kareem and offer him a cooling relief. She laid down the blazer as a blanket on the dirty ground and gently placed Kareem on it. Caliana instantly felt the relief from having held a hot, sweaty nine-month-old baby for a few hours. Her arms were cramped and covered in sweat. She yanked off her T-shirt and wiped the moisture from her body on it. She slowly massaged some stiffness out of her arms, squatted next to Kareem, and bathed him with wet wipes, followed by measured drips from the now-warm water bottle. Not wanting to dry Kareem with her dirty T-shirt, she used her breath on him as a fan.

Kareem, who had been an absolutely still observer of the day's events, seemed to have an innate ability to recognize the safety of his sole presence with his mother. He smiled and babbled "Mama," crawled onto Caliana's lap, and straightened himself by climbing on her until he had positioned his feet on the ground with an arm around her neck to support himself. He started planting wet kisses on her face. Caliana laughed at his antics and for a few seconds forgot her situation as she gave him a tight hug back.

An hour later, a female Israeli soldier pushed the curtain back as she entered the tiny room. She commanded Caliana to strip and then scanned through Caliana's and Kareem's clothing. Caliana's shoes and Kareem's sandals were thrown with dozens of other shoes in a plastic laundry basket that would undergo some scanning device. Caliana knew that in past crossings, her mother, who had refused to give up her designer shoes because it might lessen the impact of the image that she was determined to present, had had the heels ripped out to be examined and a few times had had a shoe returned with a deliberate inside-out repositioning of the heel.

Caliana and Kareem were led to a larger room to wait with the other women and children who had been physically searched. Caliana found an empty chair, fed Kareem on her lap with a bottle of formula, and rocked him until he fell asleep in her sore arms. She tried to be gentle as she placed him back on the blazer for a nap on the ground. She looked at her watch and estimated that it had been a little more than four hours from the time that she had boarded the bus. She knew that she still had to deal with the paperwork and fervently hoped the process wouldn't take more than another two hours.

For the next fifty-five minutes, she sweated and waited with all the women. Occasionally, a shoe basket would be dumped in an area and women would rummage through them, trying to match their shoes. Often, only one half of a pair arrived, and the women had to wait for the next load to be dumped to find their matching shoes.

Caliana was grateful when both her and Kareem's shoes finally arrived in the same basket. She rushed toward the paperwork section and felt the relief of being the first in line. A single Israeli officer was sitting in the caged office, reading a newspaper. He looked down at her, checked his watch, and then returned his attention to his paper. Caliana felt her anger mount. Evil thoughts flew around as she realized that he had no intention of calling her to come forward. She was stuck standing there until he deemed her important enough to waste his time by beginning his work. She seethed at the blatant disregard.

Caliana desperately needed to sit down. Her shoulders muscles were screaming for relief from the constant weight of carrying Kareem. She just wanted to sit on the ground and wait, put Kareem on her folded knees, and give her arms a tiny break, but she daren't. For forty minutes, she stood alone with Kareem. Gradually, a few people trickled behind her in line. She overheard a man complaining that the line was not moving and another man telling him to be quiet, as his complaining could only incite a retaliation of prolonged time.

Ninety-three minutes later, Caliana was suddenly screamed at to hurry up and get to the officer. She rushed forward, swallowing her raging pride. The officer asked dozens of ridiculous questions, often repeating questions, as though he may trick her into deviating from her original responses. Thirty-five minutes later, she was told to proceed to the hall and wait until she heard her name on the loudspeaker.

Caliana literally collapsed on the filthy ground of the waiting hall. She set Kareem down and cringed as she watched him crawl on the dirt. She glanced at her watch and calculated that it had been seven hours and eight minutes since she had boarded the bus. She rearranged the few items in the plastic bag. She had three diapers, one bottle with formula, and a few wet wipes left. The large bottle of spring water was half gone, and Caliana debated how to best economize the remainder. She had taken tiny sips of water, not daring to fill her bladder for the dread of having to use the nauseating toilets at the bridge.

The monotony was gruesome. Her eyelids kept fluttering shut, and she kept snapping them open. She started playing mental games, allowing her eyelids to rest for measured intervals in seconds. She gave up after a while and started pacing around Kareem to keep herself alert. The hall slowly filled with people. Caliana retreated to her corner. She promised herself that she would not look at her watch, knowing it would only frustrate her further. Kareem was getting restless, and Caliana tried to keep him entertained with songs and gestures, but he wouldn't be distracted. He wanted to roam around.

Exhausted from her efforts, Caliana gave him the water bottle to gnaw on. Kareem settled on her lap, and Caliana found herself talking to him. She thanked him for being patient and quietly started telling him about her plans for them in the next few weeks. She didn't know how long she talked before she realized that Kareem held himself in a new way. He seemed completely riveted by her words. Caliana could have sworn at that moment that he completely understood her. She realized that she had abandoned the baby talk and was sharing her innermost thoughts.

She stopped talking, and Kareem reached a hand and touched her mouth, as though signaling her to continue. Caliana laughed and started another dialogue with him. She tested Kareem by pausing every time his eyes locked into a faraway intent gaze, but he would immediately look back at her and say, "Mama."

Maybe it was exhaustion, but at that second, Caliana felt that her son was a genius. He was not able to talk yet seemed to understand words, and Caliana was thrilled to be able to safely talk aloud. When Kareem dozed off, Caliana's brain started spinning with revised thoughts on parenting him. She resolved that she would talk to him respectfully. He had given her a clear indication that he was absorbing something, and even if he only retained sounds, she would be helping him learn. A realization rocked her brain: she remembered the hours that she had spent reading to Kareem. He had had that same intense response all along. It was an affinity to words and spoken language. She had seen it but had not yet understood its implication. She had to start paying attention to clues about his development; she couldn't afford to be ignorant.

Caliana was so absorbed in adjusting her vision of parenting that she was jolted by the loud crackling that boomed out of the overhead loudspeakers. A name was repeated twice, and Caliana knew that she wasn't the only one who didn't understand it. People were looking around and repeating variations of the names they thought they had heard. Two confused males approached the line that would get them to the collection of their papers. The guard in charge of the line shouted at them both, saying that only one of them could approach. The men helplessly looked at each other, until one took the initiative to step forward.

Caliana tried to pay attention to the dialects and mispronunciation of the muffled names. She was hoping to recognize a pattern that would help her predict the possibilities of how her own name might be distorted.

Four hours later, Caliana felt her heart ready to explode from impatient frustration. She had been in restrictive confinement for more than eleven hours. The hall had gotten so crowded that even if Kareem had wanted to crawl, he wouldn't have had the space. Hundreds of people were seated on the floor, many in small groups.

Caliana gave Kareem his last formula bottle, and filled the last baby bottle with water. She now had an empty plastic spring-water bottle to use as a toy. She tried to blow various sounds into it, tap and crackle it, anything that would get a smile out of Kareem. She desperately needed to lessen his misery. She watched him literally wilt in the heat—he had been constantly sweating. Caliana wondered if she and Kareem were more uncomfortable from the heat because they were used to the luxury of air-conditioning. Caliana could not ever remember being this hot and not having a pool or some form of relief. People around her were fanning themselves and obviously suffering from the heat, but no one else seemed to be pouring out buckets of sweat. Kareem's curls were totally soaked, and she had to keep wiping his face. She had stopped throwing away the baby wipes that she used to cool his body; instead, she let them dry up and reused them as tissues to wipe his sweat.

An hour later, Caliana jumped at hearing her name called. She couldn't believe how sore her whole body was as she picked up Kareem and went to collect her papers. She stood in front of the designated officer, and when he gave her back her papers three minutes later and told her to leave, she stood frozen in disbelief. She was done, and it seemed unbelievable.

Caliana's heart started pounding as she contained herself from running through the exit.

As soon as she stepped out of the building, she saw a man carrying a sign with her name on it. Caliana gulped in the cooler air and, disoriented, walked toward the driver, who immediately took Kareem from her and expressed heartfelt sympathy for her delay. The driver, who worked for her father's company in the West Bank, was exceptionally gentle with her. He helped situate her and Kareem in the car and purposefully delayed turning on the air-conditioner for fear of making the baby sick. He lowered all the windows and told her that they needed a few minutes to cool off.

Caliana told him that she needed to stop at the first convenience store and a place to use the bathroom. She couldn't wait through the hour-long trip to Bethlehem. As the driver drove through Jericho, Caliana was yet again surprised by how identical it was to South *Shouneh* on the Jordanian side.

They pulled up to a shop in a commercial area. Caliana appreciated the fan blowing inside the small shop. She stood savoring the cool air and told the driver what she needed. He offered to carry Kareem while she used the toilette. Caliana had the urge to kiss him for his kindness.

Back in the car, she fed Kareem a jar of baby vegetables and a jar of mixed fruit. She gave him his formula bottle. He fell asleep a few sips into it. Caliana wolfed down her sandwich, drank the best-tasting icy bottle of Coke, inhaled a cigarette, and passed out in the middle of her conversation with the driver.

CHAPTER 15

CALIANA awoke in Bethlehem, feeling the excitement of her arrival. She had made it. She had escaped Rami.

The driver informed her that they were minutes from the *Sail*, the name given to their house as it had a running brook in its garden.

Her father's cousin greeted her with sympathetic inquiries and curses at the Israelis. Caliana was told that her father had been frantically calling all day, using a call-back system that rang England from Jordan and then routed the line back into the West Bank. Caliana's aunt took Kareem and called over a young girl. Caliana was told that the young girl, Aminah, would come some days for a few hours to help with Kareem, and that Aminah would now take him to give him a bath.

Caliana was grateful for the help but hated giving up Kareem to such a young girl. She was reassured that the girl, even though only a teenager, had helped raise her five younger siblings and knew how to handle a baby very well.

"First thing we need to do is contact your father, who's been worried sick, and let him know you've arrived."

Her aunt went through the process of making the complicated connection, and Caliana patiently waited. Her aunt spoke to her father for a few minutes and then passed Caliana the phone.

Her father inquired about her crossing. He told her that the driver would pick her up in the morning to take her shopping. She had access to unlimited amounts of money, whatever she needed. All she had to do was call the office and tell them the amount she required, and they would deliver it to her. He told her that his cousin had purchased necessities but that she needed to go shopping, as it might be at least a few weeks before arrangements could be made for her to leave Israel through the Ben Gurion Airport in Tel Aviv. He also told her that Rami had called dozens of times and had even attempted to come to the house but they had refused to open the electric gates for him. Her father informed her that he would be boarding a plane to London in two days and it would then facilitate communication with her.

Caliana ended her call. She thanked her aunt for her thoughtfulness and excused herself to check in on Kareem. She desperately needed to shower and to go to bed. She walked her aunt to the door and arranged to meet her in the morning, after her aunt insisted that she would accompany Caliana in her shopping to guide her to the appropriate stores.

Caliana peeked into the bathroom and smiled when she saw Kareem's familiar serious face studying the young nanny. It struck her yet again that she was looking at an old soul in a young body. Kareem, having noticed her, gave her a smile that reassured her more than any words given by the nanny. Aminah had passed Kareem's test, and to Caliana, that was better than proper qualifications.

Caliana checked out the room prepared for her. She was touched at seeing a crib, a changing table, and other baby accommodations in her room. Her aunt had even purchased her a simple, summery nightgown. Before heading for her shower, Caliana stopped again in the bathroom and politely asked the girl to keep Kareem in the bath for as long as he wanted to stay in it and told her that when Kareem was done, she could take him to the room and let him crawl around naked. Caliana emphasized that Aminah was not to dress him in his pajamas, as Caliana would attend to Kareem when she finished her own shower.

The young girl stared silently at Caliana. Just as Caliana was starting to feel uncomfortable with the muted staring, Aminah blurted, "You let him decide?"

Caliana had used the silence by preparing to repeat herself had the girl asked about any part of the instructions, but she was thrown off by Aminah's surprising question.

"What do you mean?" asked Caliana as her mind raced with the possibilities of the girl's question.

"You want your son to decide when to get out of the bath? He's only a baby. He can't tell me," she insisted disbelievingly.

"Oh! Actually, he doesn't speak yet. But he'll tell you. He'll stand up and probably try to climb, which is usually his first attempt, and then he'll figure out that he needs help, and he'll raise his arms towards you and clearly indicate that he is ready to be picked up."

Caliana was looking at Kareem, smiling at her recollections. Those were usually her favorite moments, when she watched Kareem try to first figure out how to attain his needs. He was quite smart in his self-discovery and attempts at independence. He would accept his limitations, smile, and, only recently, add "Mama" as he stretched toward her. Caliana's response was immediate and natural; she would pick him up with the towel that was always spread out on her knees in readiness, and she would use it to enfold him with lots of hugs and praise.

Caliana realized that the girl was still staring at her, and for the life of her, Caliana momentarily forgot the girl's question.

"I meant, you don't decide how long he should be in here? When I help bathe my brothers, they stay in there only as long as my mother says they should." The girl seemed genuinely confused, and Caliana was beginning to comprehend the differences.

"When he was younger, I made decisions for him, of course, but I also try to follow his lead. He's a really great baby, and you'll be surprised at how clearly he communicates his needs. By the way, thank you for arranging our room." Caliana started walking out and then remembered her own routine with Kareem's bedtime. "Are there any baby books? I didn't see any in the room."

"Baby books?" the girl asked. "Like small books?" She indicated with her hands a small size.

The poor child had probably never seen one. "Never mind, sweetheart, thank you again."

Caliana walked to the bathroom, resolved to find out the ages of Aminah's siblings and buy them appropriate baby books.

She stood under the hot shower and vigorously scrubbed every inch of her body a few times over. She washed her hair until it literally squeaked, then blasted the coldest water, and sighed in bliss. She had picked up the habit of liking ice water after a hot shower from her boarding school days. At school, after a certain amount of hot water, the water would invariably turn suddenly freezing cold. At the beginning, Caliana had jumped out of the shower when the temperature reversed, but in time, she had learned to thoroughly enjoy the sudden, refreshing chill.

Caliana found Kareem crawling naked on the king-size bed. She couldn't resist his smile, and she flung herself next to him. She picked him up and gently placed the soles of her feet on his stomach, lifting him slowly away from her and then lowering him back down toward her. Kareem burst into laughter, drooling on her. It was his favorite nighttime ritual. He especially loved it when Caliana swung him slowly from side to side, but Caliana's muscles were too exhausted that night.

"Sorry, kiddo, a short one today. But how about we get you ready for bed?" Caliana went on to tell Kareem everything she was doing as she got him ready. Every now and then, she caught a glimpse of Aminah's obvious expression of disbelief. Caliana tried to assess what she was doing and how it could possibly explain Aminah's shocked expression. Aminah stared at her routine as though she were watching a riveting adventure movie. Caliana was actually curious to know what she was doing that was so strange to the young girl, but she didn't ask.

A few days later, Caliana found out. *Um* Saleh, the young *fallaha,* or farmer, grandmother whose family had worked and lived on Caliana's family's property, told Caliana that she must not spoil her son. She insisted that Caliana was too cautious with her son and that it was hampering his natural abilities.

She showed Caliana her own grandchild, who was only two months older than Kareem and who could already run around and even grab his share of the food from the communal dish laid on the ground for the whole family. The boy walked to the dish, squatted down with his family members, and reached with his little hands for the rice and vegetables. Caliana thought it was the saddest and most endearing sight she had ever seen. Apparently, no one had the time or energy to coddle their babies as much as Caliana did. In *Um* Saleh's firm opinion, Caliana was spoiling Kareem by being with him all the time. She should just leave him alone to wander and investigate his world.

Caliana smiled back at *Um* Saleh and ended the subject firmly. The image of Kareem crawling around the huge garden unattended was absolutely crazy. Caliana saw hundreds of fatal accidents waiting for him. She started giving *Um* Saleh a morbid list of the dangers that could befall her own grandson. Caliana pointed out the unevenness of the land, the brook that could drown him, the harsh landscaping that would graze and cut him, and so on. She felt protective of the eleven-month grandchild that she had just seen eating. Caliana didn't know much about developmental abilities of a baby at that age, but she highly suspected that what she had seen was average. She also suspected that *Um* Saleh must have dozens of grandchildren and was probably incorrect about the actual age of that particular grandson.

Um Saleh simply explained that her grandson had to learn that life was hard and he would be forced to quickly learn from his mistakes if he was allowed to make them. She added that if God wished to take her grandson back to be with Him in His glorious heaven to serve Him as His angel, then who was she to know better than God His reasons for taking back any child?

Caliana was struck dumb with such logic. She finally told *Um* Saleh that in that case, she didn't mind spoiling her son while he was an angel on earth!

Even though Caliana thought the way the *Fallaheen* raised their children was absolutely preposterous, she was also fascinated in watching *Um* Saleh's grandchild. Irrespective of his real age, in many ways he had the abilities of a much older child. She even witnessed him running around while eating a slice of pita bread without anyone around to keep an eye on him to monitor the possibility of choking. Caliana would anxiously track him with her eyes, completely alert to all the possible disasters that loomed ahead.

From all the times she watched him, only once did she jerk in real fear and rush to rescue him. He had been running and had stumbled and disappeared down a small hill. Caliana ran toward him, only to find out that he had calmly climbed back up, with one knee dirty and bleeding, and continued playing. She dashed back to the house to grab a small first aid kit and was administering his wound when his grandmother came over and yelled at him for being such a baby.

That was when he cried. Caliana was shocked. She tried to explain to *Um* Saleh that he needed a disinfectant and some Neosporin to help heal the wound and prevent infection. *Um* Saleh scoffed at Caliana's nonsense and told her that God had created water to cleanse wounds.

That night, Caliana asked her aunt what the life expectancy rate was for the Bedouin and *Fallaheen* children. Her aunt laughed at her. She informed Caliana that most of them had never seen a pediatrician in their lives, let alone received the standard immunizations, and yet they thrived. They lived off the land and expected the land to fulfill all their basic needs. Their life was simple.

Caliana had never before stayed in Palestine longer than a few days. She found her stay fascinating; in many ways, watching *Um*

Saleh and her family was like glimpsing pages of a book on indigenous people coming to life. She also learned to appreciate some of their ways. *Um* Saleh had insisted that Kareem's nerves would grow much stronger if he was massaged daily with olive oil. Caliana substituted the oil for her store-bought lotions and felt Kareem get stronger.

Her surreal sense of time was especially magnified when she took Kareem sightseeing. The significance of the three monotheistic religions was nowhere as alive as in Jerusalem, the epicenter of Abrahamic faith. Historical religious events had occurred all around her, and the predominant flavor of ancient times was deeply imbedded into the city. On medieval European maps, Jerusalem had been placed at the center of the world, and Caliana marveled at the hundreds of historical monuments that had survived.

It registered with her that she was walking in the steps of history when she stood under the shining gilded Dome of the Rock, built in the seventh century at the very spot where Muhammad was believed to have ascended to heaven, and also the site of Abraham's sacrifice. Just beyond the Dome, she walked to the Church of Holy Sepulcher, believed to be the site of Christ's burial. She walked along the holiest site to the Jews, the Wailing Wall, which was the remainder of King Herod's second temple that had been destroyed by the Romans.

The section called the old city was surrounded by walls and consisted of four quarters, or neighborhoods: Armenian, Christian, Jewish, and Muslim. Caliana loved wandering through the labyrinthine paths of the heterogeneous city. The city represented a wide range of national, religious, and socioeconomic groups. The walls of the old city had eleven gates, of which seven were open, allowing for entry and exit from the old city. Each gate had a captivating historical relevance. Caliana stood at one of the main entrances to the city, known as the Jaffa Gate, built by Suleiman in 1538. Also known as the Hebron Gate, it referred to Abraham, the beloved of God, who was buried in Hebron. One of the closed gates was the Golden Gate, which, according to the Jewish tradition, was the gate that the Messiah would use to enter Jerusalem when he came. To prevent the Messiah from coming, Suleiman had ordered the gate to be sealed in the sixteenth century.

Caliana would often be jarred out of her reverie by the presence of armed soldiers. It was a rude awakening to reality and a reminder that Jerusalem was a vortex of political instability. She felt protective of the serenity assumed by the land and its inhabitants. *It should be left alone; it should belong to everybody*, she thought.

Caliana knew the city could belong equally to the three monotheistic religions and felt that world politics should not touch Jerusalem. It should be an independent theocracy like the Vatican, politically neutral like Switzerland, and governed equally by nonpolitical members of each faith.

Caliana felt that her long stay in Israel was allowing for a reprieve from the real world. In many ways, the environment around her was different from that of any other place she had lived.

She had the opportunity to experience the palpable anger of the Palestinians and their brewing discontent with their circumstances. Politics was the only subject discussed amongst the people. Caliana was amazed at the grapevine of circulating abuses that seemed to break through the numerous restrictions imposed on the Palestinians by an illegal occupation. Besides a few sightseeing trips, Caliana rarely ventured out of the house. Even though she sympathized with the Palestinian strife, she needed to step away from aggravations that were beyond her control, and focus on achieving clarity as she reevaluated the emergence of new thoughts and feelings.

Caliana spent all her time with Kareem, or reading and thinking. Occasionally, she would have short visits from her father's family, but she was very clear and respectful in establishing her boundaries with them. She needed the downtime and planned to use it well. She was finally afforded the luxury of paying total attention to her son.

When Caliana wasn't focused on her son, she experienced waves of intense loneliness. Her thoughts were often frightening; she was discovering the magnitude of the emptiness she had lived by. Her love for her son had brought her an aliveness that only enhanced the deadness of the world as she still viewed it. Loving Kareem had replenished a vast hole with an energy that fueled her desire for life and her responsibility toward it. She was able to identify that she had always been a functionally depressed person. She accepted that there were many dark holes in her soul, and every time she felt them pull her under, she fought hard with the certainty that she couldn't afford to be depressed, that she would survive. She would be a great mother. It was the only determined thought that bounced her out of her pain.

Caliana used her love for Kareem to counteract the habits of depression that she had newly seen in herself. Hour after hour, she attempted to heal her agonized feelings using positive thoughts and images of mothering. At times, no matter how cognitively she played out the optimism of the future, she felt that she was sucked under by an exhaustion that reflected an ancient weariness. She felt old at twenty-two. It was as though she carried a weariness that went further back than her present life, as though she carried the weight of so many past lives and was loaded down with their collective energy. She had read somewhere that some women experienced postpartum depression and wondered if that was what she was experiencing, this out-of-control emotional roller-coaster. It was merciless in its intensity, and Caliana could control the ride only when she focused on her son. Just the same, she could easily imagine herself lying down, succumbing to the exhaustion that was being demanded by the many bottomless holes in her soul, and just letting go.

She couldn't afford to check out from a world that never made any sense, because she had to find meaning in it, for her son. She wanted to be the steady beacon that lit his way in love and supported his development. She knew that she had a job to do, and she damn well meant to do it well. Her life was over, but her son's life had just begun.

CHAPTER 16

CALIANA'S father informed her that Rhea had managed to obtain a one-week visitor's visa and would join her in the West Bank the following day.

Caliana was staggered. She had not known that Rhea was attempting to get permission to make the crossing. The idea that Rhea was going to cross into Israel, for her, was overwhelming. She started shaking and couldn't understand her body's panicked reaction. Dreadful thoughts assumed a life of their own as they raced to keep up with her heart's fearful acceleration. She latched onto the suffocating intrusion into her space. Accepting such a huge obligation would force her to have to always interact with Rhea, forcing her to feel indebted even though she didn't need any help.

It was a paralyzing position to be in, and she felt the full force of the suffocation of being made to feel indebted to anyone. She had not asked for this, but it was being shoved at her. How dare anyone assume that she needed help! No one had bothered to ask her if she wanted or needed a visitor. Maybe Rhea had been pressured by duty to make the trip. Maybe she thought it was expected of her; maybe her parents had forced her to make the gesture because they were close friends with Caliana's parents.

Rage unlike anything she had ever experienced exploded within her. Without seeing, she walked to her room and slammed the door. She didn't trust the rage pouring out of her and the murderous scream that needed a physical outlet. She shut off her mind, letting her body pace the room.

She walked, seeing nothing, thinking nothing, focusing on the need, the demand, to move. She sensed nothing but her rage, and it sustained every movement. It locked her in a timeless zone. Evil thoughts seemed to have their own consciousness and searched for a physical outlet.

At some point Caliana became aware that she was sitting on the bed, and her mind gradually unfogged. She felt calmer. Her mind conjured a clear image of Rhea.

Her heart lurched, and she felt the contradiction of loving Rhea and having raged at her as though Rhea were her worst enemy. She felt flooded with shame at the association that she had made between her rage and one of her best, most beloved friends.

"What's wrong with me?"

Caliana implicitly understood that the question had literally bubbled from her saddest place.

After her guilt had worn away at her, she decided to understand the origin of her horrific thoughts. How could she have vilified Rhea, who had done absolutely nothing to deserve such a response?

Caliana felt compelled to understand the roots of the evil thoughts that had led her into an immediate catatonic suspicion. She felt taken aback, surprised, and utterly distrustful of her psyche, which had completely distorted her feelings. There was monstrousness inside of her, and she was determined to meet it head-on.

She closed her eyes and breathed in her loving memories of Rhea. She let the memories flood her in flashes of pictures from precious moments from her past, moments of loving kindness that had been given to her repeatedly. Moments that had struck her with the certainty of Rhea's deservingness of her love. For the first time, she really understood how much she actually loved Rhea.

Caliana focused on her certainty of Rhea's incredible heart and of having been well-loved by Rhea throughout their friendship, and she clung on to her belief with every ounce of strength. Rhea had loved her. That was real; a recognition of anything less would undermine the integrity of Rhea's love and would feed the monstrousness that could irrationally escalate and rip Caliana's friendship apart.

She opened her eyes and really looked at her fear.

No one had ever done anything of this magnitude for her. Rhea, who knew about her horrific experiences at the border, was willing to undergo a crossing to be with her! Rhea only wanted to love and support her. Caliana tried to recreate the first seconds after she heard that Rhea would be arriving the following day. She wanted to recapture those few horrific seconds when she had felt instant suffocation, followed by a rage that had exploded with distorted thoughts. She needed to understand the fear that had ignited such an immediate response. Caliana breathed into her fear, observed her thoughts, and allowed them their own unedited rationale.

She was horrified to discover that a part of her had always feared and hated loving Rhea. She resented being loved back and was petrified of being trapped by the love, of being under the mercy and control of someone else. She wanted to be able to have the *option* of retreating from the friendship at any moment and for it to be relatively easy. That Rhea mattered in her life might weaken her. Caliana had not wanted to be loved if it meant that she might start to expect, rely on, and then possibly need that love.

It wasn't that Caliana felt undeserving so much as she feared the implications of being given that much love. She wanted to honor Rhea's incredible gesture, and to do so, she had to dig out the ugliness that had infected her and made her feel monstrous toward Rhea.

All day, she vacillated between opposing thoughts and feelings, but she kept fighting her fears. She never doubted her trust in Rhea. Each realization helped her peel away yet another subtle layer of terror. That night, Caliana sweated through the fears that plagued her. She had never really processed what loving Rhea had meant to her, and she was struck by the volumes of inexplicable fears that were the direct result of loving her friend.

Sometime in the very early hours of the morning, Caliana bolted upright in bed and smiled. She had found a place of grace in accepting the love that was being offered to her. She knew that she would pay it back many times over and it would not be because she felt strangled by the indebtedness. Her obligation to give back stemmed from her *willingness* to continue to love Rhea. She would focus on loving Rhea, like she did with Kareem, and all her actions would flow from it.

Caliana felt a euphoric release of tension.

Rhea's crossing was a purely motivated loving act. Caliana thought back to the letter of condolence that Rhea had sent her in Switzerland when her grandfather had died, and she realized that Rhea's actions had always had a dynamic impact on her.

Caliana was glad for the opportunity of questioning herself about her friendship with Rhea. It reaffirmed an acceptance, a choice she had made in loving Rhea. Caliana was resolved; she would receive Rhea's loving kindness, but only because she was committed to giving it back.

Rhea arrived the following afternoon and kept Caliana laughing most of the night. Rhea's perspective on the crossing was absolutely hilarious, and she kept interrupting her retelling of the crossing by exclaiming in disbelief *"Mish tabe'e!* (It's not normal!)" after each segment of her story. Rhea was a pure Jordanian, with no ties whatsoever to Palestine, and her willingness to expose herself to the Israeli humiliation had rendered her as highly suspect.

Caliana thanked Rhea for coming and told her friend that she had spent the day waiting for her and making plans of things they could do together. Rhea, generous as ever, insisted that she was only there to spend time with her and didn't care what they did. She was happy just being with her, and she would do whatever Caliana wanted to do.

Caliana booked herself, Rhea, and Aminah to go to Herzilia, near Tel Aviv, where they would stay in a beautiful hotel by the beach. With every checkpoint that took them further away from the West Bank, they traversed into another world, another country. Both Caliana and Rhea where shocked to see how the non-Palestinian side lived. They kept commenting on how different, how Westernized, Israel was. It was disorienting to see a land so vastly divided. There was opulence on the Israeli side that didn't seem to belong to the Palestinian landscape that Caliana had imagined. Even had Palestine prospered under its own rule, she would have visualized it differently. It struck her what was missing; The place was non-Arab in feeling, in texture.

For the first time, it really registered with Caliana how hopeless the Palestinian cause of reclaiming their country. There would never be peace in that area, because the Israelis would never give that part back. The Israelis had built a country and fortified it with a solid future. They had used the Western resources to their best advantage, and Caliana had to give them credit for their speed, for they had managed to create a well-established country in only forty years. The Palestinians had better start to seriously claim the possibility of what little had been left to them after the 1967 war, she thought, before Israel swallowed up that part completely.

Caliana cringed when the driver pulled up to the five-star hotel. She felt that she was betraying her family in Bethlehem by endorsing their enemy. She remembered shopping with her aunt, who had insisted they buy only from Arab markets, thus giving the money to the people who desperately needed it to boost their tightly controlled economy. Caliana felt like a fraud walking into the fancy lobby and inwardly cringed when she registered them into the hotel. Caliana became aware of Aminah's seething anger and wanted to beg her forgiveness, but it was too late, she realized. Entering the best hotels around the world had never fazed her, yet living in utter simplicity in the West Bank for almost two months had produced a discomfort in relation to returning to her familiar world of luxury.

Aminah had been born and raised in the West Bank, in utter poverty, and had never been able to venture outside the restricted areas, preventing her from seeing the rest of her country. And Caliana had dragged her, without thinking, into her enemy's lifestyle, rubbed her face in its wealth and prosperity. The only thought that Caliana had had when she had insisted that Aminah accompany them was that she was secretly doing the girl a favor by showing her a good time at a beautiful hotel on a beach. She hadn't even thought to consider that Aminah may have feelings of anger or resentment at seeing her country so obviously invaded. She had thought to provide Aminah with an opportunity to expand her views. Caliana had made a huge mistake by bringing the girl on what she had perceived simply as a vacation.

* * *

After Rhea left, Caliana spent another two weeks in the West Bank, alone for the most part, and in many ways she felt she had fought and won a battle. She emerged again from her solitude with a deepened clarity of purpose.

Excitement at the prospect of being able to be a part of a unique experiment lifted her spirits. As a young child, she had often wondered what it would feel like to actually *be loved*. And she had been unable to imagine an answer. Now, her mothering would be the answer she sought; she would get to experience the results of a child receiving love. Kareem's happiness, she imagined, would be the natural consequence of him being well loved. And she intended that her actions would stem from her love and wisdom.

Her father finally informed her that the lawyers in the West Bank had managed to obtain an exit visa from Israel's Ben Gurion Airport. Her father emphasized, for the hundredth time, that she must not, under any circumstances, have her Jordanian passport stamped with an Israeli stamp, that she was to clearly inform every single person who touched her passport at the airport that any stamp had to be put on a separate piece of paper. Her passport could not have any Israeli stamps on it. Her father told her that she was allowed to ask for that accommodation and that the Israelis would comply, but she had to ask for it, repeatedly.

Caliana tried to be patient with her father's paranoid repetitions, for he was, after all, looking out for her. By Jordanian law, Caliana was committing an illegal act by flying out of "enemy territory." She could go to jail in Jordan if her passport was stamped by Israel. Caliana was also reminded many times that she needed to be at the airport at least seven hours before her flight time, as she would need to allow for stringent security measures.

On the morning of her flight, Caliana arrived at Ben Gurion at five o'clock. She was relieved to be entering a highly civilized facility. Even though she underwent hours of interrogations and unimaginable searching of her belongings, Caliana didn't mind the wait. She had air-conditioning, a travel stroller, a travel bag, and everything that she would have normally taken in preparation for a long trip with a baby. She could entertain Kareem with his books and toys, and, most importantly, he was comfortable. In comparison to the bridge crossing, this was heavenly.

CHAPTER 17

CALIANA flew to London and connected to Nevada. She was picked up at the airport and driven to a realty office. Her father had already made arrangements, so Caliana met with the realtor who had rented her a beautiful house in the mountains of Lake Tahoe, where she would remain for at least six weeks to establish her residency. Then she would file for an American divorce. That same morning, Caliana also met the chief of police for Lake Tahoe. She made an arrangement with the police to pay for bodyguard services directly to the officers, who would rotate their off-duty hours to work for her.

Caliana learned that Rami had revoked her application for a green card, as he had originally sponsored her through his American citizenship. Her father also informed her that he had told the lawyers in Jordan to stop engaging with Rami and to let him sweat out the waiting game. Caliana and Kareem would stay abroad indefinitely and would return only if reasonable custody was negotiated.

Caliana loved being in Lake Tahoe with Kareem. She felt safe and tolerated the discomfort of being shadowed for her safety. Caliana accepted that her primary goal was to ensure Kareem's protection at all times, and having bodyguards alleviated the anxiety at the possibility of Kareem being kidnapped by his father. She needed to focus on her son and on finding them a remote home that they could disappear to if need be.

Her father arranged to have the nanny flown in from Jordan, and Caliana appreciated the help. Leaving Kareem with the nanny and the bodyguards, she went for a short trip to St. John's Island in the Caribbean. She toured the tiny island with a realtor and fell in love with it. It was perfect; it fit with her every fantasy. She knew that she would be able to arrange an anonymous life and legal protection for herself. If Rami refused to compromise on custody, she would be able to accomplish her dream of living on an island.

She would leave the decision in the hands of fate.

Caliana began her first stage of normalcy with Kareem. Living in a safe country, she could relax and focus on raising her son. That she didn't have to worry about finances was a huge relief, and she appreciated the luxury she knew few single women had.

She was amazed at Kareem's language development. At eleven months, he was combining two and three words and easily communicating his needs. He absolutely loved to be read to and would clearly state, "Read book," to her. He was trying to walk and was able to take a few cautious steps on his own while holding onto a stablizing object. It was obvious to Caliana that her son was an eager learner who seemed to absorb new information at an incredible pace.

Her sister Deena surprised her with a visit. Deena was absolutely amazing with Kareem and supportive of Caliana. Even though Deena had been consistently kind and decent with Caliana for a few years, Caliana was still slightly wary of her. All evidence pointed to Deena having grown into a loving and generous woman, and yet Caliana was still cautious in trusting her.

When Deena had broken her first engagement, their mother had unleashed a rage so ugly that it had started Deena's awakening. And like a burst balloon, the hatred between Deena and their mother had erupted as suddenly. Prior to that, Deena had maintained a strong delusion about her mother, even with the staggering evidence of neglect. The ugliness that came out from their mother was unmistakably mean and hurtful, and its sole purpose was to destroy Deena. In her mother's efforts to pander her daughter in marriage, she literally demoralized Deena, calling her ugly and undesirable, and telling her that she should be grateful that anyone, let alone a man of wealth, would *want* to marry her.

By the time of her visit to Caliana in Lake Tahoe, Deena had gone through three other broken engagements, every single one ended by her. With every broken engagement, their mother had escalated the thrashings. Caliana was not surprised that their mother used each incident as an opportunity to vent unrestrained hatred, or that Deena had responded with affronted and justifiable fury.

Caliana admired Deena's ability to have unleashed the beast in their mother. On a perverse level, Caliana enjoyed witnessing the monstrosity that she had always told Deena their mother was capable of. On another level, she hated that Deena was the recipient of the horrendous pain. Caliana tried to bluntly point out to Deena that she needed to stop giving their parents ammunition, but Deena was on a mission to be seen, accepted, and admired by her parents. She took their assaults and tried harder to improve herself, maybe hoping that there would be less criticism in the inevitable next battle.

With each episode, Deena's awakening would further flourish. She was receiving irrefutable evidence that her mother was a mean, hollow, and vicious woman. Deena would vent to Caliana her shock and anger at the horror of the words that had wounded her and would express how unimaginable it was that any parent, especially a mother, could even utter such cruelty, yet Deena seemed driven to engage their mother in seeing her as anything but worthless. It seemed to Caliana that Deena would continue engaging with their mother because the alternative, utter neglect, was an unacceptable option.

Caliana had to admire that, in spite of their mother's verbal bombardments; Deena was able to maintain a resolved strength in investigating her life. In a sense, the verbal abuse was pushing Deena to look at herself and discover abundant integrity that had lain dormant.

Caliana couldn't understand why Deena was determined to seek affirmations from their parents. But as long as Deena felt compelled to fight for their respect and acceptance, Caliana understood that she could not be completely candid with her sister. Her distrust came from understanding that when Deena was locked in a heated fight with their mother, that Deena would spill out all the grievances that her mother had committed against all the sisters, and in the heat of the moment would not censor herself. Caliana could not risk having Deena divulge her personal information to their mother.

Caliana's respect for Deena began to flourish into love. She made efforts to judge and assess Deena as she would another friend. She couldn't conceptualize and draw on feelings of normal sibling love, as that relationship had not existed between them. She also knew that she couldn't hang on to the fear and anger that had been played out in hateful abundance in their formative years. It would be an unfair measuring tool on whom and what Deena had become, and it could distort the genuine decency that Deena was honoring her with. She needed to give Deena a blank slate that would separate her from their history yet keep alive rigid boundaries, as Deena had direct access into altering Caliana's defenses with their parents.

This budding love allowed Caliana to feel empathy for Deena in her hopeless journey to gain their parents' love and approval. It kept Caliana edited when Deena vented her anger. She heard Deena out, and empathized with her, and tried to advise her, yet she clearly understood that Deena would continue fighting and challenging their parents. Even though Deena verbally indicated otherwise, Caliana felt that she was still incapable of truly understanding their mother's depravity and inability to love.

An interesting linguistic pattern naturally developed between Caliana and Deena when any family member was mentioned. For example, when discussing their mother, they each said "your mother" to each other, as though they actually had different mothers. For years they had attributed their natural references to be based in some societal or linguistic convention. When new people met them and questioned the strange references to their family members, they would tell people that they were doing a literal translation from another language. It took them more than twenty years to realize that it had never been an actual language they had translated, but a convenient language created by two women who were trying to disown their family.

During the arguments over Deena's engagements, their father mostly stood by in support of his wife—until the very last opportunity, when he inevitably graced Deena with his decisive support. He would suddenly declare that Deena could sever the engagement. Deena would then become so indebted with guilt at the gratitude of his ultimate stance that she usually excused the misery also inflicted by him.

Caliana suspected that her father, in cowardice, had ridden the hateful tails of his wife. Caliana never understood at which point precisely her father would ultimately turn the tide in Deena's favor, but it seemed to Caliana that each incident lasted a bit longer, allowing him to practice his more subtle version of cruelty. Caliana worried that prolonging each episode was facilitating his wife's addiction to abusive behavior. His unpredictable and always abrupt switching of sides made him appear magnanimous for a few seconds with Deena while infuriating his wife, who regarded his desertion as a weakness that further spoiled his daughter.

In a way, Caliana despised her father for his passivity. She knew that eventually, either her mother would influence her father into hating Deena and completely siding with her or her father would continue to keep the war raging because of his inability to actually see his wife's manipulations.

Caliana somewhat understood and empathized with Deena's forgiving temperament toward their father. In spite of Caliana's mental clarity regarding her father's limitations, she also knew that he was capable of unwavering loyalty. He had demonstrated complete and utter support toward her decision to divorce. He had taken immediate and highly respectful actions toward her. He had fought a war on her behalf and generously financed its every possibility. He had never once questioned her decision or made her feel any shame. His actions were much more powerful than any words he could have said.

Caliana felt immensely indebted to her father. She also felt sorry for him when she watched him unravel under his wife's influence and whims, lacking the strength of character to question himself separately from her. At times, Caliana had seen crippling shyness overtake her father and turn him into a frightened boy seeking and desperately needing the love and approval of his mother—his wife. And so, in the shadow of his wife's carefully doled-out bits of restrained affection, he lived.

In the past eight months since announcing her need to divorce, Caliana had felt some stirrings of love for her father. The moments were often fleeting, and insubstantial in relation to her wider understanding of his limitations. Her gratitude, which had led to these loving feelings, was often interrupted with the image of him yanking away her crutches. That image alone hardened her heart against him. It wasn't that Caliana believed that her father was innately cruel as much as she understood that he could be led to cruelty. She viewed him as a weak man. Even though Caliana felt some emotional leniency toward her father, she still judged him by his weakness, by his dependency that kept him operating in a volatile—if inconsistent—fashion. He was still accountable for continuing to allow his wife's venom to penetrate his conduct. Observing him interact with Deena and her mother kept Caliana in absolute vigilance with him, in spite of her indebtedness, and especially during those occasional moments of loving feelings.

Caliana had once wondered if her father could have thrived with another kind of woman. With time, Caliana had watched her parents require more and more time away from people, to recuperate from their perfected façade. Everyone assumed that they were the perfect couple, and in many ways they were: They were completely devoted to each other's unconscious fears, united against the world at large.

Kareem turned one year old in August, and soon after, Rami's lawyer started to aggressively present them with a counteroffer allowing Caliana to be the custodial parent until Kareem turned twelve. Between the age of twelve to fifteen, Kareem would live with Rami. At fifteen, he would have the legal choice of deciding which parent he wanted to live with. Caliana knew Rami's mentality, that he assumed Kareem would naturally choose to continue living with Rami once Rami had taken over parenting and made his son the man he wanted him to be. Caliana also knew that Rami would never agree for Kareem to live with her past the age of twelve. That she had gotten five extra years of custody was her very best-case scenario.

As tempting as the island was, Caliana had to consider what would be best for Kareem. Could she really make him a fugitive to his culture and family? She did not want to live in the Middle East but wanted him to eventually have the choice. She also had to consider the emotional damage that she would be inflicting on Kareem by separating him from his father and his father's family. Every time Caliana weighed in Kareem's best interests she realized that she would ultimately have to agree to the contract.

Another stipulation that Rami had insisted on was that Caliana could not leave Jordan on her own for more than three weeks at a time without automatically losing custody of Kareem. Even though Caliana would never plan to leave her son behind for even three weeks, she bristled at Rami's obvious retaliatory tactics in trying to limit her and punish her by keeping her imprisoned in Jordan.

But Caliana agreed with the terms.

She returned to Jordan at the end of September and settled in to her parents' house.

A few days after Caliana's arrival, as stipulated in the contract, Kareem was to be picked up to spend a Thursday night with his father at Rami's home. Rami lived with his parents, as was tradition, and Caliana knew there would be many people on hand to care for Kareem.

Caliana stood anxiously holding Kareem and watching Rami's driver come up the curving roads of their mountainous driveway. She was braced for the awkwardness of having to engage with Rami.

When the car came into view, she was taken aback by the fact that Rami wasn't in the car. She had assumed that he had brought the driver so he could accompany Kareem in the back seat and be with him. Caliana was also surprised that a nanny had not been sent with the driver, and infuriated that a baby seat was unavailable.

She buckled Kareem as best as she could in the backseat and kissed him good-bye. As soon as she closed the car door, Kareem started screaming and crying and calling for her. Caliana had rarely heard Kareem cry. Her heart broke in response to his pain. She rushed after the slowly moving car and screamed at the driver to stop.

She yanked the door open and grabbed Kareem, who had squiggled out of the seat belt, and hugged him tight. She kept apologizing to Kareem and trying to explain that she would be with him the following day, but he was inconsolable. Every time she quieted him down, put him back in the seat belt, and closed the car door, he would begin hollering and crying with an intensity that frightened her. Caliana snapped at the driver and asked him why Rami hadn't bothered to turn up himself to collect his son. Not that Rami's presence was a guarantee for comfort, for she suspected that to Kareem, he was as good as a stranger.

Caliana rushed inside with Kareem and asked the nanny to accompany the driver to Rami's house. She wanted him to have a familiar face to help him transition. She asked the nanny if she could pack overnight clothes, as it would be best if she stayed with Kareem.

Caliana walked back to the car and positioned Kareem on the nanny's lap. The second Kareem realized that his mother was not accompanying him, he started crying again. Caliana steeled her heart and told the driver to go.

Caliana could hear Kareem's screams as the car drove down their mountain. She choked up, and her only thought was that she should have gone with him. She started running down the mountain before realizing that she couldn't catch up to the car, even though she could still hear Kareem's agonized screams.

Caliana walked back up to the house, knowing that she had made a huge mistake. She should have arranged to have dropped Kareem off herself. She called Rami's sister and awkwardly explained Kareem's agitation. She notified her that she had sent the nanny as a familiar face and that if Kareem was still miserable, he shouldn't be forced to spend the night. Caliana offered alternatives that could facilitate a more gradual transition and explained that she would be willing to bring Kareem every day for a short period until Kareem got used to them. Caliana was reassured that Rami's family would do what was best for Kareem. Caliana extracted a promise from her that she would call her and update her on Kareem's condition.

An hour later, Rami's driver returned with Kareem's nanny. Caliana was told that the nanny had not been allowed to enter Rami's house and that Rami had snatched Kareem from her and slammed the door in her face. Caliana's heart broke on hearing that Kareem had screamed for his mother the whole way there, especially when he had been taken from the nanny's safe arms.

Caliana was shaken, as Kareem had always been a sedate and happy baby. She had not expected the intensity of his reaction. Her heart was drowning from projecting his pain. She paced and fidgeted and waited for her ex-sister-in-law to call and update her.

* * *

All day, Caliana reassessed her strategies. She hoped that the novelty of having his son back with him would wear off soon and that Rami would realize that being around a baby was not something he was remotely cut out for. She knew that she would have to approach him in a manner that allowed him to save face in front of his family and friends, yet also decrease his obligation. His fight to get Kareem had been much more about pacifying his pride and his ability to control Caliana, to break her, than about having his son. She had heard that Rami had been incensed at the public humiliation of being left by his wife and publicly raged at having had his son kidnapped. He had played out the grieving father to gain sympathy in dealing with four months of intense gossip and scrutiny.

Caliana's mother, intent on securing Caliana's reputation to allow for the possibility of remarrying her in the future, had started a grapevine of gossip about Rami's drug addiction. She wanted to exonerate any blame from Caliana by clearly pointing the direction of blame for the divorce. Caliana had been angry at her mother's tactic and asked her father to exert whatever control he had over his wife's wagging tongue, pointing out to her father that even though she personally never faulted a child his parents, the Jordanian society judged a person based directly on his lineage and that her mother was in effect hurting Kareem by crucifying his father. Her father had agreed, but both were aware that it was too late to retract the damage.

Rami, having heard about the gossip, had publicly retaliated by pointing out her mother's motives: that she was clearly trying to remove blame from her spoilt daughter. It was easier for people to assume that Caliana, having grown up among immense wealth and Westernized parents, could be the product of spoiled, whimsical behavior, than that Rami had a "drug addiction," which could be excused as an indulgent, immature phase in the temptations of his youth. Either way, the gossip occupied people for many months and gave everyone a chance to show support by taking sides.

In the few days since Caliana's return to Jordan, she had been given a summary of all the variations that had resulted from the gossip. That she might be considered spoiled and reckless did not upset her, as she had never cared for anyone's opinion. She took in the information only to better understand Rami's state of mind, which would allow her to assess her maneuvers in dealing with him.

Caliana understood that she couldn't waste her energy appeasing society of their misconceptions. She did, however, mind the audacity of acquaintances who called her up, demanding to know what had happened, thus assuming license into an area of her life that was private. They assumed that because her life had become open to scrutiny and on public display, she would join them in narrating it. With those people, Caliana didn't waste any niceties in pointing out that it was clearly none of their business and that they had violated an obvious boundary.

It dawned on Caliana that by contract, Kareem would be spending every Thursday night at Rami's house. In Jordan, Thursday nights were equivalent to Saturday nights in the West, as the day off in Jordan was on Fridays. Rami loved to party, and she had never known him to miss out on a Thursday outing. Caliana had stipulated in the contract a counterpoint that restricted Rami from going out on the nights that he had Kareem. She knew that out of spite, Rami would stay home the first couple of Thursday nights and probably invite his friends over, but that eventually he would grow bored of the monotony and restrictions that prevented him from going to the parties always held on Thursday nights. Caliana would have to be diplomatic in encouraging him to drop the ordeal of Kareem spending the night with him by giving him alternative additional time with Kareem.

Caliana mentally reworked the logistics and decided to start practicing her resolve to do what was best for Kareem. The next morning, she called Rami's sister and requested a sit-down with the whole family.

As soon as Caliana entered her father-in-law's house, Kareem rushed over to her and clung to her. Caliana was overjoyed to see him and could immediately tell that he was out of his element. Everyone was focused on Kareem and his interactions with Caliana, and that seemed to start breaking the awkward tension created by her presence.

Ammo Habib, ever the gentleman, kissed Caliana and welcomed her back. Rami's sister assumed a nervous, yet jovial, role as she started gushing about how beautiful and intelligent Kareem was. Caliana used the superficial verbal chatter as an opportunity to situate herself on the couch, away from the nervous energy of the pacing Rami and his sulking mother, who had barely managed an abrupt verbal greeting. Samir wasn't there, and Caliana had mixed feelings about his absence.

Caliana asked how Kareem had fared during the night and was told that he had woken up frequently, crying for his mother. Kareem, with arms possessively clutched tightly around her neck, kept repeating, "Go home, Mama, go home. Mama, go home." There was no mistaking that her son was making it clear that he wanted to leave.

Caliana smiled at Kareem and showered him with kisses, trying to soothe him with words that they would leave soon. Caliana looked around the room and realized that it was scattered with new toys. Wanting to put Kareem at ease, she reached for one and tried to disengage him from her neck so she could play with him on the couch. Everyone in the room was focused on Caliana, and she tried to relax and engage her son so he could forget his obvious distress.

After a while, Kareem relaxed and started entertaining himself by trying to figure out the toy's complexities. Caliana took a deep breath, reminding herself to stay calm and attempt diplomacy.

"I hope that we can all agree that every decision that we make in the future should be based on what is truly best for Kareem." She paused, giving time for her words to sink in. "In the best interest of Kareem, I am ready to ignore the divorce contract, and I hope that we never have to refer to it. I am only interested in my son's happiness, and I would like to have a civil divorce whereby we can all get along, for his sake. I believe that right now, Kareem is too young to be spending the night away from me—"

Rami started to interrupt her, but his father silenced him.

"He is too young." She looked pointedly at Rami. "He doesn't understand what is happening. All he knows is that he was ripped from me, from his security, and taken to a stranger's house—"

"It's your fault that he doesn't remember me..." Rami shouted, but again, his father silenced him.

Kareem was jolted by the noise and squeezed himself back next to Caliana.

"I understand that he doesn't remember you, Rami. He hasn't seen you in four months, and for a baby, that's a long time. The reality is that you are like a stranger to him, and so is this house and everyone in it."

Caliana looked at *Ammo* Habib. "You have always claimed that, on principle, you never take on divorce cases because they pit people against each other. We also live in a world where divorce is scarce. I want to establish as much normalcy for Kareem as possible, especially under our circumstances.

"*Ammo*, I hope you know how much I respect and value you. You will always be special to me, and I hope you will listen to my advice not as a lawyer, but as a father, and as Kareem's grandfather."

Ammo Habib paused and stared deeply into Caliana's eyes. "Nothing would please me more than to forget the divorce papers and to build an understanding that would be negotiated between our families as it pertains to Kareem's best interest."

"I'm glad you feel this way. I believe that the first thing we need to focus on is to give Kareem some time to reacquaint himself with his father and your house. Instead of spending the night on Thursdays, I think he should start out by coming for a few hours on Fridays, and on another afternoon for a couple of hours. I also have to insist on his nanny being with him, as he's familiar with her and she knows his routine. In time, when Kareem is older, we can include alone, overnight visits." Caliana waited to see their reaction.

Ammo Habib and Caliana's sister-in-law heartily agreed.

"Of course, the nanny should accompany him," insisted *Ammo* Habib. "But only to help you out. Kareem needs *you* to be with him. You are his mother, and he is so obviously attached to you and we know you are a wonderful mother." *Ammo* Habib paused and made sure to look at everyone in the room. "Our two families have always been friends, and you are an integral part of our family. Nothing would make me happier than to have us continue being a family, and I insist that you must accompany Kareem every time he visits us."

Caliana believed him. She also knew that he was the ultimate authority in his household and that he was declaring a stipulation that would force his family members to comply with his wishes. He was also putting her on the spot to agree.

Caliana smiled at him. "Thank you, *Ammo*. I appreciate the offer. Let's see how Kareem adjusts. I'm not sure that I'll be able to come with him on every visit, but certainly I will at the beginning."

Ammo Habib insisted that Caliana stay and have lunch, and he made a point of focusing his energy on ensuring that she was comfortable. Caliana appreciated his decency and his attempts to resume normalcy. Everyone seemed to follow his lead, except for Rami, who barely acknowledged her presence. Rami attempted to lure Kareem away from Caliana side with pitiful and often inappropriate tactics, but Kareem wouldn't budge.

Caliana could have made it easier for Rami to engage with his son, but she deliberately held back and watched him struggle. She could sense Rami's seething resentment, and watching him make a total ass of himself was gratifying. His sister and even his mother at times interjected objections to his attempted methods and approach.

Samir joined them for lunch. There was a new awkwardness and reservation between him and Caliana, even though he had hugged her with familiar intimacy. Caliana knew that Samir had initially taken a neutral stance but that since she had disappeared with Kareem, he had shown his allegiance to his family by asking a few of their mutual friends to prove their loyalty by disengaging from Caliana.

As soon as lunch was over, Samir asked Caliana to accompany him outside for a smoke. Caliana waited until he lit his cigar before she blurted out her hurt and disappointment.

"Of all people, I didn't expect it from you. How could you have asked anyone to take a side against me?"

Samir slowly nodded his head. After what seemed like forever, he looked at her with remorse and pain and admitted, "I made a terrible mistake."

Caliana's throat constricted. She believed his vulnerability and saw that he felt contrite. She also trusted that it had been an extremely out-of-character act for Samir.

She was suddenly yanked to her feet and held in a tight hug. Samir would not let go of her, and Caliana started feeling nervous at the intensity of his appeal to be forgiven.

She disengaged from him and nervously tried to joke her way out of an emotional moment. "Okay. *Khalas*. I get it. You love and adore me! You've missed my incredible wit and charm. You couldn't live without your friend—"

"Best friend," Samir interrupted seriously.

"... whipping you into shape." Caliana smiled. She knew in her heart that everything she had believed about Samir was real.

Samir threw a party for her a few days later and made it a point to expose a declaration of his unwavering love for and support of her. He wanted everyone to clearly witness how much he still genuinely loved Caliana. That night, Caliana knew that nothing would ever come between them again, especially not Rami.

Even though Caliana and Samir resumed developing an incredibly loving and trusting friendship, and her ex in-laws were very civil and accommodating of her, and even Rami managed civility, Caliana was miserable in Jordan. She had Haya and Rhea and many other people whom she cared for, but she couldn't feel at home within the hollowness of their society. She enjoyed people but desperately missed and needed her solitude and dreamt of moving back to the United States.

Kareem was a constant source of contentment, and Caliana tried to focus on the positive aspects of her life. Her son was thriving and at fifteen months was easily able to speak. His communication skills shocked many people. To Caliana, Kareem seemed to naturally flow from using two or three words per sentence to using a more common adult language. It was a smooth, almost expected transition; he was able to put words into the thoughts that she felt she had always heard from him.

CHAPTER 18

WHEN Kareem was fifteen months old, Cindy—one of the many Persian cats that Caliana's mother kept around for aesthetic reasons— was run over by one of the family's drivers. The nanny had been outside with Kareem when the driver brought the cat he had accidentally killed to the front door. The nanny had tried to shield Kareem, but Kareem had been curious and drawn to the drama that his grandmother unleashed on the contrite driver. The nanny had told Kareem that Cindy was dead.

Kareem found Caliana reading and rushed up to her, the nanny right behind him. The nanny explained the situation, and Caliana asked the nanny to leave Kareem with her.

Kareem hugged his mother, and Caliana could tell that he felt sad, even if he hadn't really understood what had happened.

"Cindy is not moving," blurted Kareem.

"I know, *habibi*." Caliana's mind was racing with how to explain the concept of death to anyone so young. She wanted to comfort him but wanted to avoid the explanation of death. She didn't even know which version she believed, let alone how to explain it.

Kareem leaned back. Inches from her face asked, "What's dead?"

Caliana decided on a minimalist approach. "It means that Cindy will sleep for a very long time, and she won't wake up," Caliana barely managed.

Kareem considered her response. Caliana could see that his mind was not appeased.

"I can keep her in my room. She can sleep with me, okay?" he asked.

Caliana knew that drastic tactical changes had to happen.

"She can't, *habibi*. She has to go to heaven. It's a place where all dead cats go," Caliana was relieved at the simplicity of her explanation. She would focus on heaven as a *place*.

"Where is heaven?" he continued.

Caliana knew that if she described heaven as an actual place on earth, Kareem would want to visit Cindy. She took Kareem to the window and pointed to the sky.

"Up there, *habibi*. Heaven is a place that is very, very far away. It's behind the clouds. Only Cindy can go there; we can't go with her. But she will be very happy with all the other dead cats in heaven. She will play with so many new friends." Caliana was relieved that Kareem seemed focused only on trying to see cat heaven.

For days, Caliana would find Kareem looking intently at the sky. She tried to comfort him by telling him that Cindy missed playing with him and loved him and was sad not to be with him, but that she was happy in heaven. Kareem seemed to adjust to the loss of Cindy and within a few weeks stopped asking questions.

Three months later, when Kareem was eighteen months old, he and Caliana boarded a plane to London to visit Deena. As soon as the seat belt sign was released, Kareem glued his face and hands to the window. Caliana tried to distract him, unable to understand his fascination. Finally, she asked him what he was looking at.

Without looking away, Kareem answered, "I want to wave to Cindy."

Caliana was surprised that he remembered her explanation of heaven. She decided to play a game with him whereby various clouds took on animal shapes. She told Kareem that he wouldn't see Cindy as he remembered her, as she would have a cloud essence; she had become a cat-cloud, and as soon as he saw a cat-cloud, he could wave at her.

Kareem got into the game and excitedly pointed out various animals. A few times he thought he saw Cindy but decided that it wasn't Cindy but another cat. Caliana was deeply touched by Kareem's devotion and let him take his time. She understood that he needed some closure and that he would decide on the perfect cloud to say goodbye.

When Kareem finally located the cloud he thought was Cindy, he became animated and excited. He vigorously waved at her, blew her kisses, all the while shouting "Bye, Cindy. Bye ...."

Caliana looked at her son's ecstatic face and choked up. Kareem describe in detail how Cindy had also seen him and how she had waved her cloud paws at him.

"Mama, she smiled a big smile for me!" he concluded.

"Of course she did. She loves you, and she was so happy to see you too," Caliana agreed.

A few days later, Caliana and Kareem were busy taking turns playing Super Mario Brothers on Nintendo. Deena came in with a friend of hers whom Caliana hadn't met. Caliana waved at her from the floor and resumed playing with Kareem for a few more minutes.

Later, Caliana introduced herself and Kareem to Deena's friend, and Deena and her friend sat down to join the players. Kareem was intent on drawing a picture, yet Deena's friend kept engaging him in conversation. She seemed very interested in getting to know Kareem and could barely mask her surprise and excitement. She joined Kareem on the floor and immersed herself into playing with him. Caliana knew that Kareem was completely at ease and comfortable with strangers, but she was surprised by some of the questions that were asked of him, and even more surprised by his answers.

Caliana was fascinated in watching Deena's friend interact with Kareem. She had never seen anyone, besides herself, interact so well with him. Caliana was able to relate to her methods and the intelligent approach that she used with him, and found herself really enjoying the company of Deena's friend. How could she not? The woman was excellent with Kareem.

When Kareem went to take his nap, Deena's friend started gushing about Kareem's abilities. Apparently, she was doing her doctorate degree in child psychology and firmly believed that Kareem was a genius. She urged Caliana to take him to the United States, specifically to a university in Austin, Texas, where her professor could test him. She gave Caliana the professor's card and told her that anytime she wanted, testing could be arranged.

Caliana was hesitant and told her that she knew that Kareem was intelligent but she didn't see the need, or necessity, in having the fact confirmed by a doctor.

"Your son is not only intelligent, he's gifted! He's using unbelievable logic, for God's sake!" Deena's friend continued giving Caliana examples of how unique, how rare it was for an eighteen-month-old to be able to perform any of Kareem's functions. Statistics flew out of her mouth. She was determined to convince Caliana of the importance of understanding his gift.

Deena was just as excited and kept piping in with examples relating to Kareem's intelligence. She told her friend that Kareem was familiar with all the upper- and lowercase alphabet letters and that his mother was also teaching him to read.

"I knew he was a genius, I keep telling her! I'm so glad that you are telling Caliana. I don't think she really gets how smart Kareem is," Deena boasted. She urged Caliana to tell her friend the incident with Cindy, and at once, Caliana understood its immense significance.

Deena's friend dissected the mental developmental stages of growth and maturity in children, using Cindy's example to further demonstrate Kareem's incredible abilities. She pointed out that all else aside, the fact that at his age he was able to remember an incident that had occurred three months earlier and intelligently connect it to a relevant context, was staggering. She spent the next hour educating Caliana on why it was essential to determine his intelligence, and how that could positively enhance his life. Caliana appreciated the information. They parted with Caliana promising that she would try to get to Texas within the next year to have Kareem tested.

Caliana had to admit that the information she had received was extremely helpful, and she adapted some strategies that Deena's friend had recommended.

* * *

When Caliana returned to Jordan, she started paying more attention to the children around her and was shocked to discover that most normal two- and three-year-old toddlers could not even compare to Kareem's verbal abilities.

When Kareem turned two, Caliana enrolled him in the best preschool in Jordan but was dismayed by what little they had to offer her son. It wasn't only his linguistic abilities that differentiated Kareem from all the other children. It was blatantly obvious that her son did not behave anywhere near his age level. He behaved more like a seriously intelligent five- or six-year-old with an insatiable curiosity.

Caliana discussed taking Kareem to Texas with her family and her in-laws. Surprisingly, everyone was in agreement that Kareem should be tested, and Caliana was heartily supported in taking him to the United States for testing.

Caliana called Deena's friend and arranged to have Kareem tested by the renowned psychologist in October. Rami insisted on accompanying her, and Caliana knew that he wanted an excuse to spend time with her. Rami had been making obvious overt gestures regarding the possibility of remarrying her. He was also grossly dissatisfied with the restrictions that he'd faced since moving back to Jordan and was dangling the possibility of moving back to the United States as a couple.

* * *

Caliana watched Kareem being tested from behind a one-way mirror. She was grateful that it was an early morning appointment and that Rami had decided to sleep through it. He insisted that he would be at the appointment that gave them the results. Caliana focused on Kareem and marveled at his ability to attend to the testing for hours on end. He seemed to enjoy the challenging games and questions and was easily able to remain focused.

When Caliana and Rami met with the psychologist to hear the results, they were told that their son, at age 2.2 years, was a gifted boy who easily scored in the genius category. Even though the word genius was a term the doctor always used with hesitation, he felt confident that Kareem would qualify for the term. The psychologist went through the testing results and explained Kareem's advanced mental processing. He strongly recommended that Kareem be given every opportunity to develop his natural abilities and be exposed to a challenging educational environment that would allow him to learn at an accelerated pace.

Back in Jordan, Caliana tried to ask the nursery to advance Kareem's education. She offered many scenarios and options, but the reality was that they could not accommodate him. The nursery focused on socializing the children from eight in the morning until noon. They played with the children, sang with them, and did many creative art projects. Caliana tried to place Kareem in kindergarten at various other schools and was told that it would be impossible to accommodate him. Instead, she kept Kareem at the nursery but focused on spending every afternoon expanding his reading and writing skills.

A few days later, her father-in-law quoted a poem from Khalil Gibran's *The Prophet* in a conversation, and Caliana asked him if she could borrow his book. That night, she devoured the section "On Children" a few times over. She had finally read something that resonated with her idea of parenting. Like Gibran's archer, she would hold a steady loving bow and guide her son to his infinite future. She would not "house his thoughts" by limiting him with her own perceptions and thoughts but allow him to reach the house of his tomorrow—the future that she could never foresee. She needed to allow him the capability of making his own conclusions on life and let him discover his meaning and purpose. She had been his vessel and understood the honor that God had granted her.

That Kareem had arrived with evolved intelligence only confirmed his specialness and enhanced the awesome responsibility of guiding his capacity to spiritual evolvement. Caliana's understanding of spirituality was simple in that she viewed it as a reflection of pure love. She wanted Kareem to encompass her basic beliefs and also search for his own, unhindered. She needed to be able to guide him, yet she needed to assess the role and definition of guiding. Caliana spent hours pondering her exact role and questioning and reviewing the direction she had already applied with Kareem. She concluded that the best gauge would be to continue to follow Kareem's lead; when he was ready for certain information, he would ask. She needed to answer him in a way that presented him with all alternatives on any given scenario, and to encourage him to think for himself. She was resolved never to punish him for any of his mistakes but to encourage him to use each mistake as an opportunity to learn and grow. She would support him in honoring his discovery of who he wanted to become.

* * *

By June, Caliana had spent one year and nine months (minus the four months obtaining her divorce) living in frustration in Jordan. Rami formally proposed again to her father and offered to move Caliana and Kareem to Washington, DC. Her father told Rami that he would consider his request and discuss it with Caliana.

Caliana and her father engaged in a private conversation, in which they broke down the logistics of the offer. Caliana put aside any feelings that she had for Rami and began negotiating a verbal marriage contract with her father. Her father had never wanted any of his daughters to live in Jordan and had made that abundantly clear.

Caliana shared his sentiment but worried about what would happen if she had to divorce Rami a second time, as that was clearly a strong possibility. She wanted to secure her future through a new marital agreement.

Her father arranged a meeting with Caliana and Rami. He insisted that after much deliberation, he had concluded that what would be the most ideal for Kareem was to have his parents remarry. Caliana's father stated that he hoped Caliana and Rami would be able to work out their differences for Kareem's sake *but* that he was also concerned that there was a possibility that something could go wrong. One never knew what would happen in the future. Therefore, it was essential to protect his daughter. He would not object to a remarriage if certain conditions were met. They could move to Washington, DC, or anywhere else of their choosing, but it could not be in the Middle East. A signed, new contract would have to be written stating that their current divorce contract would be legally abolished and could never be legally referred to. Because Christians did not have a marriage contract, they would sign a civil and binding contract that clearly stated all the conditions for the new marriage.

The new contract would specifically state that in the case of future divorce, Jordanian law would not be applicable and could not be used in any capacity. They would follow the divorce laws of America, and both parties would adhere to the US terms of divorce. After the marriage, Rami would immediately reinstate his application for Caliana to obtain a green card and would have to stay married to her for the duration of time stipulated by the American law to guarantee that Caliana obtained her green card. If Rami and Caliana decided to divorce while her green card application was still pending, they had to both agree on a separation until she physically had the green card in her hands. Rami was to provide a separate legal document that clearly allowed Caliana to have future access to travel without any restraint from him. Caliana would carry the legal document with her every time she exited Jordan as a security measure. Rami would be giving up his legal right to block her exit from the country.

Caliana watched Rami absorb her father's lecture. Rami nodded and agreed with every point that her father made and complimented him on his wisdom and foresight. Caliana felt that she was impassively observing her future being contracted out to a man she could barely stand. She knew the terms that her father had laid out, but she was surprised when her father added that, legalities aside, Caliana would have the ultimate decision in anything relating and pertaining to Kareem's academic life.

Rami agreed with the conditions and promised her father that he was a responsible man who planned on being a great husband and father. They agreed on a joint lawyer who would draw up all the legal documents. Rami, ever so eager to leave Jordan, started discussing immediately leaving to the United States to get married. Caliana's father told him that the time for the remarriage would be determined *only* after every document was legalized and documented in the appropriate Jordanian civil courts. Meanwhile, Rami was welcome to be a constant visitor in their home, until the time they could go to the States and be married there.

When Rami left, Caliana's father gloated. He had expected some opposition, or negotiation, and had prepared for various rebuttals. Caliana knew that Rami would absolutely agree to anything to remarry her. She knew that in his distorted mind, he believed he was in love with her. She also knew that he was highly influenced by his father's and brother's respect and admiration for her. He valued their opinion and knew that they loved and admired her.

Caliana confided only to Rhea and Haya her true motives in remarrying Rami.

At the end of July, Caliana, Kareem, Rami, and the nanny boarded a flight to begin life in Washington, DC.

Caliana and Rami were married the first week in August, the same month that Kareem turned three. Three months later, to her serious surprise, Caliana discovered she was pregnant.

The next day, she received a phone call from her father informing her that Rami had called them, asking for their help in persuading her to have an abortion. Caliana's father had emphatically told Rami that he would never condone abortion, that he had financially supported his first grandchild, and that he would do so for the second grandchild. Her father reported that Rami had been extremely agitated and had threatened that he simply couldn't have another child as he was still under the pressure of trying to make his relationship work with Caliana. He gave an ultimatum: either the baby, or his marriage.

Caliana laughed when her father relayed the message. She told her father that she was going to have the baby and that there wasn't even a remote possibility of an abortion. But Rami had given her the perfect excuse to end the marriage, and she would jump on the opportunity.

Her father told her to hire a realtor and start looking for a house to buy. Rami moved out of their marital home.

The following July, Caliana gave birth to Talal. In less than a year, she had moved to the United States, been married for three months, separated, been blessed with the birth of another son, and bought a new home.

Her life as a happily divorced single mother began.

CHAPTER 19

1992–1993

CALIANA organized the space around her with everything she could possibly need for a night curled up by the fireplace. It never ceased to amaze her how much pleasure she got out of unwinding from yet another hectic day. She would have her habitual bath and would begin relaxing in anticipation of savoring the few quiet hours that would be hers alone. As much as she thoroughly enjoyed giving her abundant energy to her sons' varied needs during the day, she also appreciated the time to replenish herself. Some downtime at the end of any given day was an essential balancing requirement.

She had curtailed her personal socializing when Kareem was born and had cut it back further with the birth of Talal. It had been easy to devote her energy to her children. It seemed that every moment of every day was dedicated to being an active single mother, and it made every free moment simply precious, not to be wasted on people she did not have to engage with.

Caliana lit a cigarette, closed her eyes, and thanked God for her sons, and her life, which now felt complete. She had celebrated Kareem's sixth birthday a few days earlier, and a month earlier, Talal's second birthday. An essential aspect of Caliana's nightly routine was a treasured reflection on her life with her children, as it allowed her to consciously work on establishing her new family dynamic, as well as take the time to absorb the fullness of her blessing.

She was grateful that she didn't have a husband or live in a country that distracted her with social obligations. Her love for her sons helped to create a natural attachment that rooted her in intimacy, and to Caliana, that was an extraordinarily novel experience. It created an urgent desire to create a safe and loving world for them. She felt the need to continually inspect herself and her actions, to make sure that she lived up to the ideal of parenting that she had imagined.

As a child she had silently harbored justifiable anger at how little parenting she had received, and she was now free to indulge her deepest hunger for a family. She was determined to create a world that finally made sense and that she could comfortably live in. To Caliana's utter surprise, it had been easy to assume the management of her world. She felt confident as the sole decision maker for her children's well-being, and what continued to fuel her ability was the ease with which she trusted her intelligence and integrity. All she had to do was navigate her family into her perspective of life and decency.

The birth of Kareem had given her a strong incentive to take charge of her life, and her move to the US and the birth of Talal had validated her ability to construct a wonderful reality. She had spent the past three years carefully assimilating herself into the collectiveness of a new culture, of a new country, and it had allowed her the freedom to choose the parts of the culture to which she wanted to expose her children. She was also determined to expose them to various parts of the world to allow them to develop their cultural diversity and tolerance. She trusted and felt confident in her ability to guide them as she took charge of her life, and their lives, her way.

Caliana knew that there were still strings tying her to many dysfunctional family members, but she loved the fact that they were continents apart; they could not infect her sons with their toxicity. She had had enough engaging with the dramas that resulted from such associations. She knew that her only chance of maintaining normalcy was to be selective in choosing the people who would enter her life. That she had not known one single person in the Washington, DC, area when she had relocated there had allowed her the unlimited scope to follow her vision of parenting.

She had meticulously chosen the acquaintances she spent time with and made sure that she set very firm boundaries on planning and scheduling the times and frequencies of each interaction. After having spent a year and a half existing in the pressure of living in the high exposure of her small society in Jordan, Caliana valued the freedom that her anonymity allowed her in the States. She did not want to know many people, but she needed to have her children exposed to healthy interactions, so she focused most of her efforts on participating in events relating to activities for her children's social and school functions.

Caliana smiled, recollecting Kareem's sixth birthday weekend. She had taken him to New York for one-on-one quality time. On the train from Washington, they had gone over Kareem's detailed plan for the weekend. Caliana had booked for them a Broadway show, and Kareem wanted to tour a few sites. They had gone to the Empire State building and to the Guinness World Record exhibit, and, best of all, they had toured a few museums, where they had indulged their love of art. Kareem had discovered many new artists and decided that Titian was his new favorite. Watching Kareem's mature introspection melted Caliana's heart. His natural curiosity was engulfed in intelligence, and Caliana was intellectually stimulated by witnessing him tackle new experiences.

She had given Kareem charge of their expenses, and he had loved the responsibility of paying and keeping track of how to best budget their money. He especially enjoyed asking for the check in restaurants and calculating the percentages for tipping. Trying to encourage him to be more impulsive, Caliana had suggested a horse-drawn carriage ride through Central Park. Kareem had sat quietly throughout the ride and not shown much enthusiasm.

Caliana grinned at remembering Kareem's fascination with the Guggenheim Museum. He had been astounded with the architecture and how the spiral rooms allowed for the art to be displayed. He had drilled Caliana with dozens of question about Frank Lloyd Wright, marveling at the geometric designs and the unique use of organic forms in the architecture.

As they had left the museum, Kareem had gushed with admiration, insisting that the unqualified highlight of his visit to New York had been seeing the Guggenheim, and that the museum itself was the best artwork he had seen.

"Mom, he's a genius!" Kareem had insisted.

"Oh, I know he is, sweetheart. Actually, he's my favorite architect. You know, Kareem, some people criticized Wright because they felt he was creating a museum environment that would overpower the art, would take attention away from it. What do you think?"

Kareem had already been shaking his head in disagreement while she was talking, and Caliana knew that he was ready to defend his new champion. "That's not true. I liked the way each picture stood out because of the architecture. Every picture was on its own ... like you forget that you were in a museum."

Kareem was frowning, and Caliana knew that he was struggling with how to best express his opinion, and that he hadn't been satisfied with his answer.

"It's just not true!" he concluded emphatically.

Caliana laughed. "You're right. Actually, Wright disagreed with his critics and told them that his purpose was to make the building be something that would not interrupt the art. He wanted harmony and symphony between the art and the setting..."

"Exactly!" Kareem interrupted, excited that her explanation fit with what he had been trying to say.

"So what were some of your favorite paintings?" Caliana inquired. She burst out laughing when she saw Kareem's confused face. "You don't even remember the paintings, do you?"

"Not really," he grumbled, hating to concede the argument.

"Maybe the critics had a small point? You were so absorbed in the architecture of the building that you barely paid attention to the art," she teased. "Don't worry. I had the same reaction the first time I went. I was so excited about *being* in a Wright building that I barely remembered to look at the actual displayed art."

"I will, next time. But Mom, can I see more of his buildings? Are there more in New York?" he asked hopefully.

"I don't think so, and anyway, we don't have time. I tell you what ... we need to get our luggage and head to the station, but we'll stop at a bookstore and buy you a book that will show you different buildings that he designed."

"Are they as good?" Kareem hesitated, almost fearful that he would be disappointed. "Are his other buildings as great?"

Caliana laughed. "Where is your faith? I though you said he was a genius?" she teased. "I have many books at home that I will show you, but we'll get one for the train ride. I don't think you will be disappointed, *habibi*."

The whole trip back on the train, Kareem had been completely absorbed in reading the book that she had purchased for him. Caliana had shown him her favorite house, *Fallingwater*, and shared with him that if she could devise her idea of heaven, it would be to live in *Fallingwater* and have it located on an island. Kareem was hooked and declared that he wanted to become an architect.

"Mom, did you know that Wright died before the Guggenheim was done?"

Caliana looked up from her book and answered him, "Yes, I knew that. I remember thinking it's a pity that he had never seen it completed."

Kareem was so engrossed in contemplation that Caliana was surprised when he disagreed a few minutes later. "Maybe he didn't see it the way we saw it today, but he did see it completed in his mind." And he went back to reading. Caliana smiled, yet again, impressed by Kareeem's ability to truly consider words and ideas. He thought of everything, and Caliana knew that she needed to continue exposing his uniquely gifted mind to wondrous possibilities.

Caliana lit another cigarette and opened her daily planner. She had a busy week ahead of her. She had an open house party at Kareem's new school that she was excited to attend to learn even more. She had known within moments of first touring the school that it was a perfect fit for Kareem. Dropping Kareem off into the kindergarten class for his visiting day, she had observed other children who were similar to him in intensity and demeanor. She then had had her meeting with the owner, who was also the administrator of the school, and they had gone over Kareem's most recent testing results.

Caliana had been impressed by the owner's personal vision, which had allowed her to create a private school for gifted children. The owner had shared some of her personal history and told Caliana that she had suffered as a gifted child; she had been made to attend different grade levels in different subjects to meet her intellectual abilities. As a child, she had dreamt of creating a different educational setting, and as an adult, she had been able to realize her dream by creating an academic environment that met the needs of gifted children socially, emotionally, and academically. Her school provided a loving and supportive environment in which to challenge the unique potential of gifted learners as it accelerated the curriculum to their highest academic level. Caliana had barely been able to contain her excitement, especially when it had become obvious that Kareem was accepted based on the astounding results of his testing. According to the tests, Kareem was performing at third- or fourth-grade level in all the core subjects.

Caliana had been surprised at how comfortable she had been in discussing Kareem's abilities and intelligence with the school's owner.

She shared with the owner the struggles thus far in finding an appropriate academic setting for Kareem and how frustrating it had been to be his only real teacher.

"He is the only six-year-old that can read and write fluently in his kindergarten class, and most of the kids, not meaning to, are making him feel weird. Worst of all, he's been exposed to many adults who think they are complimenting him by referring to him as the genius. He has been stigmatized and alienated by his abilities, and I want him to feel proud and comfortable in his own skin."

Caliana had continued to pour out many worries and concerns that plagued her regarding Kareem's intelligence. She felt like she was in a confessional, spilling out every uncensored fear, and she had intuitively known that she was being heard and understood. More importantly, she had trusted that the owner had an incredible insight into providing for gifted children and that what she was hearing was not a sales pitch to get her business. Caliana was then escorted by the owner to observe parts of every grade, from kindergarten to eight.

What she saw, what she witnessed and experienced, left her breathless. Halfway through the tour, she had impulsively blurted out, "You are taking Kareem, right? This is beyond perfect. You did say in your office that you will take him and that he is a perfect addition. Right?"

The owner had smiled and assured her that Kareem was definitely accepted and all Caliana had to do was fill out some additional paperwork. Caliana had wanted to hug her. Instead, she had thanked her for having created the perfect school for Kareem and children like him.

Caliana had returned at the end of the day to pick up Kareem, and with her checkbook in readiness. She was waiting to hear Kareem's response and feedback before committing his future to the school. She had prayed that Kareem was as excited as she had been. Caliana returned to the owner's office, and together, she and the owner walked toward the classroom were Kareem was finishing his last trial class. They stood outside the glass door, observing Kareem in silence for a few minutes, and then the owner stuck her head in and asked him to come out.

It had been clear to Caliana that Kareem was disappointed to have to leave slightly ahead of the rest of the class. As soon as the door to the class closed, he had looked up at the owner and asked, "Can I come back tomorrow?"

Caliana laughed and gave him a hug. "I guess I don't need to ask you if you liked the school?" she teased.

As they walked toward the office, the owner and Kareem had engaged in a long conversation about his visit, Caliana simply observing. She had not wanted to interrupt the dialogue and was fascinated by the information that she was able to gather about what Kareem had actually done that day. For years, she had gotten his monosyllabic answers when she had asked him about his school day. Whenever she had pushed him to give her details, he would simply state that he was bored from learning "kid stuff."

"The only class that was hard was French. But the teacher was very nice and tried to help me," Kareem stated.

Caliana signed the contract and left a deposit. Her only regret was that she hadn't found that school for Kareem in time for entering kindergarten, but she felt grateful that he would be in the perfect school for the next eight years.

CHAPTER 20

CALIANA had made it a point not to compare her children, and when Talal showed signs of normal development, she was thrilled at his progress and at the pace of every step that he took. In Talal, she had felt that she would experience the wonders of all the regular stages of mothering. On a visceral level, she had sensed, from the moment she had first seen Talal, that she had been given a special angel and that they would be intrinsically entwined in his journey on earth; she understood that he was the child who would teach her the unimaginable.

Caliana had felt a loving attachment to Talal during his development in her uterus. A serene, natural flow of love had radiated from her heart toward him. She had welcomed loving her second son with an intensity that had flourished as a result of practicing as a loving mom. With Talal, she had felt prepared, excited, and curious to learn and love his journey in life.

Caliana found herself recalling Talal at the age of one. She smiled at the images of Talal following her around and his intense observations of the world around him. His hero, though, was Kareem. Talal was fascinated and drawn to his brother and worshipped him with hugs and kisses. His first word at ten months had been an attempt at his brother's name.

Caliana had been delighted at the obvious affection between her sons and was determined to encourage them to stay close with each other. Even though Kareem had started displaying some jealousy at the age of five by complaining about his one-year-old brother shadowing him, he was still an incredibly patient and loving older brother. Caliana would encourage Kareem to practice reading his favorite comic, Calvin & Hobbes, to his brother, and Talal would imitate Kareem's laughter. Caliana tried to engage them together in various activities in spite of the age and maturity differences between them. She also tried to give Kareem his own space so he could have his privacy, and she made an effort to split her time so each child had his own unique quality time with her.

Caliana scanned to the last appointment in her planner: Talal's new appointment with a speech therapist. Even though Talal's pediatrician insisted that Talal's lack of language development was normal and her in-laws had consistently reaffirmed that all their children had spoken very late, Caliana insisted on seeing a specialist and had pressured the pediatrician to give her a referral. Caliana wasn't sure exactly what a speech therapist would do for her eighteen-month-old son, but she knew that she needed to start investigating his language delay.

What was bothering Caliana was that Talal had had about twenty or so words by the time he was thirteen months but then he suddenly had crashed into silence. She was told that some children digressed, and everyone insisted that her worries were unfounded because she was worrying about things that were within normal ranges. Over the past few months, Caliana had tried to ask everyone she knew specific questions regarding language development. She had researched books and was dissatisfied with the responses, which were widely varied.

Caliana could not voice or put words to the nagging concern that there was something wrong with Talal. She had attempted to tell the pediatrician that Talal had stopped looking at her and at his surroundings; he had thoroughly dismissed her. She couldn't explain that she felt that Talal had become vacant in some ways, as though something was pulling him into a disconnected vacuum. Caliana found herself thinking that Talal was disappearing before her eyes. She would then reprimand herself for being ridiculous and raising uncomfortable fears, yet she couldn't quite stop feeling that something was off.

Earlier that morning Caliana had called Talal many times, and he had not responded, not even turned his face toward her. He had been fewer than ten feet away from her. Caliana had walked up to him, and with each step closer to him, she had progressively raised her voice while calling his name. By the time she had stood next to him, she had been trembling in utter panic as she shouted his name. At that moment, she could have sworn that he was deaf. She had been shaken enough to have called and made an appointment with a pediatric audiologist for the following week.

Caliana considered Talal's development as objectively as she could. Besides his language regression, and the limited eye contact that he now exhibited, he had quirks to his personality that she had previously considered as endearing. Now she thought them odd. For one thing, Talal was becoming almost allergic to clothing and to being touched. He seemed to react very strongly to certain fabrics and hated any tags touching his body. He preferred running around naked, and Caliana had accommodated him by keeping him outdoors and swimming as often as possible. He loved being in the water and could stay all day, yet he hated, loathed, having a drop of liquid spilled on any item of clothing. A little water spill on his sweatshirt induced a violent jerk followed by a desperate attempt to rip the offending material away from himself. He reacted as though he had been touched by fire. For the past few weeks, he had resisted her customary hugging while she read him a bedtime story and had pushed her away until she was lying down with her back completely to him. He would then entwine one hand into her curly hair and gently rub her hair between his fingers while drinking his milk bottle in the other hand. That became the only way she could put him to sleep. Caliana's thoughts spun with solutions to an incomprehensible problem. She wanted to talk to a doctor, but besides his pediatrician, who was dismissive of her worries, she had no idea which doctor she should approach.

She had researched online some neurological disorders, but none of them seemed to fit Talal's description. For the hundredth time, she told herself to stop being ridiculous, that she was overreacting purely in her typical defensive reactions; she was preparing for the worst-case scenario, except she didn't know exactly what scenario to prepare for. Her heart nagged her with worries, and she felt propelled to take some action.

A week later, she was perplexed by the negative results of Talal's testing and yet felt even more anxious. He had passed the hearing test, and the speech therapist hadn't been overly concerned, signing up Talal to once-a-week speech therapy to "help him along" with speaking. It was also recommended that only one language, English, should be spoken at home.

A few days later, Caliana was watching Talal in the backyard. She felt exhausted from her failed attempts to get him to play, to interact with her. He kept walking away and returning to his favorite corner by the brick wall in the backyard. Lost in her own thoughts, Caliana realized that she was observing Talal meticulously pick at the mortar between two bricks, and then quickly shoving pieces into his mouth. In shock, Caliana rushed to him and attempted to insert her fingers into his mouth. Talal clamped down and refused to open his mouth. Caliana had to apply pressure on his cheeks to force his mouth open, and he struggled against her. She stood stupefied, fingering the grainy sand and looking at the spot where he had been picking.

She picked up Talal, rushed inside the house, and handed him to the nanny, then raced to the computer. On her second search attempt, she discovered a name for what Talal had done; it was called Pica, the eating of nonfood items. She skimmed through the article, which spoke about the possibility of mineral deficiency. Her heart started an erratic pounding when she read about the danger of such items containing lead, which could lead to toxic lead poisoning and affect the brain....

Caliana jumped off the chair and rushed to the phone to schedule an appointment with the pediatrician. The receptionist kept putting her on hold as she conferred with the nurse regarding the relevance of what Caliana considered an emergency. The receptionist tried to convince Caliana to watch her son, and that if he continued eating nonfood items, she could bring him in for testing to determine lead poisoning.

Caliana wanted to strangle the receptionist; instead, she bullied her way into securing an appointment later that afternoon. All day, Caliana read up on Pica and was especially disturbed by the possible association of brain damage from lead poisoning. She went back outside to Talal's spot and carefully inspected all the cracks between the bricks, looking for evidence of her son, her baby, having eaten dirt. She couldn't understand any of it.

Later that afternoon, she told the pediatrician that she had seen Talal with his mouth full of sand a few weeks earlier but had attributed it to an accident in the sandbox. In retrospect, she realized that Talal had also even then resisted her attempt to get the sand out of his mouth. She insisted on the test.

All night, Caliana tossed with anger. She knew that something was wrong and was appalled that no one else sensed it. She gave up on sleeping and spent the night on the computer searching for answers without knowing the questions.

The following morning, Caliana called a famous children's hospital and made an appointment with a pediatric neurologist. She would have to wait until November, almost seven weeks, before Talal could be seen for an evaluation.

The test from the pediatrician came back negative for lead poisoning.

By the time Caliana got to the neurologist in November, she was a nervous wreck. Talal had progressively gotten worse, and Caliana was living with the utter terror of her helplessness. She had kept an accurate list of Talal's developmental issues and had a few concrete examples to help give the neurologist an accurate representation of what she clearly identified as a serious problem. Her fears in the past two months had continued to escalate, more so because she felt that her worries were justifiable. She was perplexed with the fact that she had visited many pediatricians and specialists and yet they had all been unable to easily identify or label Talal's odd symptoms. Every pediatrician seemed to be at a loss to help explain why her son had transformed into a zombie-like state, why Talal had suddenly stopped *being*.

She unloaded her nightmare onto the neurologist.

She explained to him that Talal's digression from normalcy had been rapidly escalating. Talal had started humming incessantly. Left alone, he would hypnotically hum and pace the same twenty-foot corridor, clutching his favorite toy figurine. It was intensely frightening to watch. His eye contact had completely disappeared, and when he unpurposely looked at her, she felt his disconnection. She had watched her son simply stop being her son. His intolerance to certain materials and damp clothes had escalated to include food textures. He had to smell and touch all foods and would eat only burgers, a homemade spaghetti sauce, and lots of milk. He refused to eat anything else. Yet again, she had been reassured that many children in that age group were picky eaters.

In the span of only the past two weeks, he had stopped tolerating anyone hugging him and would automatically turn his back to the person who insisted on hugging him. It was as though he didn't want to see or feel the hug. Even though he had stopped responding to clear and loud verbal attempts at getting his attention, he exhibited astounding auditory skills. Talal would look up at the sky and point his finger upwards minutes before Caliana could see or hear a plane overhead. Even then, she sometimes strained to hear the plane even when she clearly saw it, and yet knew that her son had picked up the sound from an unbelievable distance.

Everyone seemed to have an answer to every bit of Talal's individual odd behaviors. She told the neurologist that every part of Talal's symptoms could be somewhat rationalized if they were taken out of context, but if his symptoms were looked at collectively, something had to be going on.

The neurologist assured her that she had done the right thing by bringing Talal in to see him. He told her that he would have to run multiple tests to rule out brain damage such as fragile X syndrome.

The following few weeks were unbearable. In between taking Talal back to the hospital to be examined by various specialists, Caliana heard negative comments from Rami about how American doctors were basically crooks who were out for her money. She had regretted giving Rami any information, even though she felt morally obliged to share with him her worries.

After each test, Caliana met with the neurologist, who confirmed that each particular test showed that Talal was physically and mentally normal. There was no physical evidence of brain damage. Each time he told Caliana that he wanted to rule out yet another possibility, he would administer another test. The MRI, chromosomes, and metabolic tests did not show any brain dysfunction, yet the neurologist wanted Talal examined by a team of developmental doctors who would be able to determine his diagnosis.

By the end of March, Caliana, and Rami, who happened to be in town, met with the team to hear the results. Talal demonstrated developmental delays in the areas of language, cognition, and social communication. At thirty-two months, Talal's receptive language skills were estimated to be in the six- to seven-month range, his expressive skills were estimated at the twelve- to fourteen-month age range, and his social communication skills at the seven-month level. Oral motor skills and sensory processing problems were also suspect. Also, his play skills were at the pre-symbolic schemes level of 9 -15 months. Caliana and Rami were informed that Talal had Pervasive Developmental Disorder, or PDD, a euphemism for autism, and central nervous system disturbances. Caliana's heart dropped. In a daze, she heard Rami questioning the team about what autism meant. Caliana heard herself calmly asking them what could be done, what she should do.

The doctor who had taken on the responsibility of explaining the team's diagnosis recommended that Talal be placed, as soon as possible, in a clinical educational facility and gave her the name of a center in Maryland where Talal could receive intensive help. Caliana asked what the best-case scenario would be for Talal's future and was told that eventually, she might have to institutionalize him.

Caliana was grateful that she had let Rami drive her to the hospital, for she could not have driven home. Her eyes were glazed with painful thoughts, and she felt herself digressing into a familiar emotional disconnect. The pain in her heart was unbearable, and she welcomed the numbness that was removing her from her pain. Returning home after the diagnosis was a blur of intense thoughts that came and went. From a vast distance she observed Rami break down in tears as he hugged Talal; she would later remember envying his strength. She had stood shaking, afraid to look on and torn with conflicting emotions. She had clamped down on the tears and resumed the familiar numbness.

For the next few days, time ceased to matter as she operated in yet another functional depression. She noted that she was making all the appropriate decisions, and that she continued caring for her sons, but she felt nothing. She had made an appointment to visit the school recommended by the doctors and filled out the application.

* * *

Caliana entered the special education center in Maryland, stiffly clutching the application between her folded arms. She was petrified and felt her eyes mist over as though she might pass out. She had smoked heavily throughout yet another sleepless night. Nausea was burning acidic waves in her stomach. She followed other parents on a tour, barely hearing the explanations of the guide.

She was intently aware of the clinical setting and that most of the children there had physical handicaps. Many obviously had Down Syndrome. In one art classroom, she stood back, watching the multiple stations occupied by various-aged children. A staff member accompanied each child. Cynically, Caliana thought that at least they had a large enough staff to accommodate one-on-one assistance. She hated the place and refused to see Talal in it.

A child caught her eye. He was perhaps six or seven years old. At first, he looked normal, but after a moment, she noticed that he was strangely frozen in front of his easel. He was passively ignoring the assistant trying to encourage him to paint. Caliana couldn't take her eyes off of him, and she desperately willed him to look at her. She edged away from the group and closer to his station and silently stood watching him. He did not react to her presence, not even a normal flicker of his eyes to acknowledge her approach. Something about his stillness, his vacancy, struck a familiar chord.

Caliana felt the tears roll down her face. She quickly dashed out of the room. Angrily, she marched back to the main office. She hesitated only long enough to ask for a pen. In bold capital letters, she wrote on the first page of Talal's application, "My son does NOT belong here!!" before storming out.

Caliana sat in her car in the parking lot for at least an hour. Her mind was spinning with thoughts, and she tried to calm herself by slowing her breathing. She was angry at herself for having disappeared emotionally in the past few days. She berated herself for her weakness, for numbing her feelings. She had to take charge of Talal with lucidity, without being in denial of her pain.

She felt bad for the children she had seen and knew that if she truly believed that Talal was mentally retarded, she would have to place him there. Caliana flashed back on numerous moments in which she had seen Talal's nonverbal intelligence, the sparks of recognition that often lit up his eyes. He had been normal before his descent into autism, before the sudden crash. She had to fight for him, to try to get him back. She couldn't afford to give up on him; placing him in such a center would invariably be a resignation toward a fate that she was not ready to accept. Caliana started driving away and cringed at remembering her conduct. She should have simply held on to the application, not submitted it.

The following few weeks tested her resolve. She questioned herself constantly. Was she a parent in denial? She didn't think so. She understood that she may never get her son back, but she didn't want it to be from her lack of effort. She accepted that she would love and protect Talal irrespective of the outcome, but she needed to do something beyond accepting the futility of his condition and placing him in an institutionalized setting.

The doctors she had continued to confer with were adamant that there was no cure, that nobody recovered from autism. Caliana had exhausted the limited knowledge of the medical field. The doctors didn't seem to know a thing about treatments, because they had collectively decided that there wasn't one. A force larger than her under-standing kept Caliana reading and researching every alternative option. She was incapable of accepting that she could do nothing for her baby.

Very little alternative research had been given to autism. Caliana was angered by the Refrigerator Mom explanation, the theory that maternal negligence caused autism; Talal had received abundant, healthy loving from her. In her research, she came across one well-established institute for autism in California, run by Dr. Rimland. Caliana was immediately attracted to Dr. Rimland, partly because he had an autistic child, but mainly for his optimism and open approach to possible treatments. Like her, he seemed to have dismissed the futile prognosis given by the medical community. Some of the recommen-dations on his website centered on a vitamin supplement, a combina-tion of magnesium and B6. Caliana contacted the institute, ordered the supplement, enrolled in the newsletter, and purchased all the older editions of their newsletters.

Caliana pored over six years of articles from the Autism Research Review Newsletters. The articles were written by parents and professionals and provided crucial information about various treatment attempts and research. A new world was opening up to her, and Caliana planned to arm herself with every nuance related to prospective treatments. She had to become fully informed so as to start planning Talal's recovery.

Caliana remembered watching a documentary on nature versus nurture as related to developing and guiding prospective intelligence. At the time, she had watched it to learn more about Kareem and had been impressed with the simplicity of its message: Everyone, irrespec-tive of the level of genetic intelligence, could increase and enhance their intelligence through challenging mental stimulation. A great mind could also be wasted by undernourishment. Something had hap-pened to Talal, and whatever it was had resulted in autism. Caliana was sure that there had been absolutely nothing wrong with Talal's mind. She had experienced his intelligence, but she needed to discover what was blocking her from accessing it—and, more importantly, what was blocking Talal's access to his own mind. What had triggered and kept Talal in that withdrawn world? And how could she possibly nourish his mind if she could not access it?

Caliana spent every available hour researching and following up with people who dealt outside of medical conventions. Foremost in her mind, especially when she felt dejected, was the movie *Lorenzo's Oil,* about a family's real-life struggle within the world of adrenoleukodystrophy, ALD. She had seen the movie a year earlier and had been inspired by the parents' dedication in attempting to find a cure for their son's condition. They had fought with the medical professionals and had been able to extend and improve their son's life through diligence and intelligent investigations.

When Caliana mentioned Dr. Bernard Rimland to Talal's neurologist, she was told that Dr. Rimland was a quack and that it was preposterous to believe that vitamins could correct a brain disorder. Caliana retaliated by insisting that the so-called quack at least offered hope, an opportunity, unlike the medical community that had offered nothing but grimness and limited knowledge.

Caliana began the magnesium–B6 supplement as well as DMG—one article had listed a mention of a food supplement called DMG that seemed to help some children with autism. Caliana was willing to try everything so long as it wasn't a pharmaceutical (not that one existed anyway). She figured that the medical community had put her through endless medical testing to "rule out" a physiologically based factor. After exhausting all these options, she decided to apply the same efforts to investigating Talal's diet. She would apply a process of elimination and see if the culprit was food-related. She began by removing dairy completely. She met with a nutritionist, who helped her custom compound a vitamin and mineral supplement, and contacted a homeopathic pharmacy to make the supplements for her.

Caliana also immediately enrolled Talal in the Speech and Language Center of Northern Virginia, located nearby in McLean. Talal spent four and a half hours in a nursery class administered by loving professionals who focused on language development in children with developmental delays. Caliana then had him work with an occupational therapist on sensory integration issues, as it was clear that Talal was tactile-defensive. The therapists worked on Talal's neurological damage and tried to help his nervous system adjust to various tactile stimulations. They gave Caliana a few different kinds of brushes to help stimulate his nervous system while he was taking a bath. After working with the occupational therapist, Talal worked one on one with a speech therapist.

It was through the occupational therapist that Caliana heard about the Spectrum Center in Bethesda and a program there called the Tomatis Auditory Integration Therapy, combined with Sensory Integration. Caliana signed Talal up to begin an intensive listening program that required him to work on special headphones for a few hours a day. The program was supposed to help him take in, connect, and organize auditory information. Through sound stimulation, Talal would train and develop listening-related skills.

* * *

Caliana's long daily routine focused on Talal's therapies. In between, she continued her research. Exhausted, and sleep deprived, Caliana knew that Kareem was receiving far less attention from her. She stopped outside Kareem's room and quietly stood watching him read. It was hard to believe that the child sitting before her, so intently focused on his novel, was only six years old and had a few months left in kindergarten. That he was academically operating a few grade levels ahead of his peers was the least of his genius. Caliana trusted her son's emotional maturity and the healthy stability with which he continued to assimilate his world.

"Can I interrupt?" Caliana asked after a gentle knock.

Kareem looked up, and Caliana could tell from his glazed eyes that he was still in the world of the novel. They chatted for a few minutes about his book.

"I want to talk to you about Talal, *habibi*. You know he's been going to see many doctors and therapists, but I want to try to explain some things to you."

"Sure, Mom."

Caliana smiled at Kareem's recent switch from calling her Mama to Mom: the American way.

"Before I try to explain Talal's condition, I want you to really understand that it is not possible for me to love you more than Talal, or to love Talal more than you. I love each of you with my whole heart. Do you believe that?" Kareem nodded. "I have been spending more time with Talal, and will probably have to keep doing that for a while. I wanted to make sure you really know that just because I spend a lot more time with Talal, it doesn't mean that I love him more."

"I know, Mom."

"I won't be here most afternoons because I need to take Talal to different therapists. It will mean that I will have to miss out on spending time with you and doing projects together. Some days, you'll be able to come with me, and as we wait for Talal to finish, we can work together in a coffee shop or somewhere. Is that okay with you?" Again, Kareem nodded. "We'll organize a schedule so that we can all work it out and try to spend as much time together as possible."

"You could also leave me homework here, and I can work alone," Kareem added.

"Sure, I will do that. We'll see how it goes. But I want you to know that just because I am not spending as much time with you, it has nothing to do with my not loving you, or loving you any less. Got it, kiddo?"

Kareem rolled his eyes at her, and Caliana savored the hug that followed.

Kareem sat back and asked, "What's wrong with him?"

"I don't know .... I know what the doctors are saying. They say he has autism. Remember when we talked about the movie *Rain Man*? And how we looked up autism?" Kareem nodded slowly, and Caliana saw the beginning of fear. "It's not exactly like the movie, but it is similar."

Caliana regretted having given the movie as a reference. She had forgotten until that moment that Kareem had had incessant questions about autism after watching it. Ironically, she now had to alter the responses to the questions she had previously given him.

"*Habibi*, I am learning more about autism, and I will share with you what I'm learning. But the most important thing to know is that I have to help Talal, and that means spending a lot of time with him and doing things for him."

"How can I help?" Kareem asked.

Caliana's heart melted. She reached over and squeezed Kareem into a tight hug.

"You are incredible, *habibi*. Thank you for offering, and I promise I will think of ways that you will be able to. But for now, just love him the way you have all along. I know Talal hasn't been responding to you, but keep trying. I'm pretty sure he knows that you're there even if it looks like he's ignoring you."

Caliana choked up and hugged Kareem again. She did not want Kareem to feel her frustrations and sense of helplessness, and she knew that he had also been feeling the loss of Talal.

The weeks flew by. Caliana watched for signs of progress, for anything that would indicate change. Talal seemed calmer, less agitated, and at times she caught him actually looking at her for brief seconds.

Halfway through the sixth week, Caliana called Talal, fully expecting him to ignore her, but he whipped his head around in response and looked at her expectantly. It was a simple, normal gesture, yet it almost toppled Caliana's world. She abruptly stopped moving and stared at him. She repeated his name and knelt down until she had her face leveled with his. Talal did not take his eyes off of her; he had tracked her movements and was still looking at her. He showed an awareness of her presence. Caliana's heart started pounding, and tears threatened to cloud her eyes. She impatiently wiped her eyes, and she held Talal an arm's length away from her.

"Hi, *habibi*, hi Talal."

Talal's beautiful large brown eyes lit up in happiness, and he smiled and said something unintelligible.

Caliana burst out crying and hugged her son. In between sobbing, she laughed and showered him with wet kisses. The more she saw Talal's confused expression, the harder she cried and laughed. She was seeing an expression—a normal, simple, and appropriate reaction! Caliana tried to calm her excitement so as not to scare Talal with her bizarre response. She squatted down in front of him, Indian style, and stared at him.

"Welcome back, *habibi*," she whispered.

* * *

In the following few weeks, Caliana started a daily journal that listed every action and reaction that she got from Talal. She knew that gluten was a protein similar in structure to casein, so she removed wheat from his diet. She planned on giving him at least another six weeks on a dairy- and gluten-free diet before she removed sugar, coloring, and most other additives. All she knew was that removing certain foods was allowing Talal to return from a disconnected world. In her heart, she believed that he was coming out of the autism.

Intellectually, she knew that she still had a journey of intensive support that she needed to provide Talal with. She resumed the intensive therapies and started hearing back more positive responses from all his therapists. She would continue to provide him with intensive remediation and would continue to investigate his condition and learn more about the available therapies.

Caliana reread the letter from her insurance agency and felt outraged. His health insurance policy, which had been active since Talal was a week old, was declining all the services, the treatments, because they deemed his condition to be preexisting. Caliana had taken Talal to a speech therapist and an occupational therapist *before* his official medical diagnosis of PDD. Because Caliana had treated his symptoms prior to an official diagnosis, the insurance companies had created a loophole through which they could refuse to pay for treatments related to PDD. She was staggered by the logic that this insurance system used to withhold payments.

For a few weeks, she tried to fight just about everyone at the insurance company but soon gave up when she realized that she was expending energy that was needed for her son's continued care. She also realized the futility of fighting the corruption and inefficiency of the insurance system. After much research, she discovered that at the age of two and a half, her son was simply uninsurable with any other health insurance provider. No other insurance company would take him on, as his diagnosis made him a liability. Caliana swallowed her rage at the shameful conduct of a world power that not only chose not to provide free national health care but also allowed for crooked monopolized privatizations. What irked Caliana was that she was forced to maintain Talal's current policy for no other reason than to keep his standard medial coverage, in case of an emergency. She had to ask her father to continue to bankroll Talal's therapies.

Through the hours spent in various waiting rooms, Caliana spoke endlessly to mothers from all over the US who complained about their children's treatments not being covered by their respective insurance companies. Caliana knew that she was luckier than most in that she was able to pay for the multiple therapies that were needed, whereas most parents, because of limited financial resources, had to choose one therapy at a time and often worried about which to choose. Caliana knew that her son was being rescued from autism because of the intensive interventions from the multiple therapies, and it was hard to determine which one specifically helped him the most. She was convinced that each therapist was helping with an essential part of the whole. Caliana felt extremely grateful and indebted to her father for his unconditional and complete financial support. His money, after all, was allowing her son to have the opportunity for a normal life.

CHAPTER 21

CALIANA used Sunday mornings to make her international calls. Since Talal's diagnosis, she had confided only in Samir. He was Kareem and Talal's uncle, and she knew that he loved them as though they were his children. She was comfortable sharing with him every development in Talal's life. Also, Samir insisted on being there for her.

From the day that Caliana had received Talal's diagnosis, Samir had called her every day and offered his loving support while sharing her concerns. He validated her efforts and encouraged her toward all alternative treatments. Caliana had initially faxed over all reports and materials pertaining to Talal's treatments and prognosis to Rami, but he had told her that he hated reading and that he just wanted Caliana to briefly summarize the information. She had always known that Rami was a selfish and self-absorbed person, but she had also assumed that because he so clearly loved Talal, he would naturally be concerned for his well-being. She had stopped discussing Talal's condition with Rami, and he rarely asked about it. Samir, on the other hand, took the time to absorb the new information and would thoroughly underline the reports with questions and comments and fax her back in his attempts at clarification. He wanted to understand and be actively involved. Caliana gratefully welcomed the supportive actions.

Caliana especially loved the fact that Samir could have easily begged off involvement, as he had an incredibly busy life. He had fallen in love with a wonderful woman, Nuha, and was in the middle of hectically planning for his upcoming wedding in April. Even though Caliana did not know Nuha too well, she already felt love for her because she had made Samir so happy. Caliana had seen Samir pass through a series of relationships with many women and had known all along that they were not right for him. She had always wanted to see Samir with a special woman, and from Samir's detailed descriptions of Nuha's personality, she knew that he had finally met his match. He was deeply in love, and Caliana was thrilled for him.

Caliana knew that she and Samir had always shared an incredible bond, but their shared anxiety over Talal drew them even closer. With both their hectic schedules, Samir taught her to schedule "phone dates" with him and forced her to better communicate on the phone. They got into the habit of going over each other's daily schedules to settle on the following phone date. Initially, Caliana had been conscious of the fact that she might be burdening him with her worries, but Samir had called her out on these feelings and forced her to have more uncensored, authentic moments wherein she admitted to her anxieties. They spoke of Talal mainly, but made sure they still continued to share the rest of their lives with each other.

Every phone call was a blessing for Caliana. In many ways, Samir offered her a reprieve from the constant turmoil of her fears. Even though most of their communication evoked in her the pain of Talal's condition, Samir managed to steer her also into a sense of aliveness and humor within her situation. He forced her to be present to other parts of the world by continuing to share his world with her. He made her laugh; no one had ever made Caliana burst with laughter like he could. In some ways, Samir was so wholeheartedly available to her that she grew to trust and rely on his support. Naturally, Caliana's trust induced even more of her honesty to surface, allowing her to experience a wonderful new level of intimacy.

Samir understood that she could not come to his wedding and clearly demonstrated his disappointment that his best friend would not attend. At the same time, he wholeheartedly supported her decision to commit to a particularity important treatment for Talal that conflicted with his marriage date. He made every effort to include her in sharing his joy and promised her that he would bring Nuha and stay with her and the boys after the honeymoon, and Caliana loved him for it.

Caliana found herself putting off and hesitating discussing Talal with Haya. She knew that she would pour out her heart eventually but preferred to do it in person. Haya sensed Caliana's distraught state and tried to question her. Caliana promised her that she would talk to her when she saw her during the following summer break, in four months. A part of Caliana's hesitation about confiding in Haya stemmed from the fact that Haya was experiencing her first pregnancy. Caliana wanted Haya to savor the process of carrying a child to life without burdening her with her depressed worries for Talal. She knew Haya well enough to know that Haya would be unable to stay detached and would be incapable of not sharing her pain.

Haya gave birth to her son, Laith, by Caesarean on April 24. Caliana called her every day during her five-day stay at the hospital. Haya was ecstatic over her son, gushing with maternal pride. Caliana teased her mercilessly because every other word out of Haya was "*Bejanen!*": he's heavenly; he's blowing my mind and my heart; he's so perfect. Caliana couldn't help but respond to Haya's elation, and she often chuckled at her friend's deep sighs of utter contentment. Haya admitted that she couldn't bear the thought of having her son out of her sight, even for a moment, and Caliana completely related to her.

Caliana knew that Haya would be a great mother. All along, Haya had perfected those instincts by offering a maternal-like love to everyone in her life. Caliana had always viewed Haya as an extraordinarily healthy person in that she was fearless in loving and loved extremely well. At times, Caliana had wanted to shake some rational sense into Haya for being too naive in her determination to see *only* the best in everyone. Haya had the frustrating ability of genuinely empathizing with every human fault and never seemed to get annoyed by the limitations of others.

The only time Caliana had heard Haya make a negative comment (if it could be called that) was after an incident with Rami a year earlier. Until then, Haya had been a staunch believer in Rami in spite of the countless evidence that Caliana had presented. Haya had always maintained that Rami was a fundamentally good person, even when he acted crazy.

Caliana smiled at remembering Haya's shocked face. Caliana had been visiting Jordan and had dropped off the boys to visit Rami's parents one day. She had sat in her in-laws' sitting room, waiting for Haya to pick her up. Rami had been ranting and raving as he paced the floor, making ridiculous accusations about absolutely nothing that could be remotely considered significant. Caliana was grinding her teeth in exasperation when she suddenly saw Haya stride through Rami's front door. Rami, consumed in his angry erratic citations, had failed to see Haya standing inside the doorway. Haya had quickly stepped back outside and waited a few moments before ringing the doorbell.

Rami had gone to answer the door, still in a heated verbal fury. As soon as he had swung the door open and saw Haya, he had started gushing cheerful and exaggerated loving welcomes. He was exuberantly friendly and gave Haya a hug.

Caliana had never seen Haya startled, or at a loss for words. Haya didn't even know how to begin altering the frozen shock from her face, and Caliana had to suppress her urge to giggle. The only surprise for Caliana was that Rami seemed completely oblivious to Haya's horrified face and stood there chatting as though Haya was engaging him back in a pleasant conversation. Caliana had rescued Haya by insisting that they needed to leave. She literally had to nudge Haya to move her out of her shock.

As soon as Haya entered the car, she exclaimed that it was not normal the way Rami totally switched his persona. She kept repeating that something was wrong with Rami. Caliana had finally had to point out that Haya sounded like a broken record.

Haya had ignored her and resumed repeating, "I can't believe it. There is something very wrong with him!"

Caliana could see that Haya was in shock and was struggling with making sense of what she had just experienced.

"I've been telling you he's crazy!" Caliana had insisted.

After ten minutes of Haya's utterances of "unbelievable," followed by Caliana's "I've been telling you!" Haya had sunk into a subdued silence.

When they reached Haya's house, Haya had calmly apologized for not having been able to *really* understand when Caliana used to tell her stories about Rami. She admitted that she had simply been unable to imagine the extent of certain words that Caliana had used in describing Rami. She had barely been able to imagine Rami's anger as she had only had a one-dimensional, jovial image of him; all she had seen of Rami was degrees of his wildly exuberant and charming personality. What bothered Haya was not so much having witnessed Rami's rage, as much as his instantaneous switch between such vastly opposing feelings, demeanors, and affects. It was like seeing two different people; psychotic ugliness morphed into charisma in the span of a heartbeat. Haya had needed to witness it, as she had been incapable of fathoming such a distortion.

Caliana had felt grateful for having Haya validate a sliver of her life with Rami. Until that moment, Caliana had been battling with her convictions of Rami's insanity, certain of her opinion yet constantly aware that no one else could see it. Her mother had been the only one to emphatically state that Rami was "crazy," but Caliana had dismissed her opinion because her mother didn't like anyone anyway, and her venom at Rami seemed like a convenient outlet for feelings she already had within her. But having Haya understand, even if it was but just a glimpse of the truth, was validation enough for Caliana.

After the incident, Caliana had also admitted to Haya that she had given up trying to convey her certainty of Rami's unhinged mind to Haya, partly because she had accepted that Haya was incapable of recognizing it. Haya had then made Caliana retell most of the incidents that she had experienced with Rami, intently listening in a new way. Caliana could see Haya's face transform as her new perception altered her understanding.

Since the incident, Caliana had been surprised and impressed by Haya's new awareness and the actions that she took pursuant to her discovery. Caliana knew that Haya had never set boundaries with anyone and always surrounded herself with a wonderful group of healthy girlfriends. Haya had always viewed the world as a peaceful and safe haven and lived with the strong presence of faith in God's grace, which she clearly saw reflected within everyone around her.

Caliana was grateful that in spite of Haya's innocence, Haya was able to operate out of her integrity, which allowed her to hold a tough shield against Rami's repeated attempts at a continued friendship. Rami had been in the habit of occasionally trying to have Haya intercede on his behalf to get Caliana back, and Haya had obliged him with long visits whereby she empathized with him. She had tried to be supportive of his difficulties. Since the incident, however, Haya was clear with Rami that she would never again discuss his divorce, and she avoided him like the plague.

CHAPTER 22

Saturday, May 1, 1993

CALIANA was driving back to McLean after having spent an unpleasant early lunch with a friend. She had been very subdued during the meal and felt guilty enough for her demeanor that she had shared that she was unable to shake off what had woken her a few minutes past two in the morning. She had briefly told her friend that she had woken up with a feeling that one of her three best friends, Haya, was dead. She couldn't remember if she had been dreaming of something that related to the thought, but it was the first time she had experienced waking with such a strong certainty. She had tried to dismiss the feeling and managed a few hours of fitful sleep. She resisted the urge to call Haya, even though she had known that with the time difference, it would be a few minutes after eight in the morning in Jordan. Haya would most likely be awake and tending to her son.

Caliana's cell phone rang, and Jennifer, her housekeeper, asked her when she was coming home. Caliana told her that she was on her way and would be there within minutes. She meant to ask Jennifer if she had a cold, as she sounded congested, but Jennifer abruptly hung up.

When Caliana entered her house, she found Jennifer clutching a Kleenex to her mouth. Jennifer's swollen eyes clearly indicated that she had been crying.

Caliana dropped her purse on the counter and rushed over to console the housekeeper. "What's wrong? What happened?" Caliana asked.

"You have to call Jordan; something happened to Haya .... Your friends have all been calling you, but call your father. He called many times ...."

Caliana stopped hearing. She reached for the house phone and dialed her parents' house in Jordan. Her mother answered and told her that Haya had died, apparently a few minutes past eight in the morning their time.

Caliana couldn't remember what she told her mother. She hung up and called Haya's parents. Haya had moved temporarily back to her parents' house, as was customary after giving birth to the first child.

A relative answered the phone and denied Caliana access to family members. She kept insisting that Haya was in the hospital, not in a good shape, and wasn't doing well. Caliana couldn't get any details and hung up in aggravation.

Caliana's mind refused to think. She surfaced from blankness only long enough to make flight arrangements to New York to catch the Royal Jordanian flight to Amman that would get her into Jordan the following afternoon. She heard herself giving instructions to Jennifer and rushed upstairs to pack.

She noted that the empty suitcase landed on her when she fell, and observed the fact that her knees had simply given way. From a distance, she noted that she had heard of people's legs giving way but had never experienced it herself. She also noted that as she had fallen, her heart had suddenly dropped, similar to a feeling she had once experienced during a flight when the plane had suddenly plunged into a much lower attitude.

Caliana saw herself running down the stairs with a huge suitcase.

At Washington's Dulles Airport, she broke down crying when the woman at the register asked her about her final destination. Suddenly, Jordan became Haya's death, and tears exploded out of her.

Caliana next noted that she was in JFK airport, asking an airport official about directions to the first class lounge.

Caliana stood frozen at the door of the lounge, as her eyes zoomed in on Haya's brother. Caliana had always teased Haya at how much she physically resembled her brother. Caliana absorbed every detail of his drawn face.

A young woman, who had been sitting next to Haya's brother, intercepted her and started talking to her. Caliana tried to clear her foggy mind and focus on trying to identify the stranger.

Luckily, the stranger was talkative and informed Caliana that her name was Samira and that she was married to Haya's brother, that they had been in the middle of a trip in the US when they had heard the news. She gently asked Caliana to leave her husband alone, as he had not said a word since he had heard of his sister's death.

Caliana glanced back at Haya's brother. He was lost in deep thoughts, tears running unchecked down his face.

Caliana sat a few tables away and was grateful for Samira's guidance. Caliana's mind flashed to a picture of Haya telling her that she really liked the woman who was marrying her brother. The image slipped away as abruptly as it had appeared, and Caliana's mind slipped back into a shocked silence.

During the long flight, Samira played nursemaid to Caliana and Haya's brother. She alternated her time by quietly sitting by her husband, often whispering consolations and giving him loving hugs, and then joining Caliana and talking to her. She forced Caliana out of her fog by insisting on discussing Haya and what had happened to her.

Caliana found out that Haya had had a blood clot as a result of the Cesarean. That clot must have traveled in her blood stream, picking up strength, until it slammed into her heart, causing an instant, massive heart attack. Haya had less than two seconds to begin crying out in pain before she toppled over on the couch, dead. Her sister, Lara, had tried to administer CPR until the ambulance arrived, but to no avail. Haya's parents, also, witnessed their twenty-nine-year-old daughter's life extinguished before their eyes.

Haya had been getting ready to take her son to his first week's appointment with the pediatric doctor. The night before, Haya had complained to her mother that her *sidri* was hurting her. Because in Arabic the word means both chest and breast, her mother had assumed that Haya was referring to her breast and that she was sore from breastfeeding. Haya's mother had placed a pillow behind Haya's back and had ministered to her sore nipples.

Samira admitted that she didn't like the cultural tradition of not informing people who were abroad of a death in a family, instead ushering them urgently to return under the pretext of serious illness. She didn't want to expose her husband to the shock of arriving at the airport in Amman and being subjected to the traditional reception, in which dozens of people would inform him of Haya's death and escort him home. She had spared her husband by telling him the truth and thus allowing him his time of privacy with his grief.

Stunned, Caliana's imagination spun with vivid reenactments of Haya's last moments. A singular thought had been formulating and gaining power until she realized that Haya had died from exactly what had almost killed Caliana after Kareem's birth, except that her own blood clot had manifested immediately and she had been rescued because of the opportune moment of having still been in the intensive care unit and connected to wires that had alerted the medical staff.

Caliana felt a huge wave of guilt drowning her in recriminations; she should have known better and cautioned Haya. She had been naïve to assume that her near-death experience from a blood clot was a rare, freak occurrence. She had also heard of numerous incidents of horrible postoperative care in Jordan that had led to unnecessary deaths, yet she had not been concerned for Haya's life and had certainly never thought to caution her against any complications. Immediately, Caliana's mind fed into the guilty scenario wherein she had missed the opportunity to tell Haya to take a blood thinner after her surgery. An aspirin could have saved Haya's life! Caliana felt rage mounting at the realization that her best friend had died because of medical oversight. She alternated between the thought of torturing Haya's doctor, and a feeling of anguish at her failure to save Haya.

Haya's brother and his wife were the first to exit the plane, followed closely by Caliana. Caliana felt the shock of suddenly seeing dozens of people waiting outside the airplane's door to receive Haya's brother. Caliana felt gratitude for Samira, for she understood the horrific impact of the well-intended reception.

Graciously, Samira offered Caliana a ride, but Caliana declined, and insisted that she would see Samira at Haya's parents' house.

Caliana stood looking at the luggage that was coming out on the carousel, waiting for a suitcase to jog her memory. She only knew that it was large.

Caliana stepped out of the terminal, expecting to get a cab. In a very surreal moment, she saw another good friend of hers, Tala, and her mother waiting for her.

Caliana knew that her mother had cared about Haya, but the gesture of coming out to the airport to receive Caliana was extremely uncharacteristic.

In the car, Caliana learned that Tala had called Caliana's mother earlier to let her know that she would be going to the airport, and had essentially embarrassed her mother into coming along. Caliana fluctuated between anger and a strange new gratitude toward her mother. She knew her mother could have easily gotten out of being shamed into anything, let alone making a trip to the airport to receive any of her daughters in their frequent travels. Caliana also knew that even though her mother was incapable of loving anyone, she had somehow been genuinely touched by Haya. Some of Caliana's gratitude was due to her mother's honoring of Haya, in that unimaginable gesture of decency.

Caliana found herself, all too soon, in front of Haya's house. Her heart started pounding at the understanding that the car-filled street indicated crowds. She had never attended a funeral and was only somewhat familiar with the customary Arab traditions. She knew that men and women were separated in the grieving process and that she was being taken to where the women would be congregated.

Caliana fearfully climbed the stairs and walked through the opened front door. In a daze, she saw hundreds of females, mostly seated. Someone guided her arm to the right and directed her toward a section of the formal sitting room.

Caliana saw Haya's mother and froze. Haya's mother was sitting in an armchair surrounded by many quietly seated women. She was staring at her lap, lost in muttering to herself. Caliana cautiously approached, knowing that Haya's mother was oblivious to everyone around her.

Someone gently tapped Haya's mother on the shoulder and told her that Caliana was there.

Haya's mother jerked in surprise. In disbelief, she stared at Caliana and kept repeating Caliana's name, questioning her presence. She jolted out of her chair, grabbed Caliana, and burst into fresh sobs, muffled by phrases of denial. Caliana swallowed her tears and held on as the world shattered around her, again.

Caliana was dimly aware of her disconnection, and of the dull ache that barely sustained her consciousness. She had been floating away from herself, and in bizarre, clipped moments she came to, bursting with the pain. Holding Haya's mother, Caliana heard herself muttering heartfelt consoling remarks and simultaneously floated away from the unbearable intimacy of the moment. It was over-whelming, and she was colliding with forcefully opposing feelings. The part of her that was emotionally absent was aware of her dis-connect and aware of the roomful of people who were intently focused on her and Haya's mother. She felt grateful when some women eventually pulled Haya's mother from her and helped her back into her designated chair.

Caliana stood frozen. Haya's mother refused to look away from her, even as she was being gently seated. Some women were trying to distract her away from Caliana, and in a stupor, Haya's mother momentarily looked away. At that moment, Caliana became aware of how inadequate she was, and self-loathing at her utter ineptness erupted within her.

Someone helped Caliana walk away. She might have walked away on her own; she couldn't tell. She floated between the parting crowds and made herself go upstairs to Haya's bedroom and the family room that connected the upstairs bedrooms, to where Haya had died. Caliana faintly heard her name called a few times as she navigated the crowded stairway.

She reached the top floor and found herself staring back at a blur of faces staring back at her, many somewhat familiar. She stood still, stuck, waiting for someone to tell her what to do. Her ears were pounding, and Caliana had no idea what she was feeling or thinking.

Haya's sister, Lara, materialized in front of her. "Haya hated black. Please don't wear it again," Lara stated emphatically.

Caliana's vision cleared. She slowly looked down at her clothes, surprised at what she was wearing. She had on a man's black shirt, jeans, and black cowboy boots. She slowly looked up at Lara's passive face. "That's all I wear. Black. I don't know what I packed. I don't plan to sit with these people."

Caliana had no idea what she was saying, or if she made sense, and she didn't care. She was surprised at the information that Haya hated black. It was an insignificant detail, yet Caliana had not known it about Haya.

Lara looked at her intently. "Only a few of her best friends and some family can enter Haya's room. Laith is there, and if you are going to cry around him, you have to leave."

Caliana wondered if Lara knew that she in fact was one of Haya's best friends, and if so, if she would be considered as one of the ones that could enter the room. She saw suppressed rage on Lara's face and knew that Lara was barely maintaining her ability to abide by the customs of Jordanian mourning traditions. Lara abruptly spun around, motioning for Caliana to follow her.

Caliana followed Lara into Haya's room. Someone was sitting next to the crib. Lara firmly told the woman to leave and to give Caliana time with Laith.

Caliana gently approached the crib and stood staring at Haya's son. Tears flooded her eyes, and she quickly turned away, gritting her teeth against every emotion. She knew that Lara, standing a few feet away, would easily carry out her promise and toss her out. Caliana saw the strength of purpose etched into every rigid line on Lara's face.

"I don't know how long I will be here in Amman, but I plan to spend every moment in this room, taking care of Laith." Caliana stared down Lara. "And I promise you, I will not cry."

Lara nodded and left the room. Caliana stood for a few moments, looking around at familiar objects in the bedroom. Emotions and memories were flooding her. She took a few jagged deep breaths, settled herself into the chair next to the crib, and stared at Haya's tiny, eight-day-old son.

Caliana had no idea how long she sat, but Lara returned to tell her that her mother was waiting for her to take her home.

Caliana told Lara that she would return in the morning. She asked when the funeral would be held.

Caliana felt like she had been slapped in the face when Lara told her that as per Islamic custom, Haya had already been buried that morning.

Lara also informed her that she would be going the following morning to the cemetery with Haya's husband, her brother, and Samira, and insisted that Caliana should join them. Caliana responded by offering to have her father's driver take them, and made arrangements to pick them up in the morning.

Caliana couldn't remember the brief conversation that she had with her parents when she got to their house, but she knew that one had occurred.

She asked for Haya's favorite coffee, Turkish coffee, and took it upstairs to her small sitting room, where she had usually spent time with Haya.

Caliana sat on the couch, Indian-style, and stared ahead of her, unseeing. Images overflowed in her mind, yet she was incapable of transforming any of them into a thought.

Sudden sharp pain slashed across her face, and Caliana's heart lurched in reactive fear. Her temples throbbed in rhythmic sharp bursts. She clutched the sides of her head and pressed back at the magnified throbs. She felt as though her head might explode. In terror, the image of the head explosion in the movie *Scanners* flashed before her squinted eyes. Her whole face was pounding, as though massive internal energy was combusting inside her head.

Time stood still as she battled the pain with fingers racing to massage away the most horrifying pounding pressures. Tears of relief rolled down her face with each release. She tried to cling to images of her sons to soothe her turmoil, her racing heart. She stayed at it, massaging every throb, until her head rested heavily on the arm of the couch.

She slowly opened her eyes and glanced at her wristwatch, and in shock realized that it was after four o'clock in the morning.

Caliana used her hands to assist her in lifting her head, ever so slowly. Afraid to disturb the heavy dullness that had infused her head, she made her way into the bathroom. Mindlessly, she took a shower.

She opened her suitcase and stared in incomprehension at the empty interior.

At eight o'clock, she sat next to her father's driver, clutching a bottle of water. They picked up Haya's family and headed to the cemetery.

Caliana was grateful for the silence in the car. She was exhausted and could not summon the energy to interact with anyone. She tried to focus on the fact that she was going through downtown Amman, into an area she rarely ever ventured. She noted that it had grown from the last time she had been there as a child.

Ironically, the driver chose that particular moment to point to the Basha's office and to talk about how at the time, her grandfather's office had been considered the center of downtown Amman but now represented only the periphery of the area. He pointed to the expanded sections that had grown commercially and residentially in the past fifteen years. She remembered her father telling her as a child that she didn't know Jordan, as she had only been exposed to a small segment of upper-class society that did not even begin to represent the country. Caliana finally understood. The further they traveled into the downtown area, the more obvious the vast difference in class and cultural division became. It was like being in another country. The scenery, even though it had its own character, was typical of a poor, crowded third-world city with all its noises and smells.

After a while, the driver started going up a dusty and barren rocky mountain, and Caliana jerked her head upward. The driver told her that they had just entered the cemetery, and Caliana's heart lurched in disbelief. Panicked, she looked ahead and realized that the disgusting pile of rubble and barren wilderness was a cemetery. Caliana had never been to a cemetery, but she had walked by and seen countless gorgeous Western cemeteries. She was jolted from the images of lush and beautifully kept grounds to the stark scene before her.

The driver pulled up next to a shanty—a small stone structure suspended from a roof made of a few tin sheets. The peasant squatting inside wore a traditional robe, and his face was masked by a headscarf to ward off the dust. He came out with something that resembled an old notebook. When he was given Haya's name, he checked his notebook and started walking next to the car, pointing to the rows of numbers on the ground.

Caliana's anger had been mounting with the dusty climb in the car. She couldn't believe that she was sitting in a car, driving at a snail's pace, following a peasant who was reading the markings on the ground looking for Haya's grave. Caliana surveyed the rocky mountaintop and noted that nothing could live there besides the few random scrawny olive branches.

Caliana got out of the car and followed the others to Haya's marking. The graves were so close to one another that they were almost touching—each was an anonymous rectangle of stone or cement covered by dust. A few had small tombstones or markings, with a number and name. Until she saw the first tombstone, she wasn't sure if she had been walking on or between the graves.

Caliana was aware of the nonverbal agreement on who should stand next to Haya's marked grave. At some point, she stood in front of Haya's grave, alone.

Her mind raged in denial. She could not accept that Haya, with her beautiful soul, had had her body placed in such a desolate and undignified resting place. Caliana suddenly felt overwhelmed by everything around her being ugly and cruel. To counter her growing anxiety, she could only fixate on how to change this picture, how to beautify the crude finality of Haya's death.

She heard Lara telling the peasant that she had ordered a headstone and was planning to put flowers around it.

"Yes, please, Lara. This is horrible!" Caliana blurted.

The ride back to Haya's house was bizarre. They all discussed the vegetation, and what could possibly survive the heat and the barren earth. Lara insisted that she would be there all the time with fresh flowers and that she would defy nature as long as she lived. Caliana had to believe that Lara, who was an environmental engineer, would accomplish this seemingly impossible mission.

Caliana knew that Lara would deal with her immense pain in private, and she related to Lara's ability to function and go through the motions of living as best as she could. She saw Lara's anger sustaining her, the only part of the grief that she could access. Lara had just lost the most important person in her world, and Caliana could not imagine how she was able to stand it.

The next few days sped by. She spent every moment that she could in caring for Laith, focused on loving him. In between, she shared intimacy with Haya's female family members and close friends.

Lara shared with Caliana that she was trying to take comfort in the fact that Haya had done the *Haj* before she died. Caliana had known that the Islamic faith had been a vibrant part of Haya's life. Lara read Caliana passages from the Koran that explained the significance of what the *Haj* had meant to Haya. Caliana appreciated that Lara was able to explain the value and relevance of Haya's experience to her, which was a great comfort. Lara explained that Haya, and every devout Muslim, would want to complete the *Haj* process at least once in a lifetime. Haya had gone the previous summer and had returned even more inspired and at peace. Her devotion at the *Haj*, said Lara, guaranteed Haya's entrance to the kingdom of heaven.

Samira copied a video of Haya's last week on earth. She told Caliana that it had been mainly taken while Haya was still in the hospital after she had given birth. Caliana was touched by the loving gesture and tucked the bubble-wrapped tape into her purse, knowing that someday she would be able to watch it.

Five days later, Caliana got on a plane, knowing that a part of her heart was forever gone. In the past few days, she had learned much more about Haya, and her admiration for her incredible best friend had soared even higher. Even though Caliana was convinced that Haya had known how much Caliana had loved her, she regretted never having expressed to her how valuable and essential Haya had been to her. Caliana ached with loss and knew that in a strange, bizarre way, she had inherited the beginning of Haya's spiritual awareness; she had felt the presence of God every time she held Laith.

CHAPTER 23

CALIANA returned home determined to somehow survive the raw pain that infused her heart. She had never imagined such sorrow, such relentless pain. At times, she struggled to fight back the mounting panic that threatened to suffocate her. She felt petrified at how little control she had in tolerating the grief that coursed through her on a cellular level. Even if she wanted to, she had no idea how to begin to subdue the pain that took over her body. She felt bruised on the inside, as though someone had violently shaken all her internal organs and left every nerve, tissue, and muscle in various stages of sore recovery. Surprising tears spewed out of her in random bursts and jarred her sense of equilibrium. Nothing seemed real, except the constancy of the pain.

The abrupt finality of love was a tragedy she had not prepared for.

Days dragged endlessly in the wake of her grief. Caliana forced herself out of bed every morning. Dazed, she was barely conscious as her soul endured waves of fragile grieving. She felt her heart swell with the fullness of her love, as though only in pain could her heart have the courage to expand to its fullest capacity. All the love that she had been safely storing for Haya, only partially doled-out, suddenly erupted and shattered the shield Caliana had built to protect her heart. Time took on a heightened intensity as her memories stuck on fragmented reenactments of long-buried memories of Haya. Vivid images exploded from her heart, and her aggravated mind, unused to emotions usurping its command, ripped apart her resurrections.

Helplessly, she observed her mind take on a slippery life of its own as it pulled at every intimate, loving memory and tried to crush it, killing off her reliance on its beauty.

She noted that her insomnia took on an added layer; she now fluctuated either between tossing and jerking for a few restless nights or succumbing to heavy lethargic sleeping, neither of which relieved her exhausted depression. All she wanted to do was escape into the unconsciousness of a very long, deep, and dreamless sleep. She imagined this as the relief that followed death.

Caliana found a few lucid moments in which she thanked God for giving her the energy to continue on, despite her depression. For the first time, Caliana considered giving a name to the robotic part of herself that had taken over during tragedies and the events of the past weeks. This part of her was a gatekeeper, a seasoned defender who protected her and allowed her to disconnect, and she trusted it to take care of her as she survived on autopilot.

It finally dawned on Caliana that her guard was also her strongest asset. In fact, Caliana existed only because of the gatekeeper's ability to take on the awesome responsibility of problem solving, even when she was broken into pieces.

Her children were the only reason to fight her depression and ground herself more fully into the murky and senseless reality of a world that now held very little interest. As tempting as it was for her to dwell in her pain, her integrity would never allow her to shirk her commitment. She was the sole executor of her sons' world, and she could not ignore her responsibilities. Her life had to continue. Caliana realized that having chosen to be a good and responsible parent meant that she could no longer afford to self-destruct. She had to keep her heart open to her sons, and she had to exist more fully in reality— for their sakes.

Caliana knew that Haya's death had started to unravel the old hollow ache of her loneliness. She felt a gnawing need to relieve herself, to unburden the suppressed sorrow aching to spill out of her. She began to understand how the fragmentation of her segregated life had kept her isolated from everyone around her.

* * *

One day, Lydia, Caliana's closest friend in America, bluntly confronted her with the fact that she had never heard Caliana mention Haya. Lydia had known Caliana very well for a number of years and had assumed that she was Caliana's only best friend. In a tone of affronted betrayal, she reported to Caliana how shocked she had been to be told by the tearful housekeeper that Caliana was in Jordan "to bury her best friend."

Initially, Caliana was taken aback, and slightly puzzled, by the cold aggression in Lydia's voice. Almost immediately, however, the confrontation jarred her and forced her to examine how she managed her relationships with her closest friends, all in an effort to guarantee her continued solitude.

Caliana had always known and accepted that she had a distinct intimacy level within each friendship and that each level brought out a measured response from her. Because of differing trust levels, she revealed certain parts of herself to Rhea, certain parts to Haya, and so on. She had learned to safely practice heartfelt trust in each of these intimate relationships, but she could only access this intimacy when she was alone with her friends, one-on-one.

Years before, Caliana had tried meeting with Haya and Rhea simultaneously but had found that she was too aware of the shallow way that the two of them interacted, and how it had crippled her own comfort level. She had found herself thrust into superficial conversation with two of the people she loved most as though they were mere acquaintances. She had hated being forced to revert back to a neutral emotional vacancy when engaging with her loved ones. Selfishly, Caliana had been relieved that Haya and Rhea were mutually disinterested in pursuing a relationship with each other.

At the time, she had justified to herself her method of keeping her closest relationships divided. She would protect the privacy and intimacy of each relationship by not revealing details to her respective friends.

Caliana now questioned the honor behind this justification. She realized that no one really knew anything about the strong and loving framework that guided her relationship with Haya. It suddenly saddened Caliana that she had deprived Rhea from the privilege of loving Haya. Caliana was also experiencing a new sense of shame, for in not having discussed Haya with her other friends, she had unintentionally undermined Haya and somehow dishonored Haya's importance to her own life. She had devalued one of the most precious people she had ever loved, and she had not even known she was doing it.

Caliana found herself needing to purge, to unload her feelings about Haya onto someone, and to amend the shame of having devalued Haya. She found herself uncomfortably stumbling upon areas of herself that seemed inaccessible to her. Her ability to express these feelings was constrained by her inability at intimacy; she had guarded herself too well and felt confronted by her limitations: she did not know how to seek comfort.

Caliana's mind started spinning as she clinically reevaluated how she loved the people whom she loved. She wanted to detach from them all; she figured that it was impossible to stop loving the ones she already loved but that she could limit her attachment and reliance.

Caliana snapped out of this train of though, and thus from her sadness. "*Khalas!*" she admonished herself.

Her sons' lives continued, and she had many responsibilities. Caliana inhaled deeply and her body shuddered in readiness. She reminded herself that she chose to be a committed mother. She needed to focus on making sure that her every decision continued to be imbedded with her resolve to serve her sons, and serve them well. She had to continue with the best mothering that she could imagine, and she had to be at her healthiest to imagine better for them. For the past few months, she had been shocked into a disoriented grief, but she could no longer indulge her pain, no matter how tempting it was for her to disappear back into it. She loved her sons more than her attachment to her numbing depression. She had to function. She had to push down the pain that pulsed and beckoned at her with familiar tender beats.

CHAPTER 24

ONE DAY, Caliana picked up Kareem from school and was puzzled by his silence. He resisted her efforts to engage him. Caliana turned on the radio and was engrossed in the music when Kareem blurted, "What's sex?"

Caliana whipped her head around, certain that she must have misheard him yet knowing from the seriously intent look on his face that Kareem knew that he was asking an important question. He calmly awaited an answer.

Caliana inwardly cursed. She had prepared and thought out her answer but had not expected the question to come so soon. He was seven, for God's sake! Caliana reminded herself that age had never really factored into her honesty in responding to him. So far, she had followed the simple philosophy that if her gifted son was ready to ask the question, he was ready for the answer.

"Well ... it's a physical act, *habibi*, like touching, and kissing, that happens between two people. Sex can be either between a man and a man, a woman and a woman, or a man and a woman."

Caliana paused, knowing that Kareem would be busy adding this fragment of information to his data bank. She quickly glanced back at him and found him staring ahead. For a moment, she wondered if she had made a mistake in telling him her unedited version, but she couldn't for the life of her think of the childish version. She knew there were some birds or bees involved in that one ...

"Well. How come Ms. Lenox lowered her voice, and kind of whispered it to Mrs. Bell? She acted like she didn't want me to hear it. Like, it was bad, or wrong, or something?"

Kareem started picking at his full lower lip, and Caliana knew that it was a sign of focused reflection.

"Also, there are many people who kiss and touch. So why is it ... like a secret?" Kareem tilted his head and intently focused on her. "What's the big deal?"

Caliana knew that he would continue to patiently ask questions until he satisfied every illogical or incomplete thought, until he appeased his curiosity.

Caliana tried to hold back a smile, at the same time racing ahead with the enormity of the doors that she was about to open. She had already decided to unclutter her sons' minds from the limitations caused by prejudice and ignorance. She figured that even if he only understood a small part of her answers, that would be good enough. She could always reiterate and expand as he got older.

"Kareem, this is a tough topic, but I'll try to explain it some more. Basically, when the two adults are having sex, they are naked, and there is a lot of touching and kissing—all over each others' bodies. So you see, it is not something that usually happens in public. It is a very private act that gives people pleasure—it makes them feel good. Mostly, people have sex because they want to express their feelings for each other."

"But, why was she whispering? Why are children not supposed to know about sex?"

"Actually, I don't know when children should be told about sex. I think in America they teach it at school, *habibi*, but I don't know in which grade. The truth is that I didn't expect you to ask me now, at your age."

"Mom, why don't other people talk to me like you do?"

"I'm not sure. It seems to me that most people don't know how to talk to kids. Even when I was a child, I remember thinking that most adults were clueless!" *Clueless is a ridiculous understatement*, she thought.

"I try to talk to people, but only you and uncle Samir really talk to me. Most adults don't talk to me ... they don't even try. It makes me want to stop trying." Kareem's intonation never wavered, yet Caliana was used to Kareem's emotional subtleties. Her heart tightened with empathy for him.

"*Habibi*, I think when it comes to you, that sometimes people get confused because when they hear you speak they are surprised by your intelligence and maturity. They are expecting short and kind of rehearsed answers—typical and predictable answers. You do not speak to them in the way they are expecting from a child, and it disorients them. But *habibi*, don't stop talking; there are many people that will want to hear you and are fascinated by you and think you are amazing. Look at how beautifully you and your uncle communicate!"

"He's different. He's more like me."

Even though Kareem didn't say it, she knew that he must be thinking of Rami. Watching Rami and Kareem struggle to have even a small conversation was painful. Rami had always been intimidated by Kareem's intelligence and soulful maturity. With Talal, Rami was able to baby talk and play silly, which made it easier for him to express his fatherly love. Caliana had often questioned the source of Rami's immediate ability to be more expressive in loving Talal—she often suspected that it stemmed from his guilty initial response to wanting to have Talal aborted. Irrespective of Rami's inability to express his love toward Kareem, Caliana had often admonished him and had offered him specific topics that he could use to converse with Kareem, yet Rami never bothered to attempt any.

"There will be special people that will get you and love you, *habibi*. Remember, you also have a choice in choosing the people that you want in your life."

Caliana mentally noted that she would try another attempt at getting Rami to make more effort with Kareem.

A few days later, Kareem informed Caliana that he had looked up having sex and had learned that sex is a physical act that happens between a man and a woman and could result in a pregnancy. He emphasized that most of the definitions centered on the reproductive organs and the relationship between men and women only.

"Kareem, it is true that babies are born to a woman, as a result of sperm from a man. But sex is still a physical act between any two people. A man and a woman having sex can result in a baby, but two women having sex, or two men having sex, cannot result in a baby."

"Why didn't you tell me about the baby part?"

Caliana hesitated. She could see the hurt in her son, his uncertainty in this first doubtful moment with her.

"I thought it might be too much information and it could be confusing to what I was trying to have you focus on. Sorry, *habibi*, I made a mistake." Caliana took a deep breath and decided to just speak with less self-censorship. "The truth is that we live in a world that judges sex in a way that I didn't want you to judge it. Men having sex with men, and women having sex with women is called gay sex. Too many people in the world judge gay sex in a negative way, usually as wrong—and one of the reasons, or I should say excuses, that they use to judge it as bad or wrong is because it does not result in a baby."

"So the not-gay sex is done only to have babies?"

Caliana wanted to hug him. In some ways, he made her point for her. "Exactly. I mean, no …. People mainly have sex because it feels good to them. There are some things you can do so that you don't have a baby each time you have sex. Of course, there are some people who have sex for the purpose of having a baby, but most people have sex because they enjoy it—it feels good."

"So why do some people think that gay sex is wrong?"

"It's not wrong, but some people believe that only a man and woman should have sex, and that kind of sex is called straight sex."

"Who told them that? Who told people that gay sex is wrong?"

Caliana definitely did not want to get into the theological and sociopolitical agendas, but at the same time, she wanted Kareem to have a chance to foster an open-minded belief system.

"Kareem, let's just agree that ignorance makes people scared, and when they don't know or understand something, they get scared and try to destroy it, or limit it, or judge it. Many people don't even really know why they think the way they think—they've stopped asking themselves important questions. Anyway, I did not want to tell you that sex is only straight sex and can result in a baby, then wait a few years, and maybe when you're nine or ten, add something like 'Oh, by the way, sex is also between a man and a man, and between a woman and a woman, and that that kind of sex is called gay.'"

Caliana waited until Kareem indicated that he was ready to listen some more. "If I had done it that way, I would be strongly implying that only straight sex is the 'correct' or 'normal' one to have. If I omit gay sex in my introduction to sex, then I am indirectly telling you that gay sex is wrong or bad. Do you see that? I could not introduce it to you that way. I would be giving you the result of someone else's judgment, and not an opportunity for you to make up your own mind. Do you see my point?"

"I know. I'm glad you told me your way." Kareem pondered for a few moments. "But aren't you also giving me your judgment when you tell me that gay sex is not wrong?"

Caliana burst out laughing. "God, you are brilliant! Yes, *habibi*, I am." Caliana tried to gather her thoughts. "You know, I've really thought about how to introduce information and how to give it to you with the least amount of influence from me, but it's impossible to be completely unbiased. Also, I have seen how difficult it is for people to think differently from how they were taught as children. For many people, once they lock their minds onto an idea or a thought, they rarely question it, and it affects how they keep building on that first bit of information. I've come across many people who are limited in that they were not taught to think for themselves. I figured that if I *had* to actually give you the result of any judgment, then I would have to offer you more than my opinion, yet if I absolutely had to choose just *one* opinion, then I would trust my mind and my open-minded assessments and give you only my judgment."

"I get it. You didn't want me to think gay sex is wrong because when I grow up I might continue to think it is wrong because I did not think to question this judgment." Kareem was too engrossed in his thoughts to even look at her. "And because most people believe it is wrong, no one would think to give me another opinion."

"Exactly!"

Kareem had dozens of questions on fertility and hundreds of fascinated questions on how or why the majority of the world had a certain and particular unfavorable belief system regarding a segment of its society. At seven, he found the prejudiced limitations of the popular beliefs unreasonable and took the "gay side" as he played devil's advocate to Caliana's points.

Caliana had been amazed at the ease and comfort of her debating style with Kareem. She was calm and objective when she presented dreaded conservative views. In the past, whenever Caliana had argued her liberal views with people, she had always had to work hard on fighting down her passionate anger and almost always ended up blurting out her uncensored outrage.

Caliana loved experiencing Kareem in the process of thinking. She loved to witness his unbiased mind as it considered every aspect of any given perspective or idea. She listened to his analysis and how he broke down all arguments in search of the most logical and fairest to humanity. Somehow, his young soul charged him with the job of being a compassionate, moral judge as he navigated his place in the world. From the moment Kareem spoke, he expressed a deep desire to actively take charge of his growth by measuring it to his highest ideal of humanity.

Caliana could identify with Kareem, in that like him, she enjoyed concentrated thought. She told him that she would arrange for him to talk to one of her closest gay friends. Kareem was delighted. He knew and really liked this friend and felt happy that he could further interrogate him. Caliana made a second mental note to prepare her friend, who was eager to experience an in-depth gay conversation with Kareem—he had had the foresight to predict the possibility of healing some of his own childhood shame through a new educational experience.

CHAPTER 25

1997–1998

CALIANA felt centered. Kareem and Talal demanded her presence and brought out a particular aliveness in her. When she was with them, she often managed to push the rest of her life into perspective, into a less significant corner, and simply focus on being fully present. Her ability to prioritize her sons saved her; all she knew was that she was coming alive and was feeling deeper levels of love, in wondrous layers, for her sons.

A cuddle from Talal topped her list of profound moments. Even though Talal had made magnificent recoveries and Caliana had actually exhaled her last worried breath over him, she craved a hug from Talal. As a baby, he had loved nothing more than snuggling. One of the many offending side effects of the neurological injuries that afflicted Talal, however, was his aversion to being touched. Whoever tried to hug Talal would instantly get Talal's back—Talal would rotate in such a way that he would only briefly tolerate someone's contact with his back. People who were unfamiliar with Talal got Caliana's proud smile and a simple, "It's his unique way of hugging!"

Caliana knew that few truly understood how special Talal was, because no one really appreciated how hard he worked. He had never *once* complained or resisted any of his numerous therapies or medical examinations. Caliana believed that Talal understood, on a visceral level, that he needed them and was healthy enough to maximize his opportunities in therapies.

A week after Talal's seventh birthday, Caliana stopped the sensory integration therapy. She agreed with the therapist that Talal had progressed sufficiently and did not need the therapies any more. The only remaining area of "delay" was that he continued to be repelled by being hugged. At times, Caliana had been unable to resist her loving emotions and had selfishly hugged Talal against his will in quick squeezes of emotional outbursts. She felt gratified that Talal was able to tolerate her for a few seconds and delayed pushing her off. She was struggling with resigning herself with the fact that her baby could not be hugged.

Around Christmastime, Caliana started noticing that Talal had begun snuggling with her a little more, still leaning his back on her chest, but staying on her lap for longer periods. A few times, he would tilt sideways and lean his shoulder and whole side facing her. Caliana would hold her breath, scared to break the magical moments, and murmur positive endearments to him. Once, Talal had fallen asleep on her and Caliana had gently rotated him so she could carry him to bed. Talal had had his arms around her neck, and as she was climbing the stairs, he had stirred, looked at her, smiled, and squeezed her in a tight embrace. Caliana had almost fallen.

Since then, Caliana has been receiving at least one good hug a day, and she was too grateful to really question the magical transition.

At the age of six, Talal's diagnosis was officially changed to that of a severely learning disabled child. In September, Caliana and Talal started a new chapter together. Talal was finally accepted into the Lab School of Washington, the best school in the world for kids with severe learning disabilities. Caliana had tried to get Talal in the prior year and had been shocked at the ratio of applicants waiting compared to available space. To improve Talal's chances, she had enrolled him the previous summer into the Lab School's camp and made it a point to investigate the school and its creator, Sally Smith. The more she read of Sally Smith's books and toured the school, the more Caliana understood that Talal just *had* to be there—it not only was a perfect fit but had the most ingenious method of teaching that she had ever encountered. Caliana had never wanted anything as badly as to place Talal there. When she heard through the grapevine that connections helped, Caliana shamelessly pounced on the opportunity and, through her father-in-law, asked King Hussein and Queen Nour of Jordan to write a letter of recommendation on Talal's behalf. Gratefully, each of them had written a wonderful letter.

Knowing that she had been the only responsible person guiding Talal's recovery, Caliana was not willing to simply rely on the top school in the world to educate her son! She wanted to understand how to teach learning-disabled people herself. She signed up at American University to do her masters degree in Special Education for Learning Disabilities. The program was run by Sally Smith, who also taught many of its classes. Almost all the classes were taught at the Lab School, and all the students had to intern at the Lab School during school hours.

If Caliana had been impressed before she joined the program, she was in awe of the school's brilliance and creativity, which fused multisensory methodologies with the most progressive and varied teaching styles. Caliana delved into the program and at every opportunity let Sally Smith know how grateful she was that the woman had created such a school.

Caliana thought that it was ironic that both her sons were in special education—albeit in opposite spectrums. She learned that the underlying principles of special education had a universal appeal as the most effective teaching strategies. Unfortunately, the infeasibility of the cost involved would obstruct mainstreaming such methods.

* * *

Caliana thrived socially. With the weight of fear removed, she started relaxing and socializing with the Lab School staff and fellow students in her program. She loved interning at a school that was brimming with creative juices. The work was very tough: sink or swim. The masters students were suddenly coteaching in a classroom filled with children with various and multiple disabilities. Caliana had to know each child's IEP, or individualized education program, and teach accordingly. She was not only studying various methods and techniques but also applying them as she learned. It was incredible hands-on experience and training.

Caliana thought back to her very first class. The masters students had been told to meet in a large classroom at American University to meet Sally Smith, who would be teaching the course Learning Disabilities 1. Caliana had sat at her individual desk and surveyed the twenty or so other students. It was an interesting mix of women of all ages. Suddenly, Sally Smith had entered the classroom—with her eccentric and multicolored combinations and patterns, heavily trailing her signature Opium perfume—and stood on the elevated step of the podium in front of them.

"Open your notebooks," she had commanded. "You are about to take a test."

She had waited until the shuffle of panicked papers stilled.

"I will be testing you on vocabulary terms. I will only say each word and its definition *once*. Make sure you write it down, because it will be a part of your test!"

She began stating difficult scientific words. Caliana was completely absorbed in trying to figure out the third word when suddenly the classroom door opened and a barrage of people stormed in, bringing a confused assemblage of loud sounds. Someone stood at the door and randomly flicked the light switch on and off. A few girls walked around the students, carrying small handheld radios, each on a different loud station. A few other girls aggressively tried to engage the students in some form of conversation. Meanwhile, Sally Smith stood there and calmly continued with her words and their definitions.

Even though Caliana had known that this was an obvious, orchestrated gimmick, she had begun to feel the agonizing discomfort of a panic attack mounting. Her heart had raced, cold sweat had seeped through her pores, and a nauseating sense of disorientation had threatened to engulf her. She had been horrified that she would lose control and frantically bolt out of the room. The chaotic noises combined with the constant flickering lights kept on going, endlessly—far beyond everyone's comfort level. Caliana saw the girl in the desk in front of her cover her ears with both hands and drop her head between her legs.

Suddenly, at some prearranged signal, everything had stopped.

For the next few moments, no one had spoken. The electrified silence was a badly needed reprieve, and it had seemed to Caliana that everyone was recovering from their responses to the jarring experience. Caliana had tried to conceal the fact that she was loudly gulping air by quickly pretending that she had just choked on something. The stressed energy in the room was palpable.

"Welcome to the world of the learning disabled!" Sally Smith had boomed.

To Caliana, it had felt like the room exploded with collective relief and admiration. Some clapped. Caliana said, "Wow," a few times. Everyone was excitedly trying to speak, needing to share their experience. Sally had spent the remaining two hours allowing them to share their responses, to talk about all aspects of learning disabilities. Caliana had been surprised at how many of the women were drawn to the field because of their own struggles with some aspects within the learning-disabled umbrella. Caliana had admitted that she had only recently been diagnosed with ADHD combination type, and had finally understood so much about her past behaviors. She had also been able to share some of the methods and alternative treatments that had helped Talal.

Caliana had left that first session totally energized with empathy and suddenly inspired to help everyone in the world who was learning disabled. She had also known that she had been privileged to be amongst some dedicated women who seemed fascinating. Instinctively, she had known that she would form some amazing friendships.

* * *

Everything was incredible in Caliana's world, except for the constant erratic and unstable behavior of her ex-husband. Caliana could not imagine what drugs Rami was taking that could possibly justify his extreme and bizarre behaviors. She wanted nothing more than to completely cut him off from her world and he challenged her attempts at setting boundaries. He called Caliana an average of fifteen times a day. She would let the answering machine get his erratic, energetic ravings. Everything from religion to mediocre—and incorrectly paraphrased—philosophy spewed out of his mouth.

She tried to prevent him from talking to the boys, but he called so often that she was incapable of blocking his access. He would praise and glorify Kareem, who was only eleven, and encourage him to be "the man of the family." He told both boys that he was remarrying Caliana and that they would have many other siblings, even going so far as to name those imaginary siblings. Naturally, it confused and excited Talal, who believed him. Caliana had to counter many peculiar conversations that Rami had with the boys.

Thank God Samir was her daily dose of sanity offsetting Rami. Caliana felt so bad for Samir. He and Nuha had just had twins. Instead of Samir being engrossed in the happy occasion that he and Nuha had waited five years for, he was stressed and constantly worried about his brother's crazy behaviors. Samir was running himself ragged trying to do damage-control for some unbelievable irrational acts by Rami.

A few days after birthing the twins, Nuha had been rushed straight into surgery. Samir, worried sick for his wife's health, had anxiously paced the emergency corridor outside the room where Nuha was recovering from a near-death experience due to internal bleeding from the Cesarean.

Rami, operating from a distorted lens on reality, had come to the hospital and loudly proclaimed that all the doctors were idiots and that he was the son of the most famous lawyer in Jordan and would sue everyone in the hospital and personally close the hospital down!

Samir had snapped at Rami a few times to shut him up, but Rami had been determined to decree to one and all the magnitude of his power and might. He would not stop, until he pushed past Samir's calm demeanor and into an explosive fight that resulted in Samir physically lifting Rami off his feet and screaming into his face. It had taken a few of Samir's friends to physically remove Rami, still ranting and raving, from the hospital.

CHAPTER 26

Wednesday, April 8, 1998

CALIANA was in the middle of a facial when her cell phone began ringing. She glanced at it, for no other reason than to rule out any possible emergency calls from her sons' schools. She recognized the number of her family home in London on the caller ID. Caliana knew that it would be her father, and she debated ignoring him, for she had already had the perfunctory sixty-second "checking in" phone call with him first thing that morning. It was a duty that they followed religiously.

Instinct, and annoyance, made her answer.

"Where are you?" Her father's strangely strained and unusually quiet voice vibrated through her. Caliana felt her heart thud in readiness.

"Having a facial," Caliana automatically responded even as her heart fearfully registered that her father had never before asked after her whereabouts.

"Something bad happened .... I'm not sure if *Ammo* Habib was the only one ... Samir might have been with him."

Her father paused, and Caliana's heart stopped. There was no mistaking who he was talking about.

"It's almost certain that *Ammo* Habib was killed .... Samir might have been with him."

Caliana found herself in her car, driving home.

Her absolute focus was devoted to a terrorized alarm screaming in her head: Please, God, let it be *Ammo* Habib. Not Samir. Not

Samir. Please let it be *Ammo* Habib. Not Samir! God, not Samir ....
The endless prayer propelled her home, alternating from furious
affront to graceful pleading. The relentless prayers were her only way
of holding off the suffocating despair.

She stormed into her house, blinded by the intense haze of her
disorientation.

She had to get to a phone. She had to know.

She called Rami in Jordan.

A long-drawn-out inebriated "Hey!" froze her. She knew every
nuance of Rami's affects, and this one clearly told her that he was
thrilled to hear from her. He sounded in a great mood, and Caliana
was momentarily baffled.

"Did you *hear* what happened to my father and brother?"

His titillating tone of voice alone confirmed her inconceivable
fears. He sounded gleeful, almost feminine, in that he spoke as though
he were sharing shocking gossip.

Caliana shivered. She gripped the receiver to her ear, wanting to
hear his every breath, his confession. She felt the rage fully consume
her and clear her head. She deliberately held back any response; she
wanted to rattle him with her stillness. She needed his full confession.
She challenged him with her seething silence.

"They were killed. Someone is out to destroy us. They shot them
in the head. They want to wipe my bloodline ... " Rami continued,
animated in retelling his drama.

"I know you killed them." That her words came out in a calm
certainty only electrified the instant silence.

A nervous laugh emitted from him. "Ohhh, come on, don't be
stupid!"

He forcefully laughed some more, as though she had made a silly
joke, then he said seriously, "Now, listen to me. You have to protect
the boys. Where are they? Are they in school? Go right now and pick
them up. Don't let anyone touch them or come near them. They are
in danger. Someone is trying to kill them. Are you listening to me?
Hello? ... They want to dilute my bloodline!"

The dramatic shift in Rami's psychosis no longer terrified or surprised Caliana. Rami had been unfailingly confirming his insanity in
the past few months. She had fully accepted his delusional and psychotic episodes for what they were: signs of an unhinged mind. That
he had become an angry, paranoid, arrogantly demanding man in a
split second only confirmed what her gut told her: that Rami was
responsible for the murder of his father and brother.

But what if she was wrong, what if he hadn't killed them? Caliana had to allow for the slightest of possibilities. What if her children were in actual danger? She swayed with her rage and abruptly hung up on Rami.

Within seconds, Caliana was back in the car. She called Talal's school and demanded to immediately speak to Sally Smith. With a clarity that surprised her, she told the director that she wanted Talal to be escorted out of his classroom, that he was to be taken to Sally Smith's office, and that he was not to be left alone for one second until Caliana arrived because he may be in danger. Caliana explained that Talal's grandfather and uncle had been murdered, and that she had been notified that he may be in danger. She would be at the school in less than fifteen minutes to pick him up, she said, and repeated that he was to remain under Sally Smith's care and not left alone or given to anyone else. And under no circumstance, was the director to tell Talal anything.

Caliana then called the head of Kareem's school and repeated her instructions. She dialed the directory and asked for the numbers of several bodyguard services in the area. She called the first number and tried to remain calm as she explained the urgency for immediate actions. The secretary frustrated her with ridiculous questions, so Caliana hung up on her. As soon as a woman answered the second number on her list, Caliana demanded to speak to the owner or manager of the company, explaining that this was an urgent matter and she needed armed bodyguards immediately. The woman tried to explain their policies regarding armed services. Caliana was tempted to hang up. Gritting her teeth in impatience, and trying to still her beating heart, Caliana maneuvered around the woman and reached her boss. She calmly summarized the situation for the boss and asked him if he could provide immediate services. Caliana gave the necessary details and finally arranged to have an unarmed bodyguard at her house in two hours. It was the best she could do for the moment.

Tears of rage started blurring her vision, and Caliana savagely wiped her eyes.

Caliana stormed into Sally Smith's office. Three people were inside, and Caliana barely gave them a second of her time. She couldn't remember what she said to them, as her focus shifted to Talal's angelic face smiling at her. Tears choked her, and her stomach heaved at the realization that she would have to break his heart. And Kareem's. She gently guided her son to the car and helped put his seat belt on. She forced herself to breathe deeply and to calm her mind. She had to get to Kareem. She had to keep it together; she couldn't feel, she couldn't think. She had to be able to drive from DC to Herndon and then back to McLean. She had to endure one more hour.

Her vision blurred, and dizziness threatened to overtake her. She couldn't pull over and expose her son to possible danger. What if she was being followed? The possibility terrified her. She had to make it to McLean and get him home safe. Caliana fought the mounting panic attack even as it was consuming her. Shakily, she dialed Kareem's best friend's mother, who lived close to his school, and asked her to pick up Kareem for her and bring him to her home. She couldn't explain with Talal in the car and knew that any sympathy would unhinge her. She called back Kareem's school and briefly informed them of the change of plans.

Caliana then put all her energy into making it home. She refused to think of anything. She had to focus on the road, only the road. She had to ignore the pain that was threatening to obliterate her consciousness. She couldn't black out. Caliana focused her willpower on visualizing every upcoming segment of her journey home. She had to make it home. She had to hold the pain. Every turn was negotiated with concentrated dialogue. She directed her hands and legs on how to obey her and was grateful that they did. Finally, she pulled into her driveway.

As soon as they entered her house, she asked Jennifer to entertain Talal in the basement. Jennifer nervously told Caliana that her father had called many times.

The tears that had been waiting to explode shriveled up. She couldn't afford to feel, only to act.

Caliana reached for the phone and called her father in London. She informed him of her conversation with Rami and the actions that she had taken.

Her father immediately started issuing instructions. She needed to stay put at home, and he forbade her from going to Jordan. He told her that he had been on the phone with many people from Jordan and that Rami was already the prime suspect.

Caliana could hear her mother adding her opinions in the background. "I know he killed them. If you go to Jordan, he will kill you too. He did it. There is no doubt! Everyone thinks so. Everyone knows how crazy he is."

Her father went on to caution Caliana to not accuse Rami of anything. Apparently, when she had talked to him earlier, the conversation had been taped by the police, as the phones had been wired. They had heard her accusing Rami. Her accusation, combined with his manic rants, had alerted them to the possibility of his duplicity.

Her father strongly cautioned her against provoking Rami. They discussed the need for security as a safety measure. Her father pointed out that a man insane enough to kill his own father and brother could very well kill his sons.

Caliana absorbed and agonized over every bit of information. She desperately wanted to be in Jordan, to be with Nuha.

Caliana felt invaded by Rami's psychosis. All she could do was spin in reactive insanity. Opening the Yellow Pages, she started making calls and gathering information on security measures. She arranged for proper around-the-clock bodyguard service to begin the following morning.

The doorbell rang. Caliana rushed to answer the door, suddenly desperate to see Kareem's face.

"Hi, Mom." Kareem stood hesitantly before her. She could see from his expression that he was concerned for her. Her heart broke for him. Caliana choked, unable to speak. She couldn't make it real, for either of her sons. She wanted to shelter him, for just a few moments more. Pain ripped through her, and she knew that she was about to tear her son's heart.

Caliana knelt next to Kareem and told him that Samir and his grandfather were dead. Tears clouded her vision, preventing her from witnessing Kareem's immediate reaction. She wiped her eyes desperately, and no matter how hard she tried, she simply could not bring her son's face into focus. He was inches away from her, yet she felt that she was looking at him through a vast, distorted tunnel. Caliana wondered if she was in the process of fainting.

"How?" came Kareem's quiet question.

Caliana cringed. It was the first time she let herself register the idea of a bullet ending Samir's life. She felt the terror that she imagined Samir must have felt at knowing he was about to be murdered. Her head swam with horrifying images. Caliana heard herself telling Kareem that they had been shot.

Caliana became aware that the kind woman who had brought Kareem home was offering to take Kareem to her house for a few days. Caliana couldn't remember her logic as she heard herself agree that it was a good idea. Her mind swam in a dizzying empty vacuum. She vaguely heard Kareem agree to go.

Caliana watched his blurred image leave through the window and knew that she had done the right thing. At eleven, Kareem was too mature and perceptive, and she was barely hanging on. She did not want to collapse in front of him. She still had to tell Talal while she had some control.

Caliana called Talal and had him sit on the couch next to her. Her vision had cleared, and she was able to see his face. Her beautiful angel was looking at her adoringly, and she was grateful for his youth. She mustered calmness and told him that his uncle Samir and his grandfather were dead. Her heart pounded in fear, and she waited for his face to register the news.

"Who killed them?" asked Talal.

Caliana became flustered at the unexpectedness of his question. Her mind raced with alternative scenarios. None were viable.

"A car accident. No one killed them, *habibi*. It was an accident." Caliana's head started spinning, and nausea rose in her throat. The effort was killing her.

"Were they going fast?" Talal wanted to know.

Caliana started feeling lightheaded again. Her mind was woozy with cluttered, disjointed thoughts. She heard echoes but couldn't identify the words. Excusing herself, Caliana stumbled into the guest bathroom, where she collapsed on the floor.

Her body exploded.

Tears, vomit, diarrhea, and cold sweat gushed out of her.

Caliana identified that she was experiencing her most severe panic attack and believed that she was dying. She felt her heart shattering and her body complying in panicked response. Time stood agonizingly still. Caliana shuddered, heaved, choked, gasped for breath, shivered, sweated, and vomited. Unable to fathom the terror of her experience, Caliana prayed and begged for it to stop.

When it finally did stop, Caliana felt totally drained. Her body was still shaking, and her hands were fumbling badly as she peeled off every layer of clothing. She rinsed herself off as best as she could and then, checking that the main floor was empty, dashed naked upstairs and jumped into the shower.

Caliana focused on the motions of getting herself perfectly clean. Her mind became mercifully numb, and her body followed suit. She knew she had to make some dreaded phone calls, and the numbness was a gratifying reprieve.

She stepped out of the shower, wrapped in towels, and lay on the floor. She felt exhausted from the shower. She couldn't tell how long she had lain there and was jarred by the knocking on the bathroom door. Her housekeeper informed her that the bodyguard had arrived. Caliana felt the brutal ache of the reminder, and her body gave a low-level tremble. She dragged herself off the floor, using the counter to leverage herself. She had no strength. Every movement seemed to require an enormous amount of effort.

The face that looked back at her from the mirror was alien to her. Caliana stared at herself, strained, exhausted, and unrecognizable. She looked old, tired. She dressed herself mechanically and went downstairs. She heard herself having a conversation on security measures. Nothing seemed real. She was drifting into a delusional world. It was invading her every thought.

Caliana sat down with cigarettes and coffee and began making phone calls. It was eleven P.M. in Jordan, seven hours ahead of Washington, DC. Her heart insisted on beating, reminding her that she was alive and had to function.

Hearing Nuha's stunned, traumatized voice almost broke Caliana. Caliana's heart sagged even further as she registered the painful impact of the suffering of Samir's loved ones.

Their way of grieving was to piece together and exchange information that would help them understand what they both already knew, and help them solve this crime. It was an immediate bonding driven by the need to purge, the need to rationalize the unthinkable. They spoke calmly, each listening attentively to the other. The silences between the chunks of information were understood as a chance to assimilate and assess information. Their brains spun together in the hunt for the truth, and each woman wanted the other to know every pertinent detail that might help. They both knew that, together, they were the only ones who knew the whole story. Maybe they felt partly driven to avenge him. Maybe they just didn't know how to console each other. Maybe they needed to retrace the final days. Maybe they needed to keep Samir alive. Maybe they needed to torture themselves because they hadn't been able to protect Samir. They couldn't have prevented his death, but they could speak for him by solving his murder.

Nuha told her that on Monday, *Ammo* Habib had abruptly left the case that he was working on in London to return to Jordan. She knew that Samir and *Ammo* Habib had been talking to the psychiatrist in Jordan and that *Ammo* Habib had made arrangements to have Rami hospitalized somewhere in England. They had realized that his madness went deeper than drug addiction, and had discussed by phone that Rami needed urgent mental and physical care. Samir and *Ammo* Habib had had an appointment to see the psychiatrist at noon that day, to make arrangements with him to have Rami flown to England and put away.

Caliana affirmed that on Sunday, Samir had told her that he had discussed Rami with a psychiatrist and that the psychiatrist had strongly suspected that Rami might be bipolar. Samir hadn't known anything about that condition and had asked Caliana to research it for him. Samir had summarized what the psychiatrist had suspected based on the detailed information that Samir had shared with him. The psychiatrist believed that Rami's excessive drug use might have spun him into a paranoid, psychotic manic episode that had lasted for more than six months. Samir had sounded extremely upset and kept repeating that "it made sense."

Completely focused on recalling every word of her last conversation with Samir on Sunday, Caliana found herself repeating every word that had been said between them. She told Nuha that even though she and Samir had been talking every day about Rami for the past three months, Samir had never expressed real fear until that day. Samir had told her that he was going the next morning, Monday, to the bank to revoke his financial guarantee toward Rami, who had been out of control in his erratic spending. Samir had wanted to withdraw his name because he feared that Rami would ruin himself financially and that Samir would be the one responsible for his debts. He had also told Caliana that they (and Caliana had assumed that this referred to Samir and *Ammo* Habib) wanted to freeze Rami's bank accounts. Caliana choked up when she repeated Samir's final admonishment. He had ended the call with "Don't come to Jordan this summer. I can't protect you." Caliana shuddered at realizing that those were his last words to her, ever.

She also told Nuha that Samir and she had played phone tag on Monday and Tuesday and kept missing each other. She told Nuha about her conversation with Rami, and why she couldn't be with her in Jordan. Caliana had one question burning through her mind: She wanted to know if Rami knew of the appointment and of his family's plans for him.

Nuha told her that it was unclear. That day, there had been a national holiday in Jordan and everything had been closed, but Samir and *Ammo* Habib had gone to their office building to work for a few hours in the morning. Samir's office was on the top floor of the building. At eleven thirty am, Samir had gone downstairs to pick up his father to go to their appointment with the psychiatrist and had found the office empty. He had searched the building for his father, and when he couldn't find him, had gotten into his car and frantically called his mother to inquire if she had heard from his father. He had told his mother that he and his father were supposed to ride together, but his father had left unexpectedly without notifying him. Samir's mother had received another phone call from Samir at eleven fifty-five am, assuring her that he had found his father and that they were both in the waiting room of the psychiatrist's office.

Caliana interrupted Nuha and asked her how *Ammo* Habib had gotten to the office in the first place. Nuha told her that it was unclear. They discussed the possibility of him having taken a cab and debated how unbelievably out of character it was for *Ammo* Habib to have left without informing Samir. Why would he have needed a cab when his son was a minute away from him and they were supposed to be going together to their noon appointment? Nuha wondered if *Ammo* Habib had been trying to protect Samir by keeping him out of it and so had left without him. Caliana wondered if Samir had been running late and *Ammo* Habib, who was terribly punctual, had just decided to meet him there. Nuha told her "no way" would Samir run late on anything involving his father, because he had been drilled, and so had they all, on the importance of every minute when it came to *Ammo* Habib. Nuha suggested that *Ammo* Habib might have gotten a phone call from someone and been told that something urgent had happened, or that he had been picked up by someone. Caliana and Nuha both agreed that it was completely out of character for *Ammo* Habib to just leave and not say anything to Samir.

Nuha informed Caliana that the psychiatrist the men had been going to see had also been killed. The three of them had been discovered in the office around four pm. The psychiatrist had been beaten and tied up before being shot in the head. *Ammo* Habib had been shot once in the head, and Samir had received a bullet in his eye and another in his head. Caliana suddenly felt a visceral confirmation.

"Where was Rami between noon and four?" Caliana asked.

A loaded silence dragged by.

Then, Nuha told Caliana that Rami's ranting was as erratic as usual and hard to make sense. He claimed that he had gone to a part of the desert to pray, but she had been unable to discern the timing.

They were interrupted by someone who called Nuha and told her that some investigators wanted to speak to her. Caliana told Nuha to tell them everything she knew.

Caliana held it together until she got off the phone. Fierce pride for Nuha flowed out of Caliana. She understood why Samir had loved her and how special she was. Tears of sorrow finally flowed. She cried for the twins, the two-month-old babies, suddenly deprived of their father's love. She cried for Nuha, who had to bravely survive the savage brutality of her beloved husband's death. She cried for her children, who had lost their beloved uncle, the only reliable father figure in their lives, in addition to their grandfather.

Caliana's mind raced with exhausted scenarios. She told her housekeeper and the bodyguard that she was going up to her room. She called the friend who had Kareem to check in on him. The woman assured her that Kareem was fine and safe and that they would take care of him. She checked on Talal and found him absorbed in watching TV.

Weary, Caliana collapsed in bed. Her mind replayed hundreds of moments with Samir, many of which made her smile. Samir had represented life, and when Caliana had been with him, she had felt good to be alive. Caliana let the rush of loving memories cleanse her. She wanted to capture the gentle brother who had honored her with his love and devotion. She sent a prayer to Haya and visualized Haya awaiting Samir in a heavenly kingdom. Tears of pain and happiness merged at the image, and Caliana found comfort in their imagined union. The two people she loved best were sadly lost to her, but they could have each other. She was certain that they would be lovingly enveloped in a place reserved for the angels returned home. Caliana folded that image and tucked it into her heart, and with tears streaming down her face, she said good-bye.

The pain rocked her body. She sobbed and cried until she panicked that she would die.

Images of Kareem and Talal floated into her terror, and she reminded herself that she had to live for them. She didn't know how she would move forward, but she needed to imagine a way. Her tears subsided, and fear started a steady, icy crawl up her spine.

A sudden vivid image of Samir watching his father get shot in the head jerked her. The image replayed itself, and Caliana projected herself onto Samir and felt his violent jolt right after witnessing the bullet splattering his father's head. In utter horror, the torturous images kept replaying. She was in Samir's final moment.

She closed her eyes. In slow motion, she replayed every excruciating possibility. She had to feel his pain.

She felt Samir's panicked terror and his determination to save himself and his father.

She entered his spinning mind, heard the thoughts that led to strategies that failed to save them. She helped him negotiate for his life and shuddered at his certainty of death. She didn't want him to give up.

Through his eyes, she watched and heard *Ammo* Habib calmly negotiate with the killers, and heard Samir's responsive, analytical thoughts.

She felt him struggle to maintain the hope that was crashing around him.

She shuddered in horror as Samir was made to witness the execution of the therapist.

She saw Samir and his father exchange a long look that conveyed the dread, the acceptance, of their fatality. She heard their mutual unspoken sorrow, each devastated that he had failed to save the other.

She replayed Samir's horror at knowing that he was about to be forced to suffer the unbearable sight of watching his father die.

She heard his anguished scream, and felt the pain of his rage vibrate throughout his struggling body.

She crashed with him on his knees and howled his tears.

She raged with him, at the sadists who wouldn't hurry up and put him out of his misery.

She bled with him as he let himself mourn his sorrow for the loss of his children, his wife, and his life.

Caliana felt the shame of having invaded the privacy of these intimate moments and she disconnected from Samir. She looked around in total disorientation. She knew that those images had been sealed into her soul.

She stripped, and stood under the blasting shower. She tried to relax and let the serenity of the water soothe her, but a nagging thought kept creeping up on her. She felt that she had forgotten something. *Something essential...*

Rami.

Abrupt dizziness brought her to her knees.

She clutched her head.

A scream of rage bellowed out of her as rapid thoughts flogged her mind with images of Samir as he assimilated and understood that Rami was responsible—that his brother's invisible, mad hands were causing unimaginable suffering. That his brother, whom he dearly loved, was utterly insane, and capable of murder. She felt Samir's heart ripping with the unbearable agony of imagining his loved ones in danger and knowing that he wouldn't be able to protect them.

His tormented worry agonized his last thoughts. He wished for the mercy of a bullet to end it.

He got two.

* * *

Caliana's eyes snapped open, and she sat shaking in the dark. Shivering, she stood up and turned off the water. On wobbly legs, she took a few steps toward the towels. She watched her hand, ever so slowly, reach for a towel. She felt the rigid clamping of the rest of her body, as though every muscle was clenched in a tight grip.

She was incapable of wrapping the towel around her body.

She slowly lowered herself to the bathmat.

She veiled her body with the towel and, mercifully, lost consciousness.

A minute, an hour, or a few hours later, Caliana awoke. The parade of images forcefully returned. She angrily brushed away the tears and struggled with her cramped body. She quickly donned her softest tracksuit, brushed her teeth, and headed downstairs. She needed coffee. She needed to think.

At the bottom of the stairs, she was startled by the presence of the bodyguard. He explained that he would be stationed at the entrance to the sitting room, as from there he had full visual access to the front of the house. Caliana saw him clearly for the first time. She had no recollection of what he had looked like when she had met him a few hours earlier.

Caliana offered him some food and beverage, but he declined, insisting that the housekeeper had generously fed him. Caliana was grateful for Jennifer's presence of mind.

In the kitchen, Caliana was surprised to note that it was a little after one in the morning. She grabbed the largest mug and her cigarettes and headed to her favorite corner in the family room. She pressed a button on a remote control and brought a blazing fireplace to life. Caliana settled herself as close as possible to the warmth of the fire.

Her mind raced as she remembered conversations she had had with Samir regarding Khalid, the creepy companion whom Rami had adopted a few months earlier. Neither Samir nor his father had trusted Khalid, and they had strongly suspected that he was supplying Rami with a variety of drugs.

Samir had been extremely concerned with Khalid's influence and control over Rami. He had feared that in a very short time, Khalid had manipulated and ingratiated himself completely in Rami's favor.

Rami, in many paranoid rants, had repeatedly claimed that the only person he trusted was Khalid, and he had authorized Khalid to become his personal bodyguard and constant companion. Rami, with his manic spending, was handing out obscene amounts of money to his trusted bodyguard.

Samir had feared that Khalid had shrewdly "hit the jackpot" and found it easy to manipulate Rami into giving him access to everything that he owned. Caliana had been surprised to hear the frustrated hatred that Samir had expressed toward Khalid.

An evil thought crept into her mind. Caliana traced its webs. What if the murders had been planned by Khalid? What if he had realized that his financial livelihood was about to be taken away and he would then be deprived of the money and way of life that only Rami was crazy enough to provide him with? Wouldn't that have spurred him to kill the enemy who was threatening his golden egg? Rami would then benefit from his inheritance and gain freedom from the powers that could legally control him. Khalid would become the sole master of Rami and his inheritance. Samir had described Khalid as a hardened, lowlife opportunist who had blatantly, and arrogantly, assumed control of Rami. Caliana's gut screamed at her that both Rami and Khalid were involved.

If she worked really hard at exonerating Rami, she might stretch herself to imagine that his madness had allowed him to blurt out detailed information that had planted ideas in Khalid's mind to execute.

She remembered glimpses of Rami's recent ravings about his father and brother being mediocre people, and that he was the one who had achieved greatness. She tried to imagine Rami's manic fury at finding out that they had dared to plan to have him locked up.

Caliana dove further into profiling the evil. No matter how deeply she probed, the bottom line remained: Rami and Khalid must both be involved.

She was certain that Khalid had been present, that he had been one of the murderers. She didn't doubt Rami's duplicity; she was merely uncertain as to the degree of his utterly psychotic involvement.

She let the rage consume her. She understood that neither Samir nor *Ammo* Habib would have had a chance in fighting for his life. They had both been civilized men who lived by their mental power and had been unprepared to negotiate with subhuman degenerates. They had stood no chance. Caliana shivered. The only mercy that she could hope for was that from the time they had stepped into the office to the time they had died, they hadn't been tortured. She hoped they had died quickly.

Caliana shook with images of prolonged torment and sensed that Samir had been made to suffer the worst.

The murders of Samir and *Ammo* Habib remained unresolved. Through the huge public outpouring of rage, officials resorted to a secretive, speedy wrapping up of the case. Rami was put away in a hospital that treated drug addicts, where he astounded experienced professionals with his severe withdrawals.

Rumors abounded about Rami and his possible involvement, but too many of his powerfully connected friends refused to view him as a murderer and helped direct the attention away from him.

A week after the murders, a special unit was summoned from Scotland Yard to investigate the crime scene. The British criminal investigator's unit surmised that the crime scene was completely useless. It had been too badly trampled by incompetent policemen and anyone who chose to come in from the street to appease their morbid curiosity. They could not hope to obtain any viable evidence.

Even the harshest interrogative methods were unsuccessful in breaking Khalid. It was said that looking in his eyes was akin to looking in the eyes of a dead fish.

Khalid would be jailed for armed robbery a year later.

An autopsy revealed that the psychiatrist had been the first to die.

Ammo Habib had been the second killed.

Samir had been the last victim.

The estimated time of death was between three and four pm.

Caliana's tortured thoughts would continue into years of daily nightmares.

Section III

This book is dedicated to Susan.

Without her, this book could never have been written.

And in honor of her, and my journey with her, I wrote my story.

IN 2000, a friend of mine started seeing a therapist named Susan. I thought I knew about therapy—when he was five, I had briefly taken Kareem to a therapist, and therapy had helped him overcome some minor fears. I believed that psychotherapy was a science that helped people and could be beneficial. That, in a nutshell, constituted my understanding of therapy.

I lacked the personal experience and the knowledge of what therapy can really do for you if you have the courage to let it.

I had plenty of courage. Hell, I was superwoman; I didn't feel much of anything. My understanding of feelings stopped existing; "emotion" was a vague concept that people seemed to insist on talking about.

I did feel incredible love for my children; intellectual love with a few memorable moments of actual love toward my best friends; and, in the case of Samir and Haya, the agonizing pain of deep loss. I'd had fears, many of which had been physically debilitating. I had also been clearly in touch with the many layers of anger and had learned to use them as a defense toward guaranteeing continued emotional numbness.

Of course I had courage. I had survived some of the best and worst of humanity, and I emerged just fine. I had no idea what an "emotional shutdown" meant. I had long accepted that I lived for my children and that I existed only for their well-being, with no thought to my own.

So, with all the courage of my ignorance, I breezed into Susan's office expecting her to help me with my addiction to smoking. The only method of quitting that I hadn't pursued was working directly with a therapist who might help me unravel the mystery of my dependence. I figured that I'd try a couple of sessions, which would most likely fail, but I could pep myself at a future date with the comfort of having tried to quit. By then, I had spent twenty-four years perfecting my ability to distort my thoughts to suit my continued addiction.

Within minutes, we were not talking about quitting smoking, but about my life. I told her that I did not operate on an emotional level and that besides the love I had for my children, I could only identify a few emotions, namely fear and anger; I operated from the neck up. I usually spoke about my life in a polite, clipped-off way; with Susan, however, I found myself answering questions with more honesty than I was used to. This created a shift for me—something interesting happened.

By the fourth session, the original reason for coming to therapy was long gone. In fact, the first couple of years I spent in therapy, I smoked more than I ever had. I was facing unrealized fears and needed the habitual reassurance from cigarettes.

I realized that my life was spilling out unchecked. Maybe I was motivated by the relief of finally telling my whole story, of having one person really see me, even as I quaked with constant insecurities.

For months, I snuck glances at Susan during our sessions, keeping my gaze and my body primarily facing four and a half steps away from the door. My car keys were usually gripped in one hand, or within reach of the first leap that would end any session at any time, no matter how abruptly. When I made my escape, I did not want to have to come back, even for a moment, to retrieve my keys. I needed to keep the option of flight in sight.

Having viewed and lived a huge part of my life from a distrustful distance, I felt I was an excellent judge of character. I had developed the ability to easily identify all forms of insincerity. I never asked Susan about her degrees or qualification, for what I needed would not be measured by something so obvious. I was searching for the *person* behind the gifted therapist. I needed to see her and know her before I could believe her and trust her. After all, I was putting my mind, my life, under vulnerable exposure and voluntarily handing her the ability to shatter me.

Also, if this woman finally confirmed my hidden dread, that I might be crazy, then I wanted to have gathered evidence against her that would allow me to dismiss her judgment.

I wasn't going to just trust what she said, even though she had brilliant perceptions. She had to prove herself. I needed to gauge her decency. The questions she asked and the seeds she planted spun me with dizzying realizations. I understood their relevance to my healing. But I needed to know that this woman was for real, that she practiced living by the principles, the integrity, that she was asking me to delve into.

I resisted the serene and safe décor of the room. Especially because I admired Susan's exquisite taste, I was not going to let a contrived setting lull me! That she was beautiful, sexy, and elegant appealed to my sensibilities as a woman, and I resisted admiring her style for fear of letting her draw me in with superficiality. That her energy was still and absolutely focused on me was gratifying and pleasantly unnerving, so I would remind myself that she was paid to listen to me. That she held her boundaries so clearly allowed me to unravel mine, but at the time, I was too intently scared to appreciate the gift, or I certainly would have protected against it. That she was only a few years older and seemed to share a lot of commonalities with me drew me to her, so in defense, I sometimes focused on making up negative assumptions that could cause me to dislike her. Or so I justified my permission to like her. That her mind seemed to absorb my uncensored thoughts as they flew at speeds that surprised even me was simply unbelievable. She was able to follow every twist and turn that I spun and challenged my every misconception. I was too enthralled to fight her. That I felt and experienced her passionate insistence on affirming my normalcy started to unravel me. What did me in, though, was when I stopped denying the overwhelming fact that she genuinely cared for me, loved me, in spite of my total exposure—or perhaps because of it.

She shattered my world. Thank God.

She consistently proved herself to me. Six months into biweekly therapy, I realized that I trusted her as much as I was capable of trusting anyone. It dawned on me that while I had been so busy scrutinizing my demons, looking to find traces of them in her, I also had not even found a shred to support my distorted need to maintain vigilance. I felt safe. I had tested Susan with every imaginable arsenal that had dragged heavily along with my guarded soul, and she had sailed through them without even knowing that she was always being tested. I couldn't believe how much I trusted her, or the incredible relief that came from the trust.

That was when my relationship really took off with her. It was the first conscious decision I really made, my healthiest. I told myself that I would have to be the world's biggest idiot and coward if I did not trust in my trust in her and let her continue to help me. And in six years of therapy, I am proud to say that I conquered the few fears that could have hindered that trust.

I began a relationship with Susan and, in return, created a healthy relationship with myself. At the start, I was unable to imagine what a trusting, intimate relationship could be like. My imagination had been limited by the pain that had consumed my life. Susan helped me to create a healthier perspective and to feel in control of every tiny step I chose to take in constructing a new life. Her faith in me empowered me to endure, to go beyond my capabilities, and challenged me to be the highest version of myself.

She was my copilot, though she clearly intended for me to assume the reins. She paved the way for my fuller integrity to surface more completely in my everyday life. I started feeling better and happier because I had fully engaged myself in my relationship with her. I was practicing *being* when I was with her, and then would apply my newfound self outside her office. I felt at home when I was with Susan, because with her, I was at home with myself. I actually came alive in the safety of my connection with her, always knowing that I was held in gentle and loving care. She took me back to my safe, warm womb and mothered me back to my independence. I could not have asked to be guided by a more incredible mother, and that was the corrective experience that I needed. I was emotionally aborted at birth and lovingly resurrected in therapy.

My journey within my relationship with Susan grew from absolute trust. And in trust, every layer expanded my heart. With her, I had the privilege, the profound honor, of practicing being myself in a healthy, supportive, and challenging environment. She held a steady mirror, and in time, it allowed me to see my reflection and to love the parts of me that I so clearly loved in her.

I grew, because by loving Susan, I was finally able to love myself. She dismantled my every defense and freed my soul. I had no idea when I walked into her office in 2000 that I would be engaging with my angel and begin living a dream I had aborted.

There are those who believe that there are no accidents in life, that there are no coincidences, that everything has a meaning, a purpose, fate, and so on. I call my experience in therapy a divine intervention, and I make it a point to thank God every night for his gracious love in having put Susan in my path.

I do believe in reincarnation, and I survived much of this lifetime because I lived with a real conviction that I was not coming back, that this is my last lifetime! And yet, in a heartbeat, I would endure endless lifetimes if it meant that I could be there for Susan, in any one of hers. To be able to give back to her, to love her back, is the only unfulfilled intimacy that feels sadly lacking in my reality.

I could easily write a book that details my journey of loving the most incredible person I know, but I won't. This is really Caliana's story, and my emergence into Kitana is a story that may never need to be told. And I think that that is a good thing.

LaVergne, TN USA
29 September 2010
199018LV00001B/1/P